MORE ABANDONED MANITOBA

Rivers, Rails, and Ruins

GORDON GOLDSBOROUGH

GREAT PLAINS
PUBLICATIONS

ON THE COVER The one-room Gourlay School No. 695, situated a few miles northeast of Brandon in the Rural Municipality of Elton, closed in 1951. The building was still standing in June 2011, when I took a photo from which the cover illustration was created. The building has since been demolished but is commemorated by a monument. GORDON GOLDSBOROUGH

I dedicate this book to my late parents Leonard Harvey Goldsborough (1931–2012) and Joan Hodgson Goldsborough (1937–2016). Mom, I am so glad that you forced me to learn to type in high school. Dad, you were a real role model, except when it comes to the use of exclamation points!!!

Great Plains Publications
1173 Wolseley Avenue
Winnipeg, MB R3G 1H1
www.greatplains.mb.ca

Great Plains Publications gratefully acknowledges the financial support provided for its
publishing program by the Government of Canada through the Canada Book Fund; the Canada
Council for the Arts; the Province of Manitoba through the Book Publishing Tax Credit and
the Book Publisher Marketing Assistance Program; and the Manitoba Arts Council.

Design & Typography by Relish New Brand Experience
Printed in Canada by Friesens

LIBRARY AND ARCHIVES CANADA CATALOGUING IN PUBLICATION

Goldsborough, Gordon, 1959-, author
     More abandoned Manitoba : rivers, rails and ruins / Gordon Goldsborough.

ISBN 978-1-77337-002-6 (softcover)

     1. Abandoned buildings--Manitoba. 2. Abandoned buildings--Manitoba--
Pictorial works. 3. Manitoba--History. 4. Manitoba--History--Pictorial works.
1. Title.

FC3361.G653 2018   971.27   C2018-904157-9

www.abandonedmanitoba.ca

Contents

The author climbing inside the "balloon annex" of a vacant grain elevator at Tyndall, Manitoba, March 2017. MATT BIALEK

Foreword

Many of us enjoy history, but few have the ability to make it come alive. Gordon Goldsborough is one of those rare people. His stories are not only good reading but they are entertaining, enlightening and enjoyable—a perfect combination.

In his second volume of *Abandoned Manitoba*, Gordon continues to share with us his lifelong fascination with Manitoba's history. He has a unique ability to spot and then investigate unusual topographic features or examples of activities and structures that once held a prominent place in Manitoba communities in bygone eras.

Throughout a quarter century in elected public office, I often met people, who while touring me around their home community would say, "You've got to see this place (or thing) before you leave." This inevitably led to an old or remarkable structure, a failed business operation or an unsuccessful invention from times past.

When I began listening to Gordon's stories on the CBC and then reading his first book, I thought that I would know most of his revelations from my own experience. Little did I expect that Gordon's keen eye for the unusual and persistence in investigating it would far exceed my own knowledge. In fact, he provided me with a treasure trove of many more untold stories of Manitoba's forgotten past. In addition to his dogged determination, Gordon possesses the skills of a talented raconteur who is able to teach us about our history through his stories.

You will enjoy this new edition of *Abandoned Manitoba* as you read the unique and fascinating stories that conjure up images of creativity, entrepreneurship and the visionary risk takers who established and built our province.

THE HONOURABLE GARY A. FILMON
PREMIER OF MANITOBA (1988–1999)

The Manitoba 1912 license plate that
was the cause of an historical obsession.
STEFANIE GOLDSBOROUGH

Introduction

The Origins of an Historical Obsession

When I was a teenager, I spent summers living with my widowed grandfather and bachelor uncle on their farm in rural Manitoba. I worked at a country general store, driving a fuel delivery truck. I realize now that the navigational experience I gained on that job proved helpful when, many years later, I began exploring the province's back roads in search of abandoned places. This job would also prove influential in another way. Often I would notice, while talking with farmers as I filled the tanks in their yards with fuel, that nearby wooden granaries and sheds had old license plates nailed to their outsides. Why are the plates there, I asked? They are covering holes in the wood, I was told. But why use license plates, I persisted? Because they are perfectly good metal that would otherwise go to waste, and nothing is wasted here, was the answer.

Many of us have experiences that seem innocuous when they happen but, with the benefit of hindsight, turn out to have profound effects on the course of our lives. In my case, one such experience happened when my wife and I moved into a new home on the outskirts of Winnipeg. Our yard was low-lying and prone to be wet so we decided to raise it up by a foot or two. We put a "Clean Fill Wanted" sign at the end of our driveway, inviting truckers heading past with soil excavated from construction sites all over the city, on their way to the landfill, to drop them off in our yard instead. Over time, numerous truckloads were dumped and we learned by hard experience that the definition of "clean" varied enormously. Loads would frequently contain concrete chunks, scrap metal, bricks, and miscellaneous garbage. So we began to check each load as it was dumped to pull out these materials before using the soil to raise our yard. One day, as my wife suspiciously probed a newly delivered pile with her shovel, it clanked on something metallic. She pulled out a rectangular piece of flat metal, about 4½ inches wide and 10 inches long, rusty but mostly black in colour. It had mud caked all over but a large white #4 was visible on one side. Curious, she cleaned it off and found a three-digit number: 614. To the left of the number was what looked like a bison, below which were the letters M - A - N, and below those letters was another, smaller number, mostly obscured with only the number 2 visible. The numbers were not painted on the metal but were embedded into coating that looked like ceramic. She showed it to me and we were pretty sure what it was. Some online detective work confirmed my suspicion. It was a Manitoba automotive license plate from 1912.

How did an old license plate end up in soil dumped in our yard? Our theory—based on what I was told by someone familiar with road and sidewalk maintenance in downtown Winnipeg—is that in the early 20th century it was common for waste metals to be used as fill. Today, when city workers raise an old section of road or sidewalk, collectors search for treasures hidden beneath them. As well, at least two people have told me they found old license plates protruding from the banks of the Red River in the older parts of the city. Conceivably, someone had thrown away our license plate when it became obsolete, in 1913, and it was used as fill in an area that was re-excavated during some new construction project. The soil was on its way to the landfill when the trucker saw our sign and dumped it in our yard, along with a little gift from the past.

The first automobile arrived in Winnipeg in 1899. It was a three-wheeled vehicle, powered by gasoline, and brought here by a fellow named Edgar Kenrick, a chemistry professor at St. John's College. In early 1904, a dozen early car owners met at Kenrick's home to discuss the formation of a club, to be called the Winnipeg Automobile Club, a forerunner of today's CAA Manitoba. The number of cars on city streets grew rapidly as most of the wealthy Winnipeggers replaced their horse-drawn carriages with automobiles. By 1908, it was clear that some form of identification was needed on the cars so the provincial government began requiring owners to install a plate of their own design on the car, bearing a number assigned to them by the government. Many of these early plates were made of leather to which metal numbers were attached.

In 1911, the Manitoba government began to issue everyone a standardized plate. They were metal covered by blue ceramic in which white numbers were embedded. The following year, the ceramic plates were black with white numbers, then white with black numbers in 1913, and orange with black numbers in 1914. Early experience with these porcelain-covered metal plates was that they did not stand up well. Flying stones from the roads would often damage the porcelain surface, making the number illegible. Consequently, in 1915, the government went with an all-metal design. Each year, a car owner would receive a new plate bearing the same number as the preceding year. When a car was sold, the plate would typically go with it. And the numbers were issued in order so, the lower the number on the plate, the earlier the automobile had been registered.

Coming back to my 1912 plate #614, my curiosity was piqued and one of my first thoughts was "I wonder who this plate belonged to and what kind of vehicle was it on?" I resolved to check at the provincial archives, as I assumed they would have automobile registration records. Unfortunately, this proved to be a dead end. I was told that old license records were destroyed in a fire at the Motor Vehicle Branch on April Fools' Day in 1957—no joke. So I set the matter of the plate aside.

Several months later, I was pursuing an entirely different line of research for a book on the history of Delta Marsh, about a fellow named Edward Drewry (1851–1940), who had been one of the early waterfowl hunters there. Drewry was one of Winnipeg's earliest beer brewers, operating a brewery beside the Redwood Bridge. He was also an inveterate collector and, along with his son Charles, compiled 28 massive scrapbooks that contained a wealth of information about Drewry family life from 1844 to 1966. Among their

contents were Drewry's first pair of pants when he was a boy. (One wonders what motivated him to keep them.)

Not surprisingly, as a man of considerable means, Drewry was one of Manitoba's first automobile owners and he was obviously a keen automobilist. He subscribed to a local magazine for automobile enthusiasts, called *Gas Power Age*. And, lo and behold, one of the items in the Drewry scrapbooks was a 62-page booklet, published by *Gas Power Age*, dated 31 July 1912. For each plate number, up to #3999, it listed the name of the registered owner, their address, and the automobile model for which the plate was issued. The little booklet was exactly what I needed to identify the owner of my plate #614!

I learned that #614 was issued for a Franklin automobile owned by a gentleman named Elisha Hutchings (a photo of him appears on page 193). A little more research at the archives told me that Mr. Hutchings had been a prominent Winnipegger in

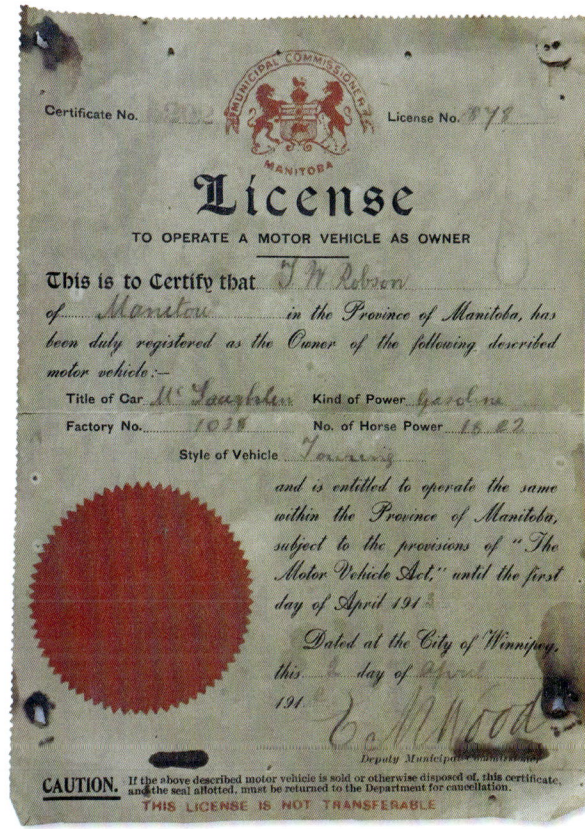

A vehicle operating license issued in April 1912 to merchant Thomas W. Robson (1878–1949) of Manitou, for his McLaughlin touring car bearing plate #878. The license is contained in the collections of the Archibald Museum near La Riviere.

his day. He came here in 1876 and established a saddlery business. He did very well in business, so much so that, by 1910, he was said to be among the city's 19 millionaires.

I thought the booklet could prove useful in other ways so I transferred its entire contents into a spreadsheet and, gradually over the next couple of years, I researched each of the automobile owners listed in it so I could learn something about these early car enthusiasts. By cross-referencing the list with census records for 1911, I could add their age and birthplace, marital status,

In early 2018, I bought this postcard online. Visual inspection tells us that it is a view of the Duke of Connaught (Canada's Governor General from 1911 to 1916) disembarking from a vehicle bearing 1912 license plate #3406. My database tells us the vehicle was registered to Robert Rogers who, at that time, was the federal Minister of Public Works. Detective work in a database of old newspapers determined that Rogers had escorted the Duke to the grand opening of the St. Charles Country Club's new clubhouse on Saturday, 13 July 1912 and the Duke had shown "great interest in the polo tournament." The building burned to the ground three months later. GORDON GOLDSBOROUGH

ethnicity, religion, and occupation. Based on data for the people I could find in the census, I calculated that the average automobile owner in 1912 was 42½ years old. The vast majority were men (but there were 66 women among them, just under 2% of the total) and 82% of them were married.

When looking at the location where the cars were located, 56% were in Winnipeg; the remaining 44% were in Brandon, smaller towns or rural communities around the province. That is interesting because Winnipeg represented only about 30% of the provincial population at that time, which means the city contained proportionately more automobiles than other parts of the province—perhaps not surprisingly given that it was the centre of industry and government. The most popular vehicle was a Ford, at 20% of the total. There were other familiar names like Cadillac, Oldsmobile, Packard, and Studebaker. McLaughlin was a predecessor to Buick. But many of the common auto models in 1912 are completely unknown today, with names like EMF, Hupp, Mitchell, Overland, Reo, and Russell. Curiously, a fellow named John Ivison had licensed a "vacuum cleaner." And today's fancy electric cars are not the novelty they may seem; there were 65 electric cars on Manitoba roads in 1912, made by at least nine manufacturers, and 12 of them were driven by women.

The 1912 automobile database has had several interesting uses to me. For example, historical photos taken in 1912 that show automobiles are often sharp enough that it is possible to read their license plate numbers. A friend of mine had an old postcard from 1912 that showed an automobile parked next to an apartment block on Hargrave Street in Winnipeg. Its plate number #112 told me the owner was John Coulter, a prominent local doctor. My research indicated that Dr. Coulter did not live in this vicinity nor was his office located here. Perhaps he was making a house call on one of his patients when the photographer took a photo of the street?

Today, early porcelain license plates are much sought by collectors, and command prices in the hundreds of dollars. I spread the word that if people having Manitoba 1912 plates in their collection would tell me its number, I could tell them about what vehicle had carried it. To date, I have heard about 153 surviving plates, or about 2% of the total issued by mid-1912. What is fascinating about these "survivors" is the demographics of where they came from. I said before that 56% of the plates issued in 1912 were in Winnipeg. In contrast, only 28% of the survivors were on Winnipeg automobiles. In other words, plates on automobiles registered in rural Manitoba are far more likely to have survived to the present than those in Winnipeg. This is probably because it was less likely in rural Manitoba for license plates to be dumped into a landfill. Instead, as I had discovered when I was delivering fuel, thrifty farmers used old license as patches for their granaries. Over the years, plates that were once viewed as abandoned garbage are now highly prized collector's items.

Looking back on the amount of work that it took me to reconstruct what I know now about automobiling in

In November 2007, retired Winnipeg firefighter Rick Northwood saw 1912 license plate #53 in a local antique shop. Without knowing its history but feeling a deep connection to it that he could not explain, he bought the plate for $100. Eventually, Northwood found me and my 1912 license plate database. I was able to tell him that, in 1912, his #53 plate had been issued to Donald MacDonald, an unmarried 55-year-old firefighter, based at Winnipeg's Fire Hall No. 2 at the corner of Smith and York, for his Ford car. Northwood researched MacDonald's history using the resources of the Winnipeg Firefighters Museum and ended up writing an article for *Manitoba History* magazine that shed light on early firefighting in Manitoba. RICK NORTHWOOD

1912, my wife has lamented several times that, if she knew then what she knows now—what that abandoned chunk of metal she found buried in our yard would lead to—she would have quietly put it back and never shown it to me. On the other hand, I choose to think that that old plate honed my detective skills and contributed to my fascination with Manitoba's past that I will share with you in the pages to follow.

Abandoned Manitoba: An Update

As some readers will know, this book is a sequel to my *Abandoned Manitoba* published two years ago which, in

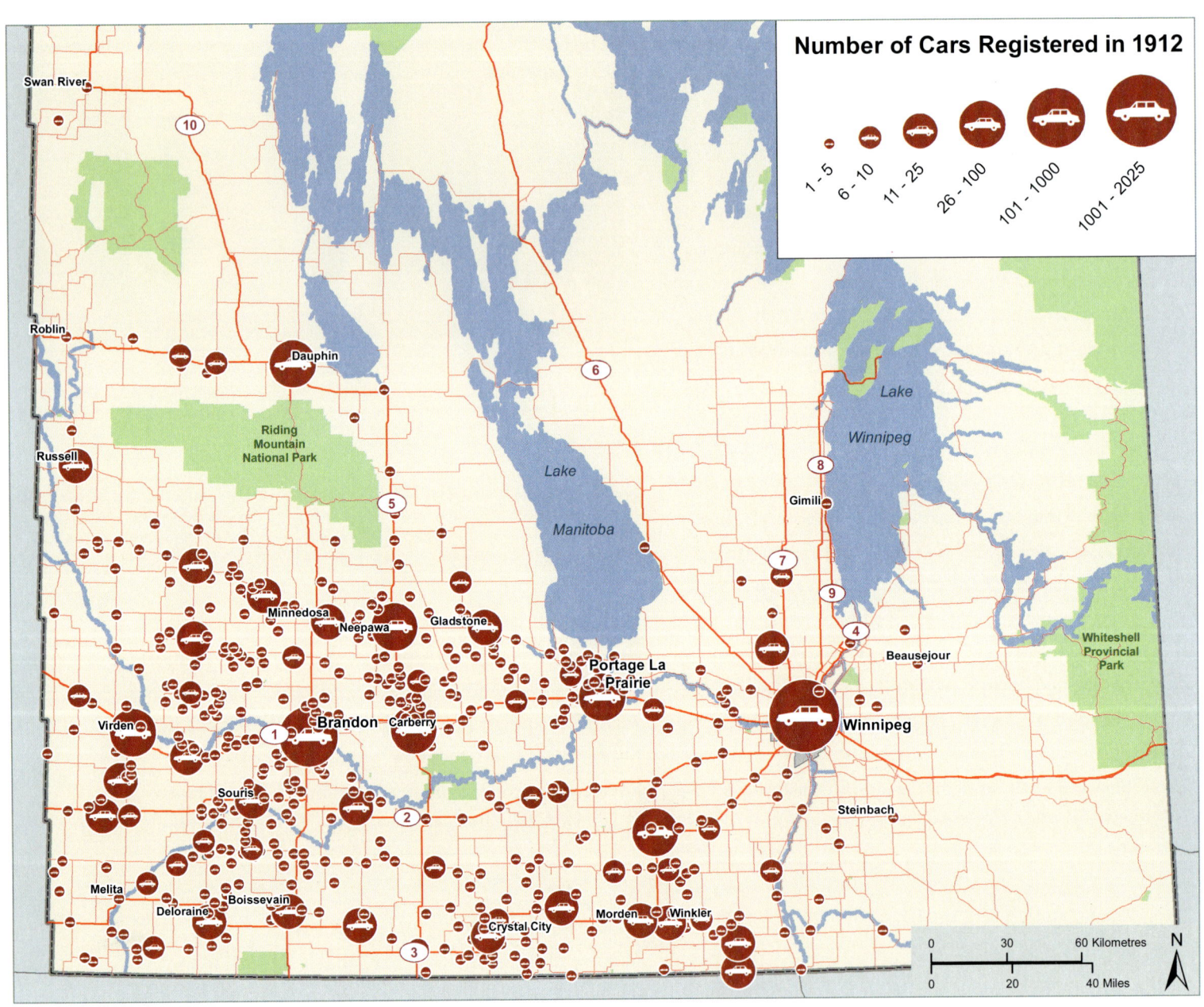

Number of Cars Registered in 1912

1 - 5   6 - 10   11 - 25   26 - 100   101 - 1000   1001 - 2025

Swan River

Roblin

Dauphin

Riding Mountain National Park

Russell

Lake Manitoba

Lake Winnipeg

Gimili

Whiteshell Provincial Park

Minnedosa

Neepawa

Gladstone

Portage La Prairie

Beausejour

Virden

Brandon

Carberry

Winnipeg

Souris

Steinbach

Melita

Deloraine

Boissevain

Crystal City

Morden

Winkler

0   30   60 Kilometres

0   20   40 Miles

N

turn, was based on a like-named weekly series on CBC Radio 1. There, I talk about abandoned places around the province. We have covered a lot of territory—literally and figuratively—in that series, and it has given me new appreciation for our province's rich history. The point of *Abandoned Manitoba* is not merely that the places we visit are no longer in use, but that they tell an interesting and important story about how Manitoba has changed through the years. For example, our visit to the former tuberculosis treatment centre at Ninette shows us how treatment for this now controllable (but as yet unvanquished) illness has evolved over the past century. Thirty-six abandoned places were featured in the preceding book and I will tell

you about another 28 sites here. As before, the three criteria for including a story here were as follows:

1. Some vestige of a site's former use should be visible. I want to know for certain, when I visit a site, that I am witnessing authentic history so I must be able to see physical remains, whether it is a stone foundation or the intact structure itself. In a few cases, the site may not be in use for the purpose for which it was originally built but is not, strictly speaking, unoccupied.

2. The site should be unique or be a good example of a wider phenomenon. For example, there were over 700 wooden grain elevators around Manitoba in the mid-20th century but they are quickly disappearing from the landscape so that, as I speak, only 132 elevators survive today. I may show you one or two of them, but hopefully your curiosity will be aroused enough that you will want to see others. I can point you in the right direction.

3. Finally, the site should have an interesting story that reveals something about life in the past and how *something* about Manitoba—our means of transportation, education, recreation, or whatever—has changed.

I have tried hard to make *More Abandoned Manitoba* a worthy follow-up to its predecessor. If anything, this book takes a more expansive view of factors that have changed in Manitoba through the years, not confining itself to the factors that caused a particular place to be abandoned, but examining the larger phenomenon of which the site was a part. For example, it seems to me that the overgrown Conestoga Campground that we will visit is a visual reminder of a major phenomenon of the 1950s and 1960s: the growth of Manitoba's road network that enabled more people to hit the roads in search of adventure … and in need of a campground by the highway. In some of the chapters in this book, I dig deeper into stories that I introduced in the first book. I have spent much of the past two years obsessing on that fast-disappearing prairie icon, the grain elevator, and have found lots of new information that allows me to put in a wider context the story of what I believe to be Canada's oldest elevator at Elva, Manitoba. I have tried to include better photographs, illustrations, and maps in this book. I have used oral history—the facts and feelings contained in people's heads rather than any book—more extensively.

In my travels around Manitoba over the past decade, I have had the opportunity to visit hundreds of abandoned places. You may wonder how I selected the specific ones to be profiled in this book. First and foremost, the site had to tell a good story. Moreover, I wanted the collection of sites to cover a wide geographic area of the province, so there would be a little bit of local interest for most readers with Manitoba roots. A practical consideration was that I could only include sites about which I could find reliable information. This meant that I had to exclude places that I thought had a good story but, for various reasons, I was unable to tell that story well. The old stone Kennedy House overlooking the Red River near Lockport was a case in point. Built between 1866 and 1870 by noted Scottish stonemason Duncan McRae, using stones quarried from the riverbank at the St. Andrews Rapids (site of the Lock and Dam), the impressive two-storey structure was later the home of Captain William Kennedy, a noted Arctic explorer. It was rescued from obscurity by a passionate history buff, the late Dr. Edward Shaw, who

bought the house in 1968 and opened it to the public as a museum project for Manitoba's 100th birthday in 1970. It was designated as a provincial historic site in 1985. Starting in 2003, it became a genteel tearoom, described in a national magazine as "one of the best places for afternoon tea in Canada." In 2015, the tearoom proprietor was abruptly evicted by the building's owner, the provincial government, allegedly based on an engineering study that found serious structural deficiencies. It has been empty ever since. Government bureaucrats were downright uncooperative in responding to my requests for information on its present and future status. They stonewalled me (pun intended). They disputed my characterization of the building as abandoned, arguing that it was merely "in pause," whatever that means. In the end, I decided that it was not worth the personal aggravation to dig more deeply into the situation at Kennedy House. Regrettably, its story will not be told here.

Inevitably, when one talks about unused places, things are bound to change so I thought you might be interested in a few updates to stories told in the preceding book. When I talked about the manufacturing plant on the eastern edge of Winnipeg where explosives were made during the Second World War, I said there had been only a single fatality at the facility during its five-year period of operation. Technically, I was right, but I could have mentioned a pair of men from Beausejour—William Wayne and Ronald Radons—who were killed during demolition of the site after the war, in late 1946. A booklet that I found in a little building at Graysville that had once housed a chapter of the Orange fraternity described the organization's rituals using a jumble of unintelligible symbols and letters. A retired military cryptographer contacted me to say that he had taken the sample page I showed in *Abandoned Manitoba* and, without breaking much of a sweat, broke the code to reveal its arcane secrets. (Contact contact me at www.abandonedmanitoba.ca if you are interested in the details.)

Within the last two years, I was able to remove a couple of items from my personal "bucket list" of must-see places, starting with the partially-constructed but abandoned site of a harbour on Hudson Bay at the mouth of the Nelson River. (The other bucket-list site is the subject of the last chapter in this book.) I had written a chapter about Port Nelson in *Abandoned Manitoba* but my narrative was based on information provided by friends and others who had actually been there. I wanted desperately to visit it myself so, when

In July 2017, a highlight of my visit to Port Nelson was an opportunity to climb inside the "million dollar dredge" shown here. Constructed in 1913 at Toronto and shipped up to the construction site for a new harbour at the mouth of the Nelson River on Hudson Bay, the dredge *Port Nelson* was lifted atop a seawall during an extreme storm in late 1924. It could not be lifted off so it was abandoned there, gradually splitting in half over the years and spilling its guts all over an artificial island that sits a mile offshore. CHRIS THOMPSON

The Lang House, built between 1896 and 1897, was finally set ablaze and demolished in early 2017 by a farmer frustrated by years of trespassing and damage to his crops. UNIDENTIFIED FARMER

the opportunity arose last July, I jumped at it. We travelled downriver on the Nelson aboard a boat that delivered us to the artificial island about a mile offshore. The weather was nasty—heavily overcast and windy with intermittent rain and sleet—but I *loved* every minute of it, taking over 300 photos in the course of a four-hour stay. I crawled all over the derelict "million dollar dredge" and noticed how much its

condition had deteriorated since my friends had visited a few years earlier. Limited time did not permit us to walk the entire length of the impressive, 17-span steel trestle railway bridge that connected the island to the mainland but I did manage to walk gingerly over the rotting wooden ties of three tilted spans. I marvelled again at how the engineers from over a century before had done such excellent work that,

despite damage from the absence of maintenance, the structure was still standing. And I wondered at the tools and materials that was strewn about the place, as though the workers had left in a hurry and had simply dumped things where they stood.

Perhaps the most sobering update is the story of the Lang House whose photo I shared near the end of the previous book. I did not name it, reveal its location, or tell its story, for fear that people inspired to visit the building would cause further grief for the farmer who owned it and the land on which it stood. The grand two-storey fieldstone structure was built between late 1896 and early 1897 by master mason Jim Willox for farmer David Lang, who had come to Manitoba from his native Quebec. Willox took stones that were scattered around the land, split each of them in half to produce two flat surfaces, placed one half facing outward and the other inward, then filled the space between them with stone rubble. The building was reported to contain some of the most beautiful woodwork and finest staircases in the area. Lang and his wife Catherine, who had no children, were famous for their house parties and dances. Catherine Lang died in 1913 and was buried in a nearby cemetery. David Lang returned to Quebec and died around 1923. The house and property was sold to a family who lived there until the late 1950s or early 1960s. I visited the old Lang House in May 2015, with permission of the landowner, long after timbers and millwork had been salvaged from its interior. The windows and doors were all gone, probably broken or removed by generations of impromptu party-goers who had ventured far out into the farmer's field to reach the old house. That was the crux of the problem. Many of the people who visited the Lang House did so without permission and would drive straight through the farmer's planted crops, trampling them in the process. Understandably, the farmer was livid at each such transgression, partly because of the loss of income from the ruined crops, and partly because he would be held responsible in the event the decrepit old building fell down when someone was inside it. To add insult to injury, the trespassers often left junk food wrappers and other garbage behind for the farmer to clean up. The farmer appreciated the historic value of the old house—that is why he had left it standing all those years—but his patience was exhausted by the spring of 2017. He set fire to the building to get rid of its wooden parts. Then a large machine set to knocking down stone walls that had withstood prairie winds for over a century. The Lang House is now only a memory preserved by some seventy photos in my personal collection. Although I regret the loss of this interesting old building, I completely understand the reasons that motivated the farmer to demolish it. The case reinforces my contention that visitors to any of the sites profiled in this book must do so respectfully, mindful of the fact that many of them are private property. While I do encourage you to venture out and explore Manitoba, I urge you to do it in a way that preserves the opportunity for explorers who will follow you.

ACKNOWLEDGEMENTS

I thank numerous collectors of 1912 Manitoba plates, all over the world, including retired firefighter Rick Northwood, who helped me to ascertain how many plates issued that year survive today. Foremost among them are a couple of fine gentlemen here in Manitoba, Ross Metcalfe and Andrew Osborne, who are even more obsessed than me with old license plates. I also thank the many readers of *Abandoned Manitoba* who contacted me about their enthusiasm for the book and shared stories about "new" places that I could visit (some of which are featured in this book) or added a detail or two to the story. Betty Anne Kilbrei alerted me to the two Beausejour men killed at the Transcona Cordite Plant while cryptographer Tim Green broke the "secret" Orange code for me. Chris Thompson joined me in exploring the artificial island at Port Nelson, and managed to climb into places in that old dredge that I could not reach. Chris also arranged a visit to Lang House for the two of us. I am grateful to the farmer who owned the now-demolished house and who shared a photo taken during its final moments.

Crabby Steve's Dance Hall

Manitoba had an eight-year fling with Prohibition, from 1916 to 1923, during which police vigorously sought out violators of the Temperance Act. This photo, taken by Winnipeg photographer Lewis Foote in September 1922, shows an illegal still found at 521 Boyd Avenue. ARCHIVES OF MANITOBA

his chapter might make some readers nostalgic, but others might get a little crabby. Our focus shifts to a building in the Interlake along Highway 7—about two miles north of Komarno and forty miles north of Winnipeg—that was legendary in the mid-20th century. It was a place where one could find flirtation with the opposite sex, public inebriation, and conflict in equal measure. The place: a dance hall operated by the late Steve "Crabby" Maksymyk.

In the days before vehicle ownership was common-place and public highways were extensive, the options for recreation in many parts of rural Manitoba were severely limited. The solitary pleasures of reading a book or a newspaper did not appeal to everyone. Radio reception was spotty, television was non-existent, and only the larger towns had movie theatres. Seeing an opportunity, entre-preneurs around the province built halls where people would come from far and wide to dance to "old time" music played by live bands. Admission was as little as five cents so that, as historian Norm Larsen has observed, even during the depths of the Great Depression, most everyone could come up with a nickel to attend the dance on a Friday or Saturday evening.

Born in the Interlake community of Malonton in 1924, Steve Maksymyk left home at the age of 15 and joined the merchant marine, travelling the world over the next seven years. After returning home in 1947, he decided the

OPPOSITE Aerial view of Crabby Steve's Dance Hall, April 2017. GORDON GOLDSBOROUGH

community needed more recreational opportunities so he built a dance hall on his property and named it after Crabby Joe's Bar that he had frequented in San Francisco. Crabby Steve's was an immediate success, so much so that within a year it had competition from another dance hall a few miles to the north, run by businessman Walter Lake. It was the perfect foil to Crabby Steve's, known as Jolly Wally's Rangeland.

People came from far and wide to attend dances at Crabby Steve's hall, including military men from the nearby Gimli Air Base who had time on their hands and

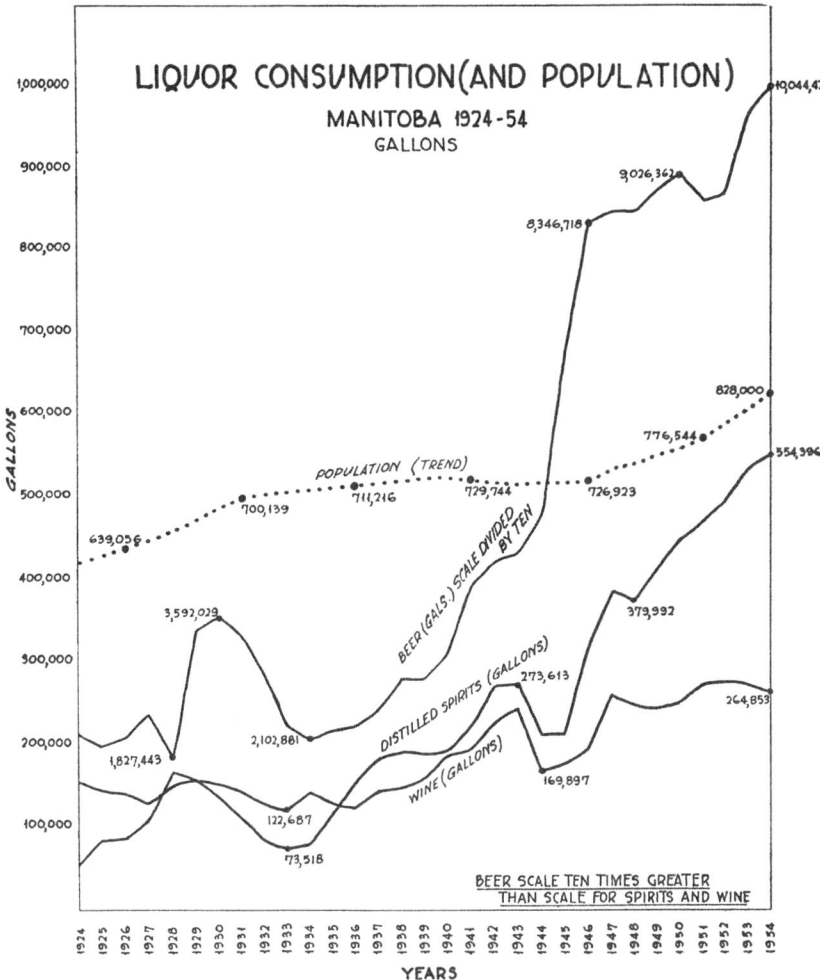

LIQUOR CONSUMPTION (AND POPULATION)
MANITOBA 1924-54
GALLONS

GALLONS (y-axis): 1,000,000 / 900,000 / 800,000 / 700,000 / 600,000 / 500,000 / 400,000 / 300,000 / 200,000 / 100,000

10,044,424

9,026,362

8,346,718

828,000

776,544

POPULATION (TREND)

711,216

700,139

729,744

726,923

554,396

639,056

BEER (GALS.) SCALE DIVIDED BY TEN

3,592,029

DISTILLED SPIRITS (GALLONS)

373,992

273,613

2,102,881

WINE (GALLONS)

264,853

1,827,443

122,687

169,897

73,518

BEER SCALE TEN TIMES GREATER
THAN SCALE FOR SPIRITS AND WINE

YEARS: 1924 1925 1926 1927 1928 1929 1930 1931 1932 1933 1934 1935 1936 1937 1938 1939 1940 1941 1942 1943 1944 1945 1946 1947 1948 1949 1950 1951 1952 1953 1954

This chart of statistics on the annual consumption of wine, beer, and distilled liquor by Manitobans, between 1924 and 1954, shows the marked increases that occurred in the late 1940s, disproportionate to provincial population, as wartime rationing ended. REPORT OF THE MANITOBA LIQUOR ENQUIRY COMMISSION, 1955, PAGE 239, LEGISLATIVE LIBRARY OF MANITOBA

ample disposable income. It was a chance to meet local girls and unwind. In preparing to write this chapter, I spoke with numerous people with fond memories of Crabby Steve's in particular and the dance hall culture in general. There were common elements to many of their stories. The code of conduct seems to have been that, like in Las Vegas, "what happens at Crabby's, stays at Crabby's." Hijinks and uninhibited behavior occurred on the dance floor and also outside behind the hall. Fistfights broke out spontaneously over romantic complications, masculine posturing, or perceived slights over one's place of residence or ethnicity. Fights were usually fuelled by generous consumption of beer dispensed from the trunk of someone's car, as well as locally produced moonshine. The highly alcoholic, distilled liquor goes by numerous nicknames—including Hooch, Stone Pile's Finest, Apple Pie, White Soup, Baba's Medicine, and many others— and was usually made in someone's home or barn. The making of moonshine was illegal but widely tolerated and enjoyed. According to family members, Crabby Steve did not make moonshine but his dance hall sat at an epicentre of moonshining in Manitoba.

For generations, Manitobans have held firm views, pro and con, on alcohol consumption. Provincial votes in favour of Prohibition, in 1892 (the first in Canada) and 1898, had not been enforced, partly because the government received considerable tax revenue from the sale of liquor, and a third referendum in 1902 was narrowly defeated because advocates from such organizations

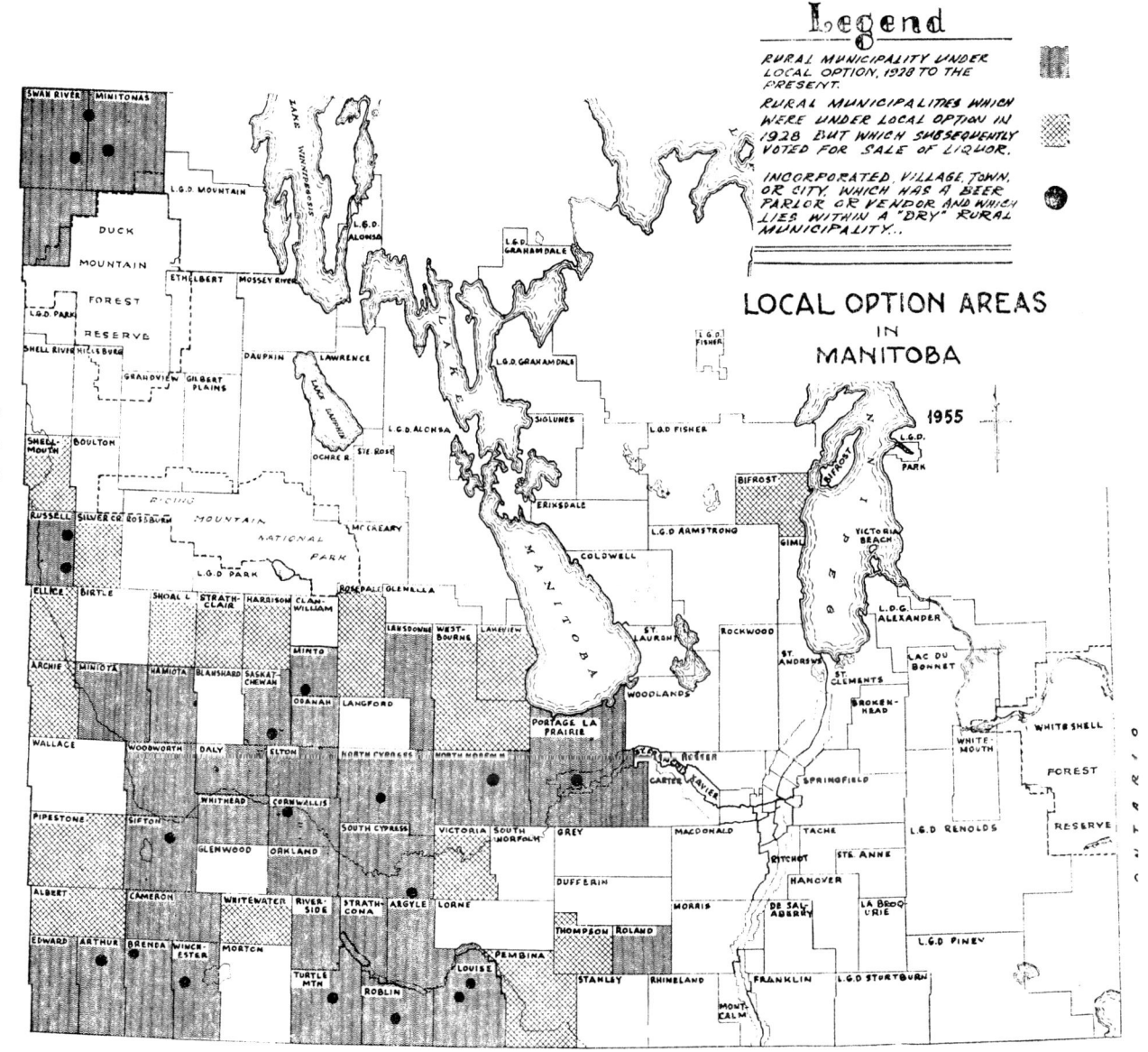

LOCAL OPTION AREAS IN MANITOBA

1955

In June 1927, Manitobans in 23 municipalities—mostly in the southwestern part of the province—voted to ban the local sale of liquor. Some of them subsequently rescinded the vote and became "wet." By 1955, when this map was drawn, several municipalities that were officially "dry" contained towns that were wet. REPORT OF THE MANITOBA LIQUOR ENQUIRY COMMISSION, 1955, PAGE 262, LEGISLATIVE LIBRARY OF MANITOBA

as the Women's Christian Temperance Union and the Royal Templars of Temperance boycotted it. Through the late 19th and early 20th centuries, women (who typically bore the brunt of alcoholic men's behaviour) became an increasingly powerful political force, especially after gaining the right to vote in provincial elections in 1916. That year, the government of Tobias Norris finally enacted legislation to enforce, with a few carefully worded exceptions, Prohibition throughout the province. Prosecutions under the Manitoba Temperance Act put numerous Manitobans behind bars (for example, 117 of them in 1923, roughly one-tenth of the total prison population) and generated substantial revenue for the government from the levied fines ($188,035 in 1923). Alcohol was only permitted for "industrial, scientific, mechanical, artistic, sacramental or medicinal" purposes, although interpretations of these uses were defined liberally. In the seven-year period before the legislation was finally repealed in 1923, and liquor sales resumed under tight government control of sales, advertising, and pricing, there was never any real shortages in the supply of alcohol, mainly because there were so many points of illegal production.

Making high-strength alcohol at home is fairly easy. According to my friend "Alfred," an avid distiller who will, for obvious reasons, remain anonymous, you add five kilograms of refined, white sugar to a pail of tap water then add bread or brewer's yeast. At room temperature, over a period of ten to fourteen days, the yeast converts the sugar to ethanol (aka grain alcohol). Then, a simple

distillation apparatus made from two nested pails uses electric heat over a period of 24 hours to boost the alcohol content of the raw ethanol "mash" until it is 50 to 60 percent pure. An optional second distillation step, taking another 24 hours, removes further impurities that impart undesirable flavours. (The home distiller must be careful not to allow methanol, also known as wood alcohol, into the final product, as it can cause blindness and even death.) This double-distilled stock is usually diluted down to 38 to 40 percent ethanol—about the same as commercially-produced liquor—using purified water then, as desired, flavouring agents can be added. Otherwise, the new brew, made in sixteen days at a cost of $10, produces about 5 litres of mostly colourless, mild-tasting liquor that reminds me of vodka. In the old days, the source of sugar might have been potatoes, barley, or other plant material, and the distillation step involved more complex hardware, but the basic process—and the end result—was the same. The economic motive to make your own liquor is obvious, especially if you are intending to take the highly illegal step, as many did, of selling it.

A retired Winnipeg police officer (who I will call "James" to preserve his anonymity) told me racy stories of moonshining in the Interlake. He recalls a magazine article from the late 1940s in which the village of Meleb was dubbed the "home brewing capital of North America." He contends that many a house was built, store was bought, or children were sent to college from the proceeds of moonshining. His grandfather had been among those

Crabby Steve's Dance Hall, May 1981. ED LEDOHOWSKI

who made a tidy living through the production and sale of moonshine. Some of his product was sold directly to consumers, in the form of stubby six-ounce pop bottles of moonshine sold for a dollar apiece. It was sold while he and his aunt peddled farm produce door-to-door to cottages in Gimli. Occasionally, one of the cottagers would ask if they had something "a little stronger." His grandfather also sold moonshine intended for resale. He might deliver, for example, two gallons of brew to a hotel owner in a three-gallon jug, for which he would be paid four dollars per gallon. The hotelier would then add a gallon of water to dilute the product and increase the profit margin. His grandfather had a strict policy, however, against selling his product to Indigenous people, arguing that "they have enough trouble already," though they were unable to consume liquor in licensed premises (until 1960) and legal consumption was not permitted on reserves (until 1985).

Interestingly, despite the widespread home-brewing phenomenon in Manitoba, there have been almost no scholarly studies on the practice. One of the few was a paper written in the 1970s by James, then an undergraduate student in geography at the University of Winnipeg.

The dance floor was full when a reunion at Crabby Steve's hall in February 1984 was filmed for a CBC television documentary. Crabby Steve is in the centre of the photo, dancing with the woman in blue. CANADIAN BROADCASTING CORPORATION

record, all copies of the student paper have disappeared over the years. However, concrete documentation of the RCMP's actions to curb illegal brewing come from a series of maps made using James' research by his academic supervisor, Dr. Jim Richtik, and a small collection of RCMP Annual Reports held by the Legislative Library of Manitoba. Those maps and reports provide fascinating insight into the practice of moonshining and measures taken by the police to thwart it.

Manitobans have had a longtime love for moonshine, which may explain why, when the provincial government held a Commission of Enquiry on the state of alcohol consumption in the mid-1950s, the annual totals for wine, beer, and spirits were all lower than the national average—the statistics did not include illicit consumption for which Manitobans were renowned. The RCMP Annual Report for 1954 provides supporting evidence. At that time, Manitoba was the number one moonshining province in Canada

He was given unprecedented access to notes taken by officers in the RCMP's D Division (whose jurisdiction covers Manitoba and northwestern Ontario) in the course of their investigations of moonshining around the province. (The RCMP and Winnipeg Police's morality squad took over responsibility for enforcing liquor laws from the provincial government in 1942.) Unfortunately for the historical

and "seizures in those two provinces [Manitoba and Quebec] accounted for 49 per cent of stills, 76 per cent of the illicit spirits and 83 per cent of the total gallonage of beer and mash seized." Between 1952 and 1972, police officers investigated over 4,000 cases of illegal moonshining in Manitoba, averaging some 350 cases a year. They seized 976 illegal stills around the province, including 347 in 1966 alone, representing up to nearly one-third of the *national* total of seizures. During the same period, they confiscated 6,989 gallons of illicit spirits. The lengths to which Manitoba moonshiners would go to conceal their operation can be inferred from a case described in the RCMP's 1968 Annual Report:

On Jan. 10, 1968, RCMP seized a commercial-type still at St. Vital, Manitoba, situated in a building which appeared to be a commercial garage. The building was divided into three separate rooms. The first served as a garage while the latter two were used to store farm produce. On visual examination there was no indication of a still in the building, but during the search it was noticed that a freezer along the east wall of the garage was mounted on rollers. Moving this freezer out from the wall revealed a hole in the cement floor leading to an underground room housing the still. This discovery was made even more difficult as the chimney pipe from the oil burner of the still and the "wash fumes" were drawn into the main chimney for the oil furnace which heated the building proper. This of course, accounted for the lack of odor. The residue from the cooker was pumped out of the building by means of

a sump pump through a hole in the wall approximately three feet underground and eventually fed to a nearby river. Three persons arrested at the site were convicted and fines totalling $6,000 were imposed.

The RCMP statistics do not reveal *where*, and by *whom*, the moonshining was being done. The James and Richtik maps fill in these details, showing a possible ethnic and cultural dimension to moonshining in Manitoba. Taking 1954 as a representative year, the map of still seizures by the RCMP shows five areas of greatest concentration: 1) southern Manitoba centred around the Rural Municipality of Stuartburn, 2) south of Lake Winnipeg in the RMs of St. Clements, Brokenhead, and Springfield, 3) the Interlake in the RMs of Rockwood and Armstrong, 4) a wide swath south of Riding Mountain National Park in the former RMs of Rossburn, Shoal Lake, Strathclair, and Harrison, and 5) most of the RMs surrounding Lake Dauphin as far north as the RM of Mountain. These areas correspond almost perfectly to the parts of Manitoba settled predominantly by Ukrainians and Poles. These country-folk brought to Canada a tradition of moonshining and the remoteness of their new farms in Manitoba (meaning a limited police presence and access to legally sanctioned alcohol sources), combined with an abundance of raw materials for brewing, fostered the tradition in the New World.

Just as the socially conservative area of southern Manitoba is sometimes referred to as our "Bible Belt,"

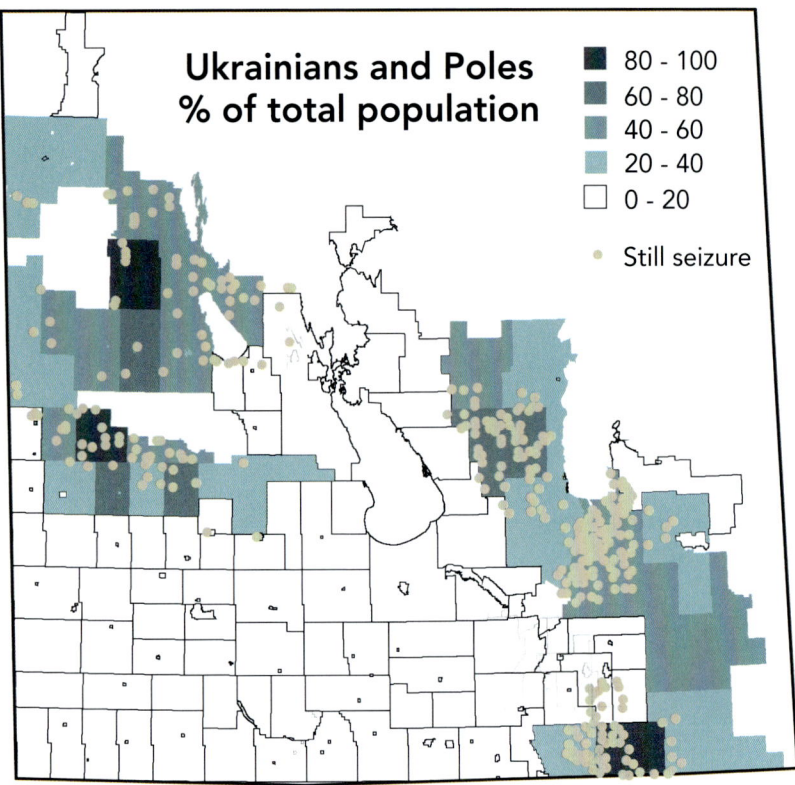

Ukrainians and Poles % of total population

- 80 - 100
- 60 - 80
- 40 - 60
- 20 - 40
- 0 - 20

• Still seizure

Where you had Manitobans of Ukrainian or Polish descent, there was homemade liquor. The greatest concentrations of illegal stills seized by the RCMP in 1954 correlated with the regions of rural Manitoba settled predominantly by Ukrainians and Poles, based on ethnicity data from the 1961 Canadian census. Crabby Steve's dance hall was smack in the middle of a cluster of seizures in the Interlake region. REDRAWN FROM A MAP COMPILED BY JIM RICHTIK, DANNY HUTCH, AND GEOFF THOMPSON, FROM RCMP FILES

we might call these five regions of Manitoba our "Booze Belt," for its permissive attitude about liquor in general and moonshining in particular. This view seems to have been different elsewhere in the province, especially in the areas settled by Anglophone Protestants. In a referendum held

by the provincial government in 1927, all of the constituencies in southwestern Manitoba voted to go "dry" while the Booze Belt resolutely remained "wet." Southwestern Manitoba would remain mostly dry well into the 1950s, at least in principle, although several dry municipalities contained separately incorporated towns that voted to go wet so thirsty country-folk could simply head into town to wet their whistles. Looking again at that map, however, I have a hard time believing that no moonshining occurred anywhere in "dry" parts of Manitoba, as suggested by the absence of still seizures in the region outside of the Booze Belt. I wonder if the correlation between seizures and the predominance of Slavic settlers is the result of what we now call racial profiling? If everyone, especially the police, assumed that Slavs were avid moonshiners, the only places to be searched might have been those occupied by Slavs. Even today, this biased view of Slavic Manitobans persists; nearly everyone to whom I showed a draft of the map said they were not surprised by it.

By the 1980s, diverse new opportunities for public recreation, combined with diminished interest of a youthful generation in dancing as a social form, contributed to the demise of public dance halls. In February 1984, Crabby Steve held a reunion dance for 350 people from far and wide who came to renew old acquaintances and refresh memories of youthful good times. Hot dogs and soft drinks were ten cents each and entertainment was provided by a local band called the Brushcutters (probably named for their haircuts). A crew from CBC Television was on hand to capture the event for a documentary that aired in March 1986. The reunion was one of the last events held at Crabby's place. A final dance in November 1987 raised funds for development of a public park in nearby Komarno around a monument of a metal mosquito that riffs on the fact that settlers to the area gave it a Polish name translating to "full of mosquitoes."

Time has not been kind to Crabby Steve's dance hall over the 34 years since the reunion in 1984. By the time that I visited it early last spring, the building looked as though a giant had used it as seat that could not support his weight, and squashed it flat. Jolly Wally's dance hall fared even worse; it is gone altogether. Fortunately, in early 2015, soon after Steve Maksymyk's death at the age of 91, CBC's documentary was made freely available online. In it, we see a middle-aged Maksymyk standing with a broad smile on his face as dancers propel themselves around the floor to the lively tunes of a fiddle-and-accordion band. We observe people "seeing old friends, exchanging old lies, and talking old romances." Inevitably, we see a few revellers sneaking swigs of "liquid courage" from a flask concealed in a coat pocket. As long as that wonderful video survives, along with the remains of Crabby Steve's along Highway 7, the role that dance halls once played in the social lives of rural Manitobans will live forever in our collective memory. Meanwhile, the proud tradition of moonshining lives on. My friend Alfred—along with many of his neighbours—distills his own spirits despite its continued illegality in an era of relaxed regulation of rules on commercially-produced beer, wine, and hard liquor. He does it not because he cannot afford higher-cost commercial booze, but because he enjoys the challenge of making his low-cost alternative for his family and friends (free of charge, I must stress). What frugal Manitoban does not like a good deal, regardless of their ethnicity and views on booze?

Jolly Wally's Rangeland, June 1978. ED LEDOHOWSKI

ACKNOWLEDGEMENTS

This chapter benefitted enormously from numerous shares. Many people of a "certain age" shared their stories about good times at Crabby Steve's and other dance halls around Manitoba. Ed Ledohowski shared his photos of abandoned dance halls. Alfred and James shared their experiences, good and bad, with home-made liquor. Retired geographer Jim Richtik shared his exceptionally rare maps of still seizures by the RCMP while his colleague Jock Lehr shared a great, albeit macabre, story about a flock of domestic geese near Stuartburn—one of five regions in the Booze Belt—that ate grain from fermenting mash. Several friends familiar with moonshine (wink, wink) shared some of its many nicknames.

Emerson
Fox Barn

Several years ago, I found an arresting photo at the provincial archives. Taken somewhere in Manitoba around 1910, it showed a man proudly standing on a piece of farm machinery behind a shiny new tractor. Three horses lay on the ground in the background, their heads drooped in what seemed like a sad, dejected pose. I wondered if they realized that the tractor meant their necessity in farm operations was nearing an end? By this time, Manitoba farmers had begun to seek ways of farming with greater efficiency so they could produce the maximum amount of food per acre. One way they achieved this efficiency was to replace horse-drawn equipment with machinery powered by steam or gasoline engines. Unlike horses, tractors could work all day, never needed to rest, and had a longer lifespan. This trend toward increasing farm mechanization is illustrated nicely by that great photo, but also by a curious little barn that stands forlornly near the Red River at Emerson. It existed, in part, because of a glut of horses made obsolete by tractors.

In 1920, Manitoba had 306,329 horses, compared to the human population of 610,000, or about one horse for every two people. As the pace of farm mechanization quickened through the 1920s and 1930s, fewer horses were needed on the farm. A 1948 Annual Report from the Manitoba Department of Agriculture and Immigration observed:

Horses are becoming fewer and fewer each year, with less than 200,000 horses on Manitoba farms, and a large percentage of them in the upper years bracket, and correspondingly few in the lower years bracket. One wonders if we are not fast approaching a horseless farm practice. I still feel there is a place for a horse or two on an average farm. Most certainly that is true during the winter months, when snow renders mechanical travel quite impotent.

Manitoba's horse population peaked at 419,789 in 1921 then began a slow decline through the 1930s, rebounded slightly during the Second World War—when horses were put back to work to save fuel for the war effort—then plummeted. As of 2010, there were around 58,000 horses in Manitoba, a decline of 80 percent from 1920. What happened to all the unneeded horses? Along with old horses that were no longer able to work, they were

Horses reclining near a tractor, circa 1910. ARCHIVES OF MANITOBA

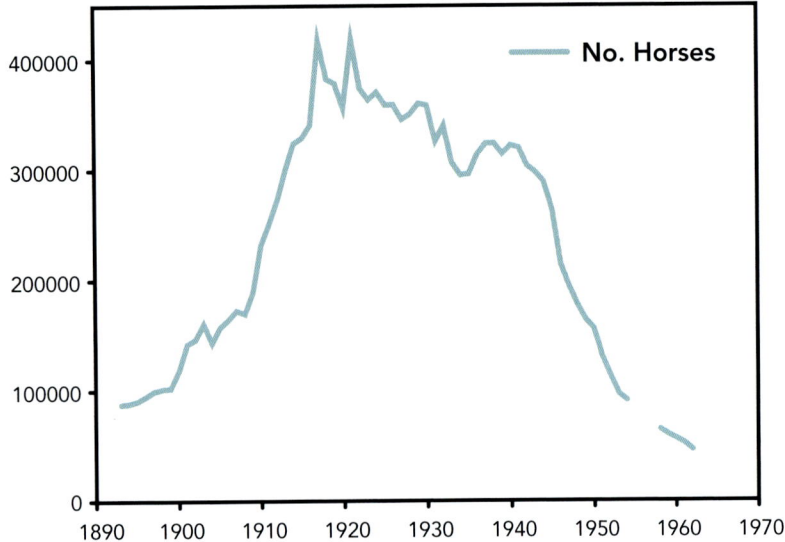

Horses were once an essential part of Manitoba agriculture. From around 100,000 horses in 1900, their numbers grew dramatically through the 1910s, peaking in 1921, then declining slowly until 1940 when their numbers plummeted. DRAWN FROM ANNUAL REPORTS OF THE MANITOBA DEPARTMENT OF AGRICULTURE AND IMMIGRATION, LEGISLATIVE LIBRARY OF MANITOBA

"put out to pasture" which, in most cases, meant they were sold to slaughterhouses. Most of the resulting horsemeat was not intended for human consumption—there has been a long-standing taboo against it, at least in much of Canada and the US—but as food for other farm animals.

Manitoba has a long history in the fur trade, going back to 1670 with the establishment of the Hudson's Bay Company. In those early days, the fur came from wild animals trapped by indigenous people as a source of income and food. In the early 20th century, entrepreneurs saw an opportunity to raise wild animals in captivity as a way of supplementing the fur supply. They began to raise fox

(a relative of dogs and wolves) and mink (in a group with weasels, otters, and ferrets) on farms where they could breed them in much the same way as domestic livestock. In 1920, there were two fur farms in Manitoba, containing 152 animals in total. By 1933, there were 328 fur farms. One of these farms, in the RM of Hanover, had 100 female foxes, each in a wire-enclosed pen that gave it some degree of freedom to run around. Amongst the pens was a small building with a tall, narrow tower protruding through its roof. During the breeding season in late January or early February, fox farmers sat in these fox towers to keep watch on their breeding programs. Each morning, a male fox would be moved into a female's pen and, if mating occurred, he would be moved to another pen the next morning. If mating did not occur, he would stay to try again. The breeding season ended about one month after it started. Born in the spring, the young fox would be turned into a pelt by December of that same year.

Manitoba's fur farming industry thrived, peaking at 996 farms in 1940. In the mid-1920s, top male and female breeding stock was being exported from Manitoba farms to Sweden for as much as $1,500 per animal ($21,000 in today's dollars). Prime fox pelts were commanding prices of up to $300 and $400 each ($4,000 to $5,500). To support the growing industry, in late 1936 the provincial government established a Fur and Game Experimental Station at the University of Manitoba, one of only two in Canada (the other was at Summerside, PEI) to research disease control and animal nutrition. By that time,

fur farms generated one-third of Canada's total fur sales. In 1946, the station's staff of pathologists and veterinarians helped to host a week-long Manitoba Open Live Fox and Mink Show in a building in downtown Winnipeg where farmers displayed 1,100 of their top animals.

Unlike cattle and other domestic animals, which are herbivores and can therefore be fed grain and hay, fox and mink are carnivores. A 1962 report to the Manitoba government noted that farmed mink were fed a diet of 70% meat (10% liver, 20% fish, 20% packing house scraps, and 20% horsemeat) with the remainder made up by oatmeal, cracked wheat, and corn meal. Just before they were pelted, foxes were fed whole chunks of meat—heart, tripe, or horsemeat—to improve the lustre of their coat. It took 7,000 tons of meat to produce 200,000 mink pelts in a year. That is a lot of meat … and a lot of bones to discard. At Delta Marsh, where I used to work, there is a small body of water called Bone Pile Pond, so called because, many decades ago,

Winnipeg socialite Della Lemon took this photo of fox at a Manitoba fur farm in the early 20th century. ARCHIVES OF MANITOBA

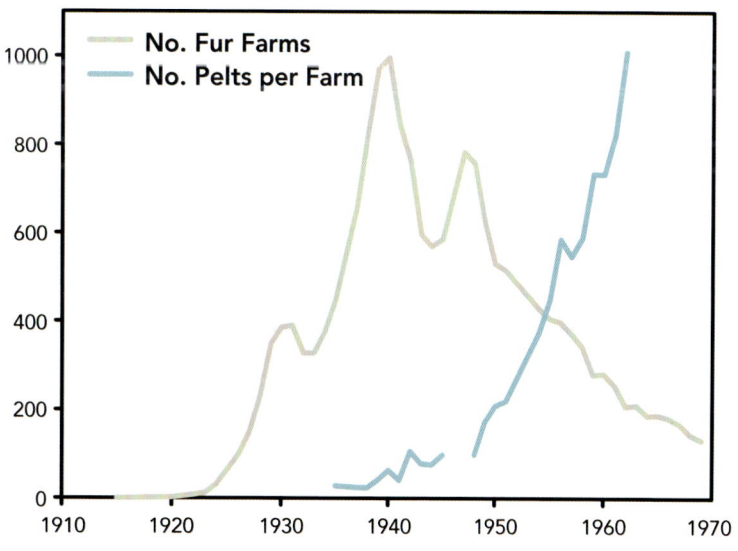

The number of fur farms in Manitoba declined with "bad news" events such as the start of the Great Depression and the outbreak of the Second World War, but peaked in the late 1930s and following the war. Through the 1950s and early 1960s, fewer fur farms produced more pelts until the output stabilized in the late 1960s. DRAWN FROM ANNUAL REPORTS: 1930–1969, GAME (WILDLIFE) BRANCH, MANITOBA DEPARTMENT OF MINES AND NATURAL RESOURCES, MANITOBA LEGISLATIVE LIBRARY

Disappearing Prairie Barns

At one time, many Manitoba farms raised livestock in addition to whatever crops they might grow, what is known as a mixed farm. A visible sign of a mixed farm was a farmyard containing granaries for storing the crops and a barn for the animals. Crops provided revenue while the animals provided essential labour (for example, horses pulled farm equipment), meat (chicken, pork, beef), and other food products (eggs, milk, butter). Barns provided a place where farm animals could be housed during adverse weather or when females were delivering their young, or when predators were present. Barns also provided a place to store food for the animals. Both sides of my family were mixed farmers and most of their neighbours were mixed farmers too. My grandparents were largely self-sufficient, needing only a few store-bought products such as coffee and sugar that they could not grow in their fields or garden. Today, however, farms often have granaries or barns, but not both, as the nature of agriculture is changing.

In the early 1980s, a weekly series in the *Manitoba Co-operator* farm newspaper featured photographs of photogenic or historically interesting barns around the province taken by journalist Bob Hainstock, along with

Recent photos of four barns featured in Bob Hainstock's 1985 book *Barns of Western Canada*. The unique twelve-sided Hill Barn west of Portage la Prairie was built in 1907 for Kansas-born Armand Hill. Before returning to the USA, he sold it to the Batters family. Re-sold to the Bruce family in 1943, it was still in their hands when I visited in July 2014. GORDON GOLDSBOROUGH

information on the barn's architecture provided by historian Ed Ledohowski. In 1985, Hainstock published the best-selling book *Barns of Western Canada* that included barns from the *Co-operator* series along with ones in Saskatchewan and Alberta. A few years ago, I learned that an acquaintance from my work life was related to Bob Hainstock, now living in retirement in eastern Canada, and she put me in touch with him. I spoke with him about my admiration of his book, and we mutually speculated on how many of the barns were still standing. He suggested that I contact the editor of the *Co-operator* to see if they would be interested in re-running photos from the series with a "Is it surviving?" tag line, and generously shipped me a large collection of colour

The Izon Barn west of Dauphin, seen here in May 2014, was built in the early 1920s by Hubert Izon, an English First World War veteran who had been gassed and wounded in France. Timber came from the Riding Mountains to the south and spaces between the logs were filled with a mixture of lime and horsehair. The barn was sold to municipal reeve John Potoski in 1959. GORDON GOLDSBOROUGH

One of Manitoba's largest barns at 14,000 square feet was built in 1915 near St. Jean Baptiste for American land developer John Kane. Cattle were housed on its lowest level. Horses were on the second level and hay was stored in the top level. Later purchased by the Hamblin family, the barn was owned by the fourth generation when this photo was taken in June 2017. ERIC DE SCHEPPER

photographs for digital scanning. The *Co-operator* was interested and the series began in late 2014.

Over the course of the next 15 months, we featured photos of 85 barns, of which we were able to learn what happened to just 28, or about one-third. What about the other two-thirds? Maybe those barns have disappeared in the past 35 years since they were photographed by Bob Hainstock. Of the 28 barns whose fate we learned, two-thirds were still standing and one-third had either collapsed under their own weight or were demolished. What this tells us is that the era of the family mixed farm is coming to an end as farms become increasingly specialized to produce a narrower range of products: crops or animals but not both. Increasingly, farmers are getting their food from the same places as the rest of us: grocery stores.

The Reeves Barn in the Municipality of Riverdale was built of fieldstones in the late 19th century. Owned initially by Ernest Reeves, a wealthy Englishman, it was taken over by Thomas Sibbald and his family around 1910. Still standing proudly when photographed in 1990, when it was designated as a municipal heritage building, the barn was mostly fallen when I was there in May 2013. GORDON GOLDSBOROUGH

there was a mink farm nearby. The farmer used a disproportionately large amount of horse meat, obtained from other farmers that had mostly converted to tractors, to feed his animals, and the leftover bones were discarded near the pond.

Foxes were expensive to raise, about four to five times as much as mink, needing more food and space. Over time, fox farmers began switching to mink, which furriers and fashionistas seemed to prefer. The number of fur farms declined through the 1950s but the number of pelts they produced increased proportionately. By 1960, there were 242 mink farms in Manitoba, producing about 950 pelts each, and mink accounted for over 99% of the fur. By the 1980s, there are only seven fox fur farms still operating in Manitoba: at Arborg, Cartwright, Gilbert Plains, Leaf Rapids, Lundar, Lynn Lake, and Sperling. In October 1987, on what came to be known as "Black Monday," the stock market crashed and destroyed much of the discretionary income that drove the fur market.

By 1995, few fur farms were left. However, the cause of the "fur crash of 1987" was not purely financial, which probably explains why the fur industry never fully rebounded. The demand for fur fell due to a growing public perception that trapping or rearing wild animals solely for their fur was inhumane. Today, Manitoba has a handful of mink farms and no fox farms. In fact, there are few fox farms anywhere in North America. The greatest concentration of them is in Scandinavia.

There is nothing left of the mink farm near Bone Pile Pond. Of the once abundant fox farms that existed around Manitoba, I have found only three fox towers during my travels in search of historic places. One, built in 1919, is near Stonewall in the Rural Municipality of Rockwood, on what is now the site of a family-owned berry farm. A second tower in the Rural Municipality of Hanover was built in 1936 and the third, near the Assiniboine River, immediately north of Emerson, is perhaps the oldest surviving fox tower in Manitoba, built in 1911. Wayne Arseny, an historian at Emerson who has made a special study of the fox tower there, has been unable to identify who built the tower, only that he believes they farmed fox in Nova Scotia, where there was an abundance of fish to feed their stock, before coming to Manitoba. Whatever the origin, the Emerson fox tower is a curiously striking building, different from most other farm structures, and it reminds us of a bygone time when wild animals were farmed for their fur.

OPPOSITE A chimney inside an abandoned fox barn near Emerson, July 2017. GORDON GOLDSBOROUGH

ACKNOWLEDGEMENTS

Wayne Arseny is a force of nature when it comes to promoting the history and heritage of the Emerson area. I would have never known about the Emerson Fox Barn—and a lot of other sites—if not for him. Glen Suggett and Dean Berezanski of the Wildlife Branch at Manitoba Sustainable Development provided historical data on fox pelt sales in Manitoba. I thank Bob and Meagan Hainstock for their help in documenting the decline in Manitoba barns between the early 1980s and now.

Bowsman
Biffy Burn
Monument

Abandonment can take many forms. In most cases, an actual structure or site is involved and there is a general sense of sadness or remorse for what has been lost. But sometimes the abandonment is a symbol for something we have left behind and it can be a joyful experience. The best example I can offer is a monument at Bowsman, a pile of simple stones topped with a model of a small building. When I rolled into Bowsman a few years ago, intent on mapping the locations of all monuments in the area, it caught my eye and I walked over to find out more about it. The little building was especially curious. What was it? As I looked more closely, I realized it was an outhouse, known by some as a privy, or, as my grandmother used to call it, a biffy. These small buildings, where people would go to "do their business," were once ubiquitous throughout Manitoba. Regardless of subzero weather, hordes of mosquitoes, or cloying stench, everyone had to patronize the biffy regularly. On realizing what I had found, my first thought was "Why would someone dedicate a monument to a stinky outdoor toilet?" Therein lies the story of sewage treatment in the early 20th century.

In 1873, when Winnipeg was founded, modern sewer disposal was nonexistent. Inside their homes, Winnipeggers (and other Manitobans) typically had a small ceramic pot with a lid, called either a "chamber

In 1906, workers installed cast-iron sewer pipes under the 700 block of Rosser Avenue in downtown Brandon. MCGUINNESS COLLECTION, S. J. MCKEE ARCHIVES, BRANDON UNIVERSITY

pot" or, in more colourful language, a "thunder mug," stored under their beds. Outdoors, there was a biffy. It was usually built for as single occupant but occasionally sported multiple holes for several simultaneous users, and wastes were collected in a hole in the ground that, when full, was covered over with soil. Then, the biffy was moved above a newly dug hole nearby and the filling process began again. Several year ago, I was reminded of how common biffies had once been in Winnipeg when I was involved in a construction project at a residential property in a downtown part of the city, within eyesight of

Children play around an open "box closet" on Winnipeg's Jasper Avenue in 1906.
CITY OF WINNIPEG ARCHIVES

the provincial Legislative Building. As the workers dug a hole to construct a building foundation, they encountered extremely foul-smelling "soil" at the bottom of the hole. We concluded that the workers had broken into a buried biffy pit dating back over a century.

Thousands of Winnipeg residences and businesses had a biffy. In July 1883, Winnipeg's City Engineer, after carrying out a thorough survey, proposed to the city council the construction of a sewage system to supplement an existing line that ran down Main Street. Additional lines would be run along Assiniboine Street, Bannatyne Avenue, Logan Avenue, Selkirk Avenue, Higgins Street, and Spence Street. All of them would discharge raw sewage into the Red or Assiniboine rivers, to be whisked away, eventually into Lake Winnipeg and ultimately into

Hudson Bay, relying on the old maxim that "the solution to pollution is dilution." The very same rivers, along with public wells, were the primary sources of the city's drinking water. Infectious diseases such as typhus, associated with inadequate sanitation, were common. Between 1900 and 1904, the number of reported cases of typhus in Winnipeg ranged from 349 to 1,276, or about 110 cases per 10,000 residents. One-tenth of those cases resulted in death, a rate roughly triple that of cities in the US and Europe. I have always thought it ironic that Professor Edgar Kenrick, a chemist who did water testing of the Red and Assiniboine rivers for the federal government (and who, coincidentally, has a place in history as owner of the city's first automobile), died in January 1905 from typhus contracted from river water that he had tested.

Kenrick's death might have been the "final straw" that motivated the City of Winnipeg to address its typhus problem. Chicago-based bacteriologist and public health scientist Edwin Jordan was brought in to study the matter and suggest remedies. His report, tabled with the city council in February 1905, observed that:

> [T]he numerous outside privies, loosely constructed and with the contents freely exposed both to insects and to larger animals is a constant menace to the health of the city. … Children play in the alleys upon which these privies abut, and may readily soil their shoes, clothing and even fingers with infectious material. Dogs and other animals may convey infection into houses in ways that need not be specified. Perhaps the most mischievous carrier of

infection under the circumstances described is the common house-fly. It has been shown on more than one occasion that this pestiferous insect is a common purveyor of infection.

The Jordan report recommended the "abolition of the open outhouses" and avoidance of drinking river water. In response, the city council passed a new public health by-law in April 1906. It required all buildings on city streets serviced by water and sewer mains to be connected to them. Biffies at these buildings would henceforth be banned. (Buildings on streets not so equipped were, for the time being, exempt from this requirement.) The by-law also specified that each building must have at least one sink and one toilet, with an additional toilet (but, curiously, not

A map of the Greater Winnipeg Sanitary District, provided at the official opening of the city's sewage treatment plant on 25 October 1937, shows how the main sewer lines were in close proximity to the Red and Assiniboine rivers. MANITOBA MAPS BY LARRY LALIBERTE, HTTPS://WWW.FLICKR.COM/PHOTOS/MANITOBAMAPS

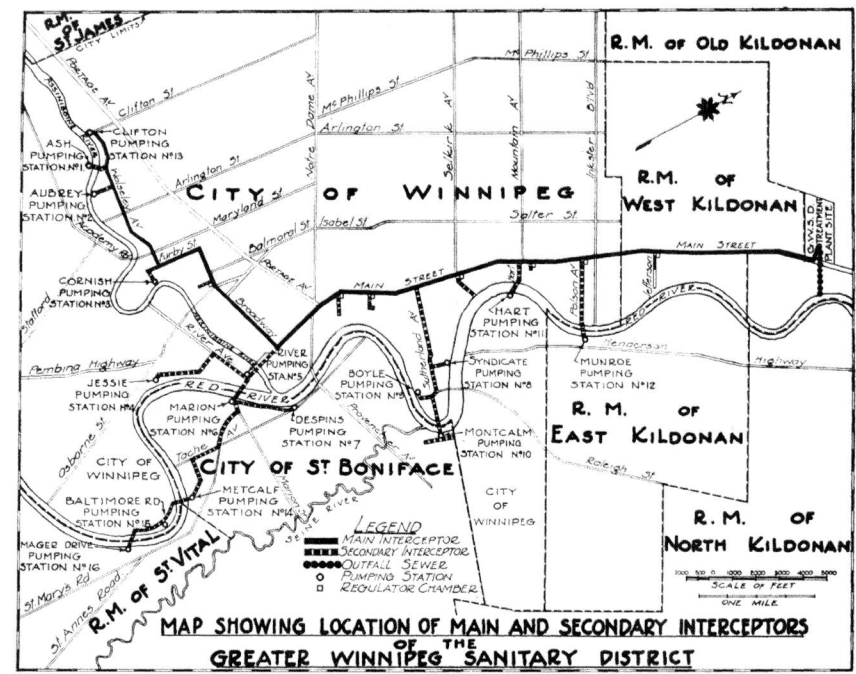

MAP SHOWING LOCATION OF MAIN AND SECONDARY INTERCEPTORS
OF THE
GREATER WINNIPEG SANITARY DISTRICT

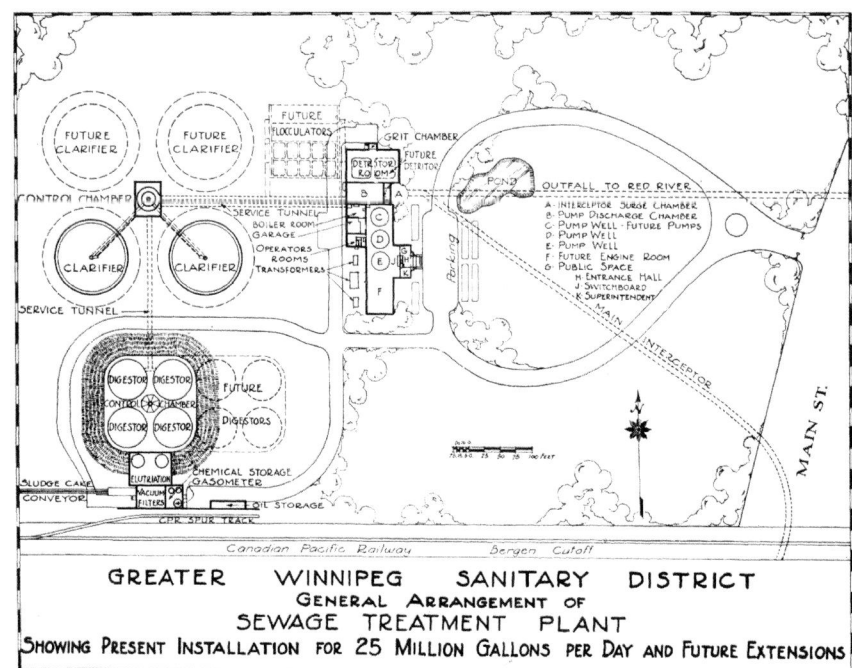

GREATER WINNIPEG SANITARY DISTRICT
GENERAL ARRANGEMENT OF
SEWAGE TREATMENT PLANT
SHOWING PRESENT INSTALLATION FOR 25 MILLION GALLONS PER DAY AND FUTURE EXTENSIONS

Headquarters of the Greater Winnipeg Sanitary District opposite Kildonan Park in northern Winnipeg, built between 1935 and 1937, seen here in July 1966. CITY OF WINNIPEG, HISTORICAL BUILDINGS AND RESOURCES COMMITTEE

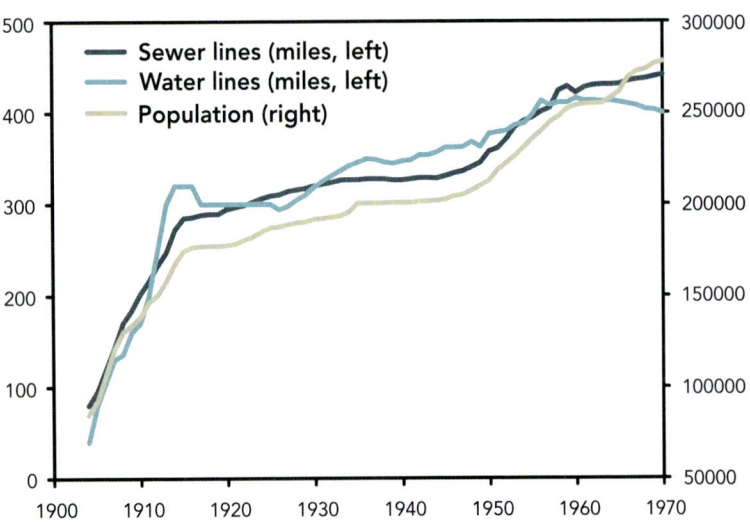

Miles of sewers in the City of Winnipeg, between 1904 and 1970. DRAWN FROM WINNIPEG MUNICIPAL MANUALS, 1904 TO 1971, CITY OF WINNIPEG ARCHIVES

an additional sink) for every twenty occupants. Owners of tenements, houses, boarding houses, hotels, restaurants, workshops, factories, stores, and offices were required to provide sinks and toilets for the use of tenants, lodgers, boarders, and workers. The facilities were required to be kept in "such cleanly and wholesome condition as not to be offensive, dangerous or detrimental to health." Conformance with the new rules was to be monitored by Health Officers having the power to levy fines. Ultimately, the system only ensured that sewage did not accumulate in back yards but was instead conveyed to the rivers, where raw untreated sewage continued to be dumped. This practice continued for the next 24 years. However, the new measures, combined with the construction of the Shoal Lake Aqueduct between 1915 and 1919 to provide the city with pure water, did address the typhus problem. From a high of 1,606 cases in 1905, the incidence of typhus dropped to an average of about 360 per year.

In 1930, Winnipeg's water pollution problem came to a head, so to speak. Residents began to complain that the Red and Assiniboine rivers stank because water flow had dropped during a period of drought so there was not enough water to dilute the sewage. In 1931, the city government hired engineer William S. Lea of Montreal (who also assisted in the design of the Slave Falls Generating Station on the Winnipeg River) to report on the problem. As the condition of the rivers grew worse in 1932 and 1933, the Manitoba government brought together representatives of the various municipalities surrounding

Winnipeg for a conference on sewage disposal. The group devised a plan for the disposal of raw sewage and a system to treat it. Through 1933 and 1934, engineers working under Lea's supervision studied the situation thoroughly. Finally, in March 1935, a bill to create the Greater Winnipeg Sanitary District (GWSD) passed the Provincial Legislature and was proclaimed into law that June. It was the first inter-municipal corporation established in Canada for the treatment of sewage. The GWSD included the City of Winnipeg and all of the contiguous municipalities, but the Act permitted any of them to withdraw within thirty days of its proclamation. Six municipalities opted out of the plan but three of them soon rejoined. The other three holdouts were forced to rejoin in 1955. By 1959, the GWSD consisted of the sister cities of Winnipeg and St. Boniface along with the Rural Municipality of Assiniboia, Village of Brooklands, City of East Kildonan, Rural Municipality of Fort Garry, City of St. James, Rural Municipality of North Kildonan,

In December 1966, the residents of Bowsman drove around town, picked up all the outhouses, and brought them to a central spot. GORDON GOLDSBOROUGH PHOTO COLLECTION, 2014-0021

Rural Municipality of St. Vital, Town of Transcona, Town of Tuxedo, and Rural Municipality of West Kildonan.

In July 1935, the provincial and federal governments commenced the project as an unemployment relief measure during the Great Depression, with the costs to be shared by the two governments and participating municipalities. The federal government contributed 40% of the cost while the Manitoba government kicked in 20%. The municipalities came up with the remaining 40% and had to assume 100% of costs for the purchase of land, administration, interest, and preliminary work. The first contract issued by the new GWSD, for a portion of the main interceptor sewer line— cast-iron pipes ranging in diameter from 2½ to 7½ feet—to run along Main Street, was awarded in August 1935. A few days later, Winnipeg Mayor John Queen broke ground for the line at the corner of Main Street and Pritchard Avenue. Other components of the main interceptor sewer network ran under Broadway, Furby Street, and Wolseley Avenue, with secondary interceptor lines following River Avenue, Tache Avenue, Sutherland Avenue, and Polson Avenue. Sixteen pumping stations were to be built at strategic spots to keep the wastewater flowing to a new sewage treatment plant, known today as the North End Water Pollution Control Centre. This plant, the showpiece of the system, was to be built on the west side of Main Street opposite Kildonan Park. Initially capable of handling 25 million gallons of sewage each day from the GWSD, it was designed with future expansion in mind. However, it provided only primary treatment of the sewage, essentially removing about half of the solid particles and a third of the dissolved organic matter. The "purified" water was dumped into the Red River, at the northern edge of the city, for the "enjoyment" of communities downstream.

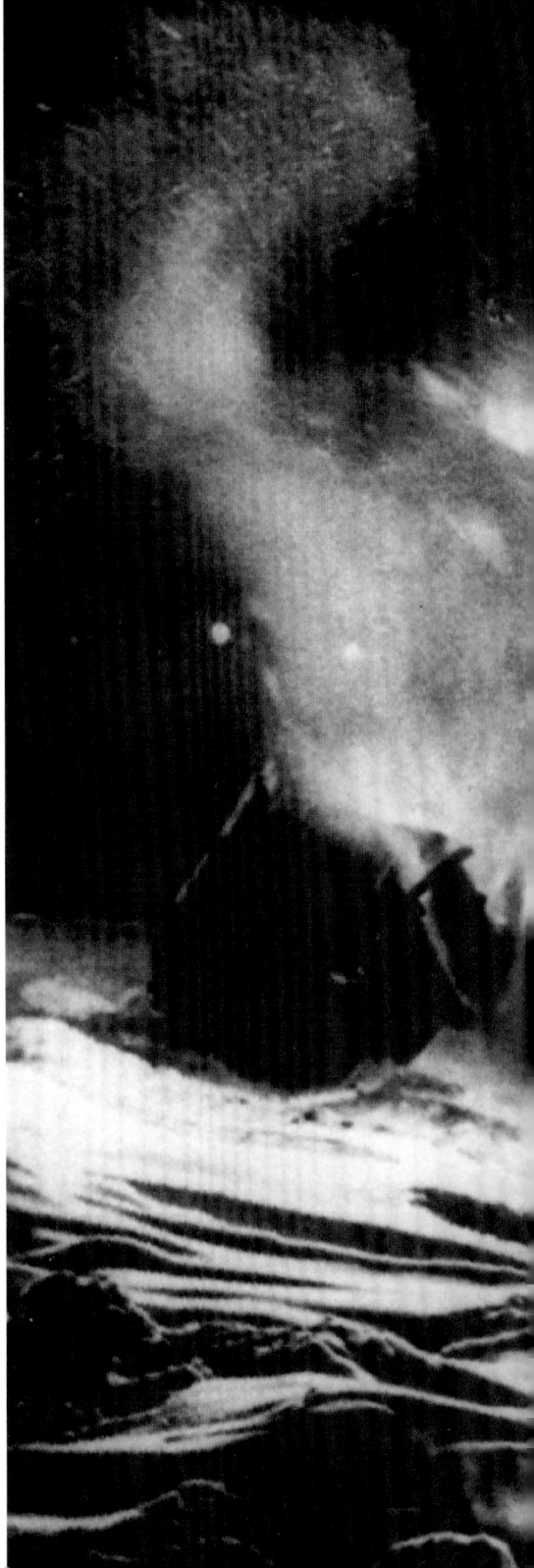

The Bowsman outhouses, collected near the new sewage treatment plant, were put to the torch to celebrate the town's leap into modernity. GORDON GOLDSBOROUGH PHOTO COLLECTION, 2014-0020.

By the end of the Second World War, the growing city was beginning to exceed the capabilities of its sewage plant, and the plant was having difficulty treating industrial wastes, especially those from the city's several meat packing plants. Engineers recommended that the plant be upgraded to handle up to 35 million gallons per day, thought to be sufficient to meet demand up to 1965. Expanded between 1953 and 1954, secondary treatment of sewage entailed aeration to introduce oxygen into the sewage. This stimulated bacteria and other microorganisms to break down more of the organic material. Methane and other gases emitted by the sewage was captured for use in heating the plant buildings and sewage-digester tanks. The plant also began to air-dry the digested sewage sludge at a site north of the city. A second plant, the South End Water Pollution Control Centre, was built on the south side of Winnipeg between 1972 and 1974 to receive 10 million gallons per day of wastewater from the southern parts of the newly-amalgamated Unicity, formed in January 1972. Like its northern predecessor, the southern plant used secondary treatment prior to discharging water into the Red River. Having spent my childhood in the Charleswood suburb of southwest Winnipeg, I can attest to the joys of a west wind that carried aromas emanating from five open-air sewage lagoons—three primary cells and two secondary cells— at the West End Water Pollution Control Centre. Built in 1964 to redirect raw sewage from the Assiniboine River, the lagoons have since been covered to the everlasting gratitude of noses in Charleswood. By the 1970s, there were 35 pumping stations pushing sewage through the lines to one of these three treatment facilities.

I compiled statistics on the extent of Winnipeg's sewer and water pipe networks from 1904, when the Jordan report drew attention to the necessity of better public sanitation, to 1971, when Winnipeg expanded through its merger with outlying municipalities. Not surprisingly, these statistics show that sewer and water service increased throughout this period, from a mere 70 miles in 1904 to 459 miles by 1971. The fastest rate of increase occurred in the first few years of the twentieth century when the city's population exploded. From 1914 onward, the expansion of the sewage collection system was more gradual, being more or less synchronized with growth in the city's population. The number of Winnipeggers served by one mile of sewer pipe has diminished somewhat over this period, from a high of 1,071 in 1905 to around 550 by the time of Unicity. Since then, the extent of Winnipeg's system has continued to increase so that, by 1999, the total stood at 3,427 miles of pipe or about 180 sewage-producers per mile. Winnipeg still employs secondary treatment of its wastewater and is balking at the enormous cost of tertiary treatment under which nutrients contributing to the massive growth of algae in Lake Winnipeg would be removed.

Numerous other communities in Manitoba have installed sewage collection systems, sometimes overcoming serious engineering challenges along the way. For example, at Flin Flon, collection pipes were installed in the late

1920s to replace "honey wagons" that had plied the streets to collect sewage manually. Because Flin Flon is underlain by solid rock, it was impossible to bury the sewer lines underground, as most communities do. This meant the lines would be subject to freezing during the cold Flin Flon winters. So engineers built a system in which above-ground pipes were housed in an innovative heated "sewer box" system that is still in use today, nearly a century later.

Let us return now to Bowsman, to the monument with a little biffy on top. Despite my initial scorn, I began to realize that I should not cast aspersions on the good folks of Bowsman. In October 1966, the 558 residents had proudly unveiled a new $350,000 sewage treatment plant. This meant they now had sewer lines that enabled most (but not all) homes in town to have an indoor toilet. Effective immediately, the biffies in town were rendered obsolete. On the 31st of December 1966, on the cusp of Canada's 100th birthday in 1967, trucks drove around Bowsman and collected 26 biffies, bringing them to a spot near the new sewage treatment plant. Then, townspeople cheered as their biffies were burned, symbolically eliminating these reminders of more primitive times. Three years later, for the 100th anniversary of Manitoba's entry into Confederation, Bowsmanites commemorated their leap into modernity. On Canada Day 1970, they erected the monument on the site of the biffy burning. If anyone understands their joy, it is me. Nearly 50 years later, I live on the edge of Winnipeg within city boundaries, but my home has neither municipal water nor sewage lines. The houses on my two-mile-long street are widely spaced and there simply are not enough of us (by my estimation, about 120 residents) to warrant the cost of installing the lines. Instead, I have two large, concrete tanks buried in my yard, one containing fresh water (hauled from a public filling station by truck) and one for sewage (whose contents are trucked to the south-end plant). I am continually worrying about them. Is the pump running? Has the pipe become clogged or frozen? When was the last time the tank was pumped? I have come to realize that Bowsman's Biffy Burn monument symbolizes an important transformation of life through the twentieth century. As more and more communities improved their sanitation systems, they gradually abandoned the biffies in the backyard in favour of convenient, clean flush toilets inside the house. This little cairn symbolizes the civic pride of the people of Bowsman when they abandoned the ways of the past and embraced modern sewage treatment, enjoying a luxury that many of us take for granted nowadays.

ACKNOWLEDGEMENTS

Sarah Ramsden of the City of Winnipeg Archives provided me with great information on the city's sewer system, starting with the 1905 Jordan report and the Municipal Manuals that the city has published annually since 1904. I love statistics, and those piles of slim little booklets provided a wealth of them. Jim Smith drew my attention to a great map of Winnipeg's sewer lines in 1937, a copy of which is available online thanks to the Herculean efforts of former University of Manitoba librarian Larry Laliberte.

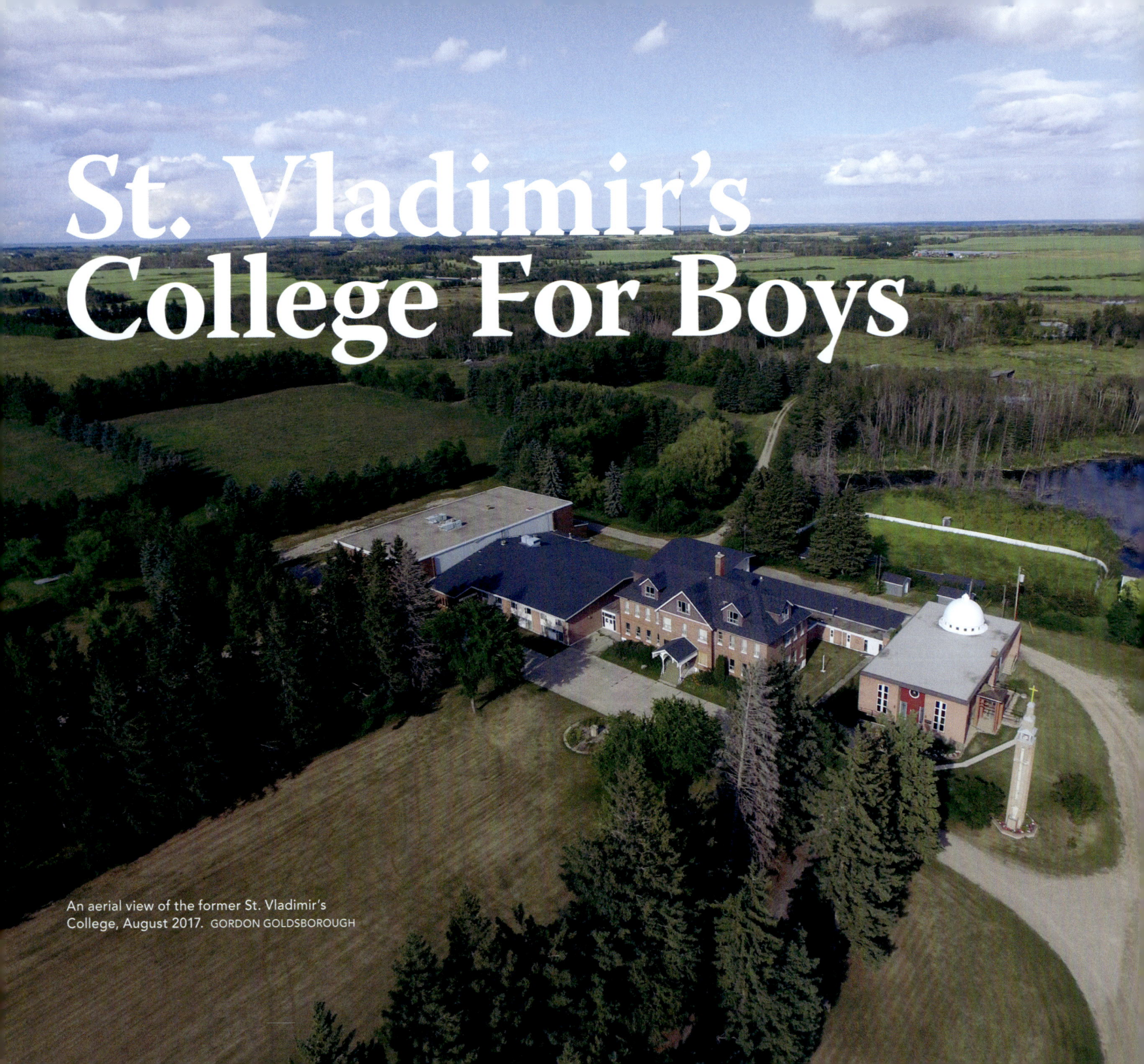

St. Vladimir's College For Boys

An aerial view of the former St. Vladimir's
College, August 2017. GORDON GOLDSBOROUGH

I attended public school for grades 1 through 12. So did my wife and our two kids. However, those wanting an education that is more grounded in culture or faith have, since before Manitoba was born, attended private schools. For 60 years, the St. Vladimir's College for Boys, known popularly as St. Vlads, operated in the town of Roblin. It was the only Ukrainian Catholic minor seminary (a facility for training teenaged candidates for the priesthood) and boarding school in Canada, and the only Catholic high school in Manitoba outside of Winnipeg. After St. Vlads closed in 2002, plans to turn it into a facility for English language instruction for international students never quite panned out. It is presently vacant and awaiting some new use.

In 1941, a group of Redemptorists, an order of Ukrainian Catholic priests and religious brothers of Ukrainian ethnicity, left their seminary at Yorkton, Saskatchewan to seek a quiet spot away from "the hustle and bustle of the big town." They travelled 50 miles east, to the smaller town of Roblin, where they purchased 160 acres of land nearby. They built a modest two-storey brick building at a cost of $40,000 (about $660,000 in today's dollars), and named it the Redemptorist Fathers College. The school opened in January 1942 with a group of seven students, in grades 8 to 10, transferred from Yorkton. Classes were instructed by the priests, who also conducted masses for several surrounding Ukrainian Catholic parishes, while the brothers made meals using products from their garden and farm (supplemented with perogies

and other fare donated by local parishioners) and cut trees in the surrounding woods to heat the building. Students paid $12 per month (today, about $180) for tuition, board, and room. During its first nine years of operation, until 1951, the college operated without formal accreditation and, as a result, its students were unable to graduate with a recognized high school education. Realizing this as a long-term impediment to its success, the college closed between 1951 and 1956 to enable a new group of Canadian-born priests to get teaching degrees needed to gain the accreditation. This allowed instruction using the standard provincial curriculum to be held in grades 9 to 12. When it reopened in 1956, the facility was renamed

Students play hockey on a rink behind the St. Vladimir's College, circa 1974. *OMICRON 1974*, ARCHEPARCHY OF WINNIPEG ARCHIVES

The original building of St. Vladimir's College, built by the Ukrainian Redemptorist Fathers in late 1941, as it appeared when I visited the site in June 2016. GORDON GOLDSBOROUGH

St. Vladimir's College in commemoration of the man who brought Christianity to Ukraine in 988.

The students of St. Vlads came from all over Manitoba and occasionally from other provinces, and in a few cases from New Jersey where the Redemptorists operated another college. Most of the classes were in the usual secular subjects— biology, chemistry, mathematics, geography, history, English, and social studies, but students could also take classes in "Basic Christian Themes," "World Religions," and "Christian Living." Although there was no requirement for students to be of Ukrainian descent, there was Ukrainian language instruction and Ukrainian dancing and folk arts. Music was an important part of the curriculum, and the school's choir toured widely in a used bus bought by a group of parents. The students were encouraged to be well-rounded physically as well as mentally, and to participate actively in track and field, soccer, basketball, volleyball, and badminton. The hockey program was especially prominent. The Fathers had hopes of imitating the success of a private, faith-based college at Wilcox, Saskatchewan that produced several NHLers. Initially, the boys skated on a nearby pond until, in the 1950s, a rink and changing room was built behind the college buildings. The present hockey rink dates to the mid-1970s. From the 1960s to 1980s, the St. Vlad's annual enrollment ranged between 40 and 50 students, peaking at 65 in 1975, with 13 to 15 graduates each year. An average of one student each year proceeded to the priesthood. The grade 9 program ended in 1981, after which instruction was only in grades 10 to 12.

Major expansions to the school's campus occurred in 1961. Early in the year, the first service was held in the newly constructed Holy Redeemer Ukrainian Catholic Church on the south side of the original building. In the fall of 1961, Premier Duff Roblin cut a ribbon to open a new two-storey wing on the north side where the boys would spend the majority of their time, either in classrooms on its main floor or in the large, barracks-style dormitory, recreation room, and communal washrooms on its upper floor. For meals, they trooped back into the original building, where a kitchen and dining room were located in the basement. They would rarely, if ever, see the upper floors where administrative offices and a small chapel for staff occupied the main floor, and the second and third floors had staff living quarters. Around 1969, a former one-room schoolhouse, taken from a site twelve miles north of Roblin, was moved beside the hockey rink

to be turned into a small museum. The school's library was enlarged in 1977. Between 1985 and 1987, a large expansion on the north end of the facility, connecting to the 1961 wing, included a gymnasium, stage-theatre, new washrooms, and change rooms. The gym was large enough for a full-sized basketball court or two volleyball courts or four badminton courts. The stage was to be used as a studio for dancing practices. The college's library was renovated and expanded at the same time.

The gymnasium and classroom annex of the former St. Vladimir's College, constructed between 1985 and 1986 to commemorate the millennium of Ukrainian Christianity in 1988, as it appeared in June 2016. GORDON GOLDSBOROUGH

Other renovations included a new computer room, typing room, audio-visual room, and a bigger, commercial-grade kitchen. Designed by Winnipeg architect Victor Deneka and built at a cost of $1.3 million, the expansion was dedicated to the 1000th anniversary of Ukrainian Christianity in 1988.

The daily routine of students at St. Vlads started at 7:00 AM when they were awoken from their bunks by gentle music playing from speakers in the dormitory. They dressed in the school uniform consisting of a pair of dress slacks (blue jeans were not permitted), a shirt, and a blue wool cardigan bearing three yellow stripes on its left sleeve (the colour scheme of the Ukrainian flag) and the letters SVC over the heart. After morning prayers in the nearby church, everyone had breakfast in one of the dining halls. Meals were served by a single group of boys for a week, with groups cycling over the course of a month. Another group was responsible for cleanup afterward. Following light domestic chores such as cleaning the communal bathrooms and mopping floors, the boys gathered at the front of the school to sing "O Canada" and raise the flag. The morning was spent in classes and, before lunch, there was choir practice. After lunch had been eaten and cleaned up, mail collected from Roblin's post office was handed out. There were more classes in the afternoon then sports activities. After supper at 5:30 PM, there was a mandatory two-hour study period, discretionary time for reading, watching television, or playing games in a recreation room in their dormitory. Promptly at 9:45 PM,

A hockey rink and warm-up shack behind the St. Vladimir's College, built in 1974, with the former Hillcrest School building, used for a time as a small museum, August 2017. CHRISTOPHER STEELE

Inside the abandoned gymnasium of St. Vladimir's College, August 2017. CHRISTOPHER STEELE

St. Boniface Normal School

An unassuming yellow-brick, two-storey building at the corner of Rue Aulneau and Rue Masson in Winnipeg, now vacant, was once home to the St. Boniface Normal School. A normal school is one specializing in the training of school teachers. It is called a normal school because its intention is to "to instill and reinforce particular norms within students," so they get a basic education. By the early 20th century, there were six other Normal Schools around Manitoba, at Brandon, Dauphin, Gretna, Manitou, and Portage la Prairie. The largest one, the Central Normal School, is still standing and is now a residential building on William Avenue near the old Carnegie Library.

Prior to 1890, Manitoba had a dual educational system based on religion, with schools being either Catholic and Protestant depending on the community. In 1890, a new Manitoba Public Schools Act was passed by the provincial legislature. Faith-based schools were prevented from receiving public funds, and a Department of Education was created to administer schools where English was made the sole official language of instruction. This change caused considerable anger, especially in German- and French-speaking communities who wanted their children to

The former St. Boniface Normal School, a centre for Francophone education in the early 20th century, was boarded up and awaiting demolition when I took this photo in January 2018. GORDON GOLDSBOROUGH

be educated in their native languages and faiths. The incident became known as the Manitoba Schools Question. In 1896, the matter became an issue in the federal election. The following year, the Act was amended to include a clause stating that "where ten of the pupils speak the French language (or any language other than English) as their native language, the teaching of such pupils shall be conducted in French (or such other language) and English upon the

bilingual system." This change meant it was now desirable to have bilingual teachers, who could teach in two or more languages.

The Gretna Normal School, which trained German-speaking teachers, had been operating for a half-dozen years by this point but most of the other normal schools had yet not been built. In 1905, the government established a "Ruthenian Training School" for training bilingual English-Ukrainian teachers.

First located in Winnipeg, the school was later relocated to Brandon and it operated until 1916. For a while, the Francophone community of Manitoba organized a bilingual teacher-training course. To meet the need for a more formal facility, the St. Boniface Normal School was built in 1903. It was a modest, one-storey building, constructed at a cost of $20,000, with four classrooms on the main floor along with a library, laboratory, parlour, kitchen, and dining hall. In its basement was a recreation room and mechanical systems. A shorter second storey with residential space was added later. The school opened in January 1904. The minimum requirement to attend was a grade 10 education and, if a person had grade 11 or grade 12, they were given higher levels of certification that enabled them to teach higher grades of students. The school offered a "long course" program of study of a year in length and a "short course" of a few months duration.

In 1916, the provincial government repealed the part of the Public Schools Act that permitted bilingual education, so henceforth teaching was to be done only in English. This may have been a measure aimed at promoting loyalty to Britain at the height of the First World War, especially among German-speaking Manitobans, given that the enemy was German-speaking.

It was probably also a measure for assimilation, to "Canadianize" the foreign-language students of Manitoba. The St. Boniface Normal School remained open as a unilingual English facility, under the direction of the staff of the Central Normal School, until 1923. At that time, it was sold to the Oblate Sisters, a Roman Catholic order of nuns, and converted into a residential school for boys. A two-storey brick addition on its west side was made in 1928. Ten years later, it became a domestic training centre for girls that operated until 1972 when the building was converted into housing for seniors. The Oblate Sisters sold it in 1980 and it was subsequently connected by a one-storey addition to a large residential complex to the west.

The building has stood empty for a number of years. Its windows have been boarded over and the door connecting it to the adjacent building is blocked. Most of its original interior is gone. I am told there is a problem with water leakage, as evidenced by hoses extending out onto the lawn in a few places. There are plans to replace it with a multi-storey residential building, but the timeframe in which the demolition will occur is unknown. At least for a while longer, the old Normal School reminds us of the history of minority language education in Manitoba.

music over the speakers alerted the students to the approaching bedtime and, after evening prayers, lights were out by 10:15 PM. Students who lived reasonably close to the school went home on weekends. Those living farther away had a weekend routine that was somewhat more relaxed than weekdays but still consisted of meals at set times, morning and evening prayers, and a mandatory study period.

I spoke with one of my friends, a Winnipegger who I will call Taras, who attended St. Vlads for a few years in the 1970s, about his experiences. He was encouraged, but not coerced, to attend the school by his parents, who were divorcing at the time. Admittance was predicated on the payment of fees for tuition, room, and board—although Taras suspects that no boy was ever turned away for financial reasons—and an interview with the school's Director to ascertain that his motivation to attend was genuine. Taras' experience in the first two years was mostly good. It was a close-knit community and he felt that the priests and brothers of the school were sincere, pious men who were nurturing and supportive. He enjoyed the discipline and order that it brought to his life. He joined the running club, loved performing with the choir, honed his photographic skills in the school's darkroom, and worked on the student yearbook. Things went downhill for Taras in his third year when the friendly atmosphere was poisoned by a single student who, he thinks, sold drugs and formed an exclusive clique around himself. That student was eventually expelled, but for Taras, the damage was done. He left St. Vlads at the end of grade 11 and returned to Winnipeg to attend a public high school. Taras said that he experienced more "culture shock" going from a small, rural school to a large, urban one than he had going from his small Winnipeg elementary school to St. Vlads. There was much more diversity in ethnicity and manner of dress, and of course there were girls! In retrospect, nearly 40 years later, Taras looks back on his

experience with bittersweet fondness. He thinks the construction of the gymnasium complex in the 1980s was bad for the school in two ways. It consumed vitally needed resources that could have been used better in other areas. More importantly, it disconnected the school from the local community. Previously, he and his classmates had used the gym in Roblin's Goose Lake High School for their physical activities. There was a link, real and symbolic, to the local community. Once they had their own gym, he thinks that St. Vlads became isolated.

The teaching staff had traditionally come from the ranks of the Redemptorist Fathers, but in 1995, with dwindling numbers of priests to fill teaching positions, management of the facility was transferred to the Archeparchy of Winnipeg, the regional administration of the Ukrainian Catholic Church. The last two Redemptorist Fathers at the school left as teaching duties were assumed by lay teachers. In its final few years of operation, student

enrollment at St. Vlads dwindled below the 35 needed to cover the costs of operating and maintaining the buildings and paying the salaries of 15 teachers and administrative staff, five cooks, and three custodians. After the last class of seven students graduated in June 2002, the college closed. The Archbishop and Metropolitan in Winnipeg, Most Reverend Michael Bzdel, observed that:

> For seven years we tried to maintain the school. We failed miserably. At no time was the enrollment and tuition sufficient to balance the budget. We had to come to the realization that the era of all-boys residential schools was gone.

The school's contents were sold at auction in October 2004 with the auctioneer advising people to "bring your trucks and trailers, you won't go home empty handed, something for all." The buildings, except for the church (where regular Sunday services continue to be held), were purchased in early 2007 by an entrepreneur from Vancouver.

In collaboration with the local Mountain View School Division, he planned to use it for a high school specializing in university-entrance and English-language instruction to students from South Korea. He reportedly spent a million dollars on renovations and equipment, and the first group of students arrived in the fall of 2008. At its peak, up to 30 international students came to Roblin for their high school education. He bought a local motel and a local restaurant. Ultimately, however, things did not turn out as he planned. Instead of using the former St. Vlads facility to the fullest, students attended classes in Goose Lake High School and were billeted with local families or lived in his motel. In 2013, the businessman put the St. Vlads buildings and property up for sale and, two years later, auctioned off its remaining contents.

In June 2016, while checking out the miscellaneous junk in the old Hillcrest schoolhouse near the college's overgrown hockey rink, I happened to meet the owner. He told me the last cohort of students had just departed. Since then, I have learned that he too has left Roblin. A pair of urban explorers were able to peek inside the building during the summer of 2017 and shared their photos with me. The roof seems to be leaking in numerous places, with garbage pails put in strategic spots to catch the incoming water. So far, the damage does not seem so severe that it could not be repaired and the building put to some good use. It seems a shame for a relatively new building to be sitting unused.

In addition to the St. Vlads student alumni over 60 years—who number nearly 1,000, including some 40 who became Ukrainian Catholic priests and who have dispersed around the world—there is at least one other tangible reminder of the private school's legacy besides the vacant buildings in Roblin. In 1969, a group of former students formed the St. Vladimir's College Alumni Choir. Six years later, they merged with a dance troupe and band, also with roots at the college, to become the Hoosli Ukrainian Male Chorus. Today, its members are drawn from a wide stratum of society, not all of them from St. Vlads, although the connection to Ukrainian culture and language remains strong. They have performed across Canada, recorded ten albums to date, and will celebrate their 50th anniversary in 2019.

ACKNOWLEDGEMENTS

I thank Gloria Romaniuk of the Archeparchy of Winnipeg Archives for giving me access to archival information on the St. Vladimir's College, and David Lisowski, David Yun, Orest Kinasevych, and "Taras" for providing additional details. Christopher Steele and Rémi Tellier shared photos taken in and around the former St. Vlads campus.

Caddy Lake
Emergency Airfield

W e take for granted that we can board an aircraft in Manitoba and, within a day, disembark on the other side of the planet. By comparison, our ancestors accepted that travel over great distances required a substantial commitment of time. In the early 20th century, a voyage from England to Winnipeg entailed crossing the Atlantic aboard a large ship, typically taking about a week to reach Montreal. Then, boarding a train, the intrepid traveller might spend another week to reach Winnipeg. The revolution in our expectations came with the invention of aircraft that travelled far faster than any ship or train, in straight lines between two points. A secluded spot in the forest near Caddy Lake, in the Whiteshell Provincial Park of eastern Manitoba, reminds us of this revolution by telling a story about the development of commercial aviation in Canada.

Our story begins in 1933, when the federal government of R. B. Bennett began to enlist able-bodied men left unemployed by the Great Depression to build public infrastructure. In return for their labour, each man was provided with food, shelter, and 20 cents per day. In Manitoba, among the many works done by these men were roads and buildings in the newly-established Riding Mountain National Park. On the eastern side of the province, three work gangs in the Whiteshell

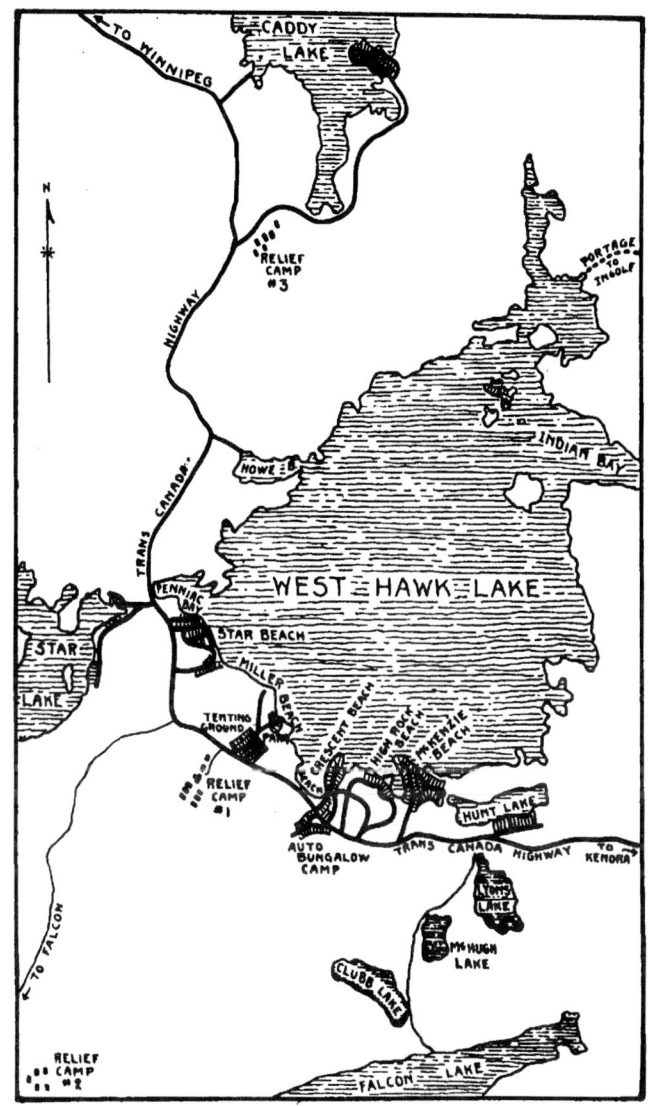

This map from early 1933 shows the locations of three camps in the Whiteshell Forest Reserve (today's Whiteshell Provincial Park) where unemployed men lived while working on public projects such as construction of an emergency airfield near Caddy Lake. *WINNIPEG TRIBUNE*

OPPOSITE The concrete basement is all that remains of the caretaker's residence at the Caddy Lake emergency airstrip, July 2017. Its age is attested by the imprint in the concrete of horizontal wooden boards used for the forms, rather than sheets of plywood that are typical in more recent construction projects. GORDON GOLDSBOROUGH

ABOVE Between fall 1933 and spring 1934, a work crew made up of unemployed men cut down the trees near Caddy Lake to make an emergency runway for aircraft that were beginning to carry mail, passengers, and cargo across Canada. In this view from April 1935, the three runways were plowed to make them smooth enough for an aircraft to land. I found no evidence the airfield was ever used for emergency purposes; it seems it was only used recreationally by a few small, private planes. LIBRARY AND ARCHIVES CANADA

RIGHT Advertisements such as this one in the *Winnipeg Tribune* during the Second World War reminded Canadians of the speed with which aircraft could convey mail, passengers, and cargo that were vital to the war effort, and made a subtle appeal for civilian use of these services after the war's end. *WINNIPEG TRIBUNE*, 29 DECEMBER 1942

Serves THE NATION
IN WAR AND PEACE

Trans-Canada Air Lines are an indispensable arm of transport to a nation at war. In peace, they accelerated the tempo of Canadian life. Now they operate over a 5,000-mile route from the Atlantic to the Pacific, from Newfoundland to British Columbia, to speed men, materials and mails, essential to victory.

They fly 8,250,000 miles a year, and carried in 1942 2,260,000 pounds of air mail, 106,000 passengers and 396,000 pounds of air express.

In addition to a great transportation task, T.C.A. repairs and overhauls military aircraft, including engines, propellers and instruments. T.C.A. crews are making flights across the Atlantic as part of the war effort, and T.C.A. ground crews overhaul and maintain the trans-oceanic transports from Canada.

Winnipeg is operations headquarters for T.C.A., and as the men and machines of T.C.A. are dedicated to the Nation's war effort, Winnipeg and Trans-Canada Air Lines work together for Victory.

In peace and war alike, Trans-Canada Air Lines have one constant, unvarying objective—to serve the nation.

TCA TRANS-CANADA AIR LINES
CANADA'S NATIONAL AIR SERVICE

Forest Reserve—today's Whiteshell Provincial Park—built roads to enable the development of tourism in this previously secluded part of Manitoba. Between fall 1933 and spring 1934, one hundred men from the Caddy Lake Relief Camp, under Colonel Logie Armstrong of the Department of National Defence, built an emergency airfield about 1½ miles west of the Ontario border. They cleared trees by hand and levelled the terrain with horse-drawn plows, then built three runways in a triangular layout so that aircraft could land under any wind conditions. An east-west runway was 0.6 miles in length while southeast-northwest and southwest-northeast runways were each a half mile long. The facility was not intended for regular use. It was meant only to be used by aircraft that encountered mechanical problems or bad weather as they were passing over.

Aircraft were becoming an increasingly common sight in Canadian skies through the 1920s

and 1930s. In 1926, Winnipegger James Richardson helped to establish Western Canada Airways and, in 1929, merged it with other companies into Canadian Airways Limited. Trans-Canada Air Lines (TCA, forerunner of today's Air Canada) was established by the federal government in 1937, building on the Trans-Canada Airway System designed to improve infrastructure for commercial aviation. On the first of March 1939, TCA initiated cross-country delivery of mail by aircraft. One month later, passenger service began.

Emergency landings of civilian aircraft were not especially difficult on the flat, featureless prairies, but much of the Canadian Shield covering eastern Manitoba and western Ontario was blanketed in a vast expanse of boreal forest that provided no places for aircraft to land. Under the Trans-Canada Airway System, emergency airfields were built every 25 to 100 miles, generally following railway tracks. Government plans called for three

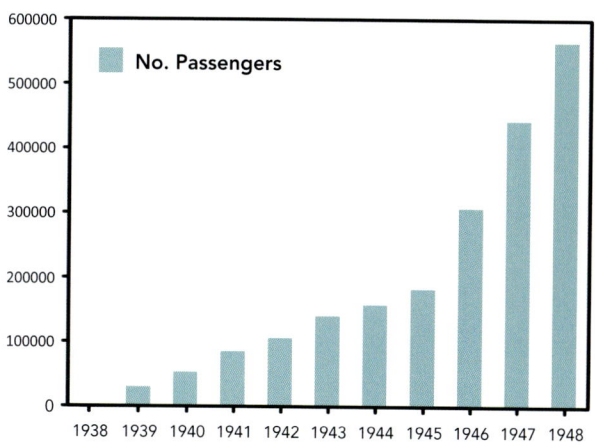

The annual number of passengers aboard Trans-Canada Air Lines aircraft increased steadily during the Second World War then began to rise rapidly in post-war peacetime. GORDON GOLDSBOROUGH, DRAWN FROM DATA COMPILED FROM HISTORICAL NEWSPAPERS.

emergency airfields in eastern Manitoba: one at Lac du Bonnet, a second near Whitemouth, and the third near Caddy Lake. Flight crews and passengers forced to land at the Caddy Lake airfield would have to leave the aircraft on the runway and walk to the Canadian Pacific Railway main line about a mile to the south and flag down a passing train.

The airfield in the Whiteshell was never used for an emergency landing but this was not the case for all airfields in the system. In

February 1941, the airfield at Armstrong, Ontario (about 270 miles east of the one in the Whiteshell) was the site of a crash in which twelve people were killed, including several Winnipeggers, among them a noted economics professor from the University of Manitoba. From scant information that I found, the Caddy Lake airfield was used only for landings of small, private aircraft belonging to people who owned recreational cottages in the area. The runways stopped being cleared of trees in the early 1950s and were abandoned completely around 1968. An aerial photo from 1970 shows numerous trees growing on the runways. If you look at the area in satellite imagery taken in the past few years, you can make out the east-west runway and a portion of the southeast-northwest runway, but the third runway is completely overgrown.

I visited the airfield site last summer and could find little evidence of it, though I knew from the coordinates on my GPS receiver that I was standing at the right spot. A forest fire in May 2016 had destroyed most of the trees in the area, making it difficult to tell where the runways had once been. I did find a 900-square-foot concrete basement for the residence of the airfield's wartime caretaker, a fellow named Charlie Brinkman. Four concrete blocks stood on a rise of land near the basement, probably used at one time for the foundation of a communications or fire observation tower. A portion of the Mantario Trail runs

There are several abandoned emergency airstrips around Manitoba, including ones built during the Second World War for use by training aircraft that might be unable, due to mechanical failures or bad weather, to return to their main bases. This aerial view shows the remains of Service Flying Training School No. 17 Relief Field south of Hartney, consisting of three concrete runways in a triangular configuration, as it appeared in July 2015. GORDON GOLDSBOROUGH

through the former runway area and passes right by the old caretaker's residence. Hikers who were likely unaware of the site's history had used the tower site for campfires.

Aircraft technology has reached a high level of mechanical reliability, and modern planes fly above the weather, so a network of emergency landing sites is no longer required. Today, most long-distance travel is done by air—to the regret of ship lines and railways—and every large community in Canada has an airfield of some type. We tend to forget a time when air travel was a novel enterprise that might require plucky travellers to include a hike through the forest near Caddy Lake in their itinerary.

ACKNOWLEDGEMENTS

I thank Judy Tyson and her son Dave who first made me aware of the emergency airstrip near Caddy Lake. Former Manitoban Kyle Daun, whose family has a cottage in the region, provided additional details. I dedicate this chapter to my wife Maria who accompanied me on a grueling, miserable walk to the site (21,127 steps, as recorded by her FitBit) on a hot July day.

Grainfields
School

I have spent many enjoyable days on country roads in search of one-room schoolhouses. At one time, there were over 2,000 of them spread across the province. After most closed due to school consolidation in the 1960s, some were turned into people's homes, granaries, or stores. Others were simply abandoned, and some were demolished or burned. In 2012, I was in the area southeast of Roblin, about sixty miles west of Dauphin, looking for what I had been led to believe were remains of the former Grainfields School No. 2186. I had found geographic coordinates for it at the provincial archives and I went to those coordinates using my trusty GPS receiver. I could see nothing but a tangle of low bushes and taller trees. I walked around the outside of the bush but it was so dense that it did not seem possible there had ever been a school there. Thinking my coordinates were wrong, I made a note in my trip log and continued on my way.

Later, when I was looking at a satellite photo for that area, I zoomed into where Grainfields School was supposed to be and, lo and behold, there it was, a rectangular shape of what looked like a building. I made a note to check it out again during my next visit to Roblin. When I did a year later, I was confronted by the same dense foliage. This time, I was not so easily dissuaded. Instead of walking around the area, I bushwhacked into it. After

OPPOSITE The roof of the former Grainfields School is barely visible in this aerial view of its shelterbelt in June 2018. GORDON GOLDSBOROUGH

An Arbor Day tree-planting party at Winnipeg's Manitoba College, 10 May 1887. Visible among the planters, at the right side, were the Reverends George Bryce (wearing a top hat and carrying a young child) and Thomas Hart (to Bryce's right), both of whom taught at the college. GORDON GOLDSBOROUGH PHOTO COLLECTION, 2006-0002.

stumbling through numerous bushes covered in sharp thorns, I found it. The building was so tightly encroached by caragana bushes that it was completely invisible from the road.

Grainfields School opened in the fall of 1928, operated for just 31 years, and closed in January 1959 after which local students went to a school in Roblin. The building sat vacant, filled with junk, and shrubs and trees completely overgrew it. In all my travels, I had never encountered an abandoned building so near a road yet so well concealed by vegetation. It had a great shelterbelt, doing what it was designed to do.

This photo of Grainfields School, taken in 1930 by school inspector Harold Albright, shows the early beginnings of its shelterbelt that, in time, would completely hide the schoolhouse. ARCHIVES OF MANITOBA

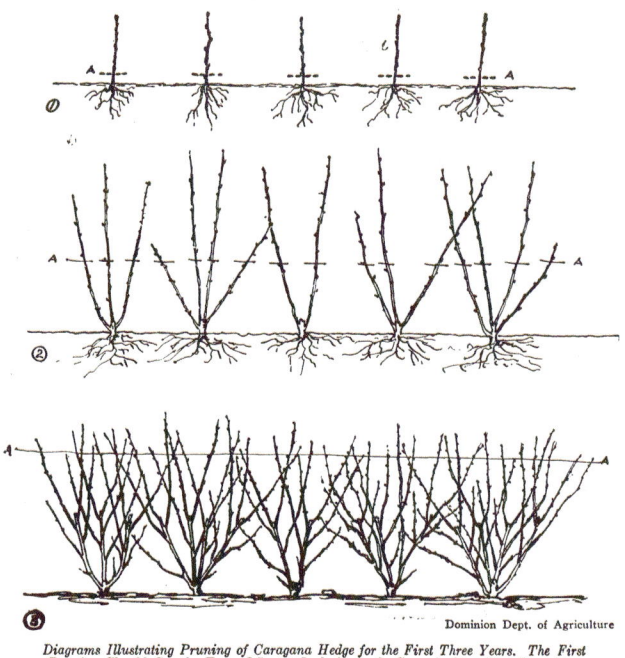

Diagrams Illustrating Pruning of Caragana Hedge for the First Three Years. The First Pruning Should Cut the Trees Off at 1 Inch Above the Ground. Note That Branching Takes Place at Point of Pruning.

Dominion Dept. of Agriculture

A diagram in a 1938 pamphlet from the Manitoba Department of Mines and Natural Resources showed farmers how to prune a Caragana hedge during its first three years to encourage the plants to become more bushy, providing the best possible cover in the shortest time for farm buildings on the wind-swept prairie. MANITOBA LEGISLATIVE LIBRARY

Visitors to Winnipeg admire the beautiful mature trees that line many of its streets. It is worth remembering that these trees are the result of a conscious program of planting that goes back to the city's early days. In 1884, picking up an idea started in the American prairie states in the mid-1870s, the Manitoba Legislature gave Lieutenant Governor James Aikins the power to establish a new public holiday, to be observed throughout the province, for the planting of trees. The holiday in early May

was to be known as Arbor Day. Experts provided advice on which tree species would survive in Manitoba's climate and parents were encouraged to involve their children in tree planting. Nurseries around Winnipeg offered a variety of trees for sale, promising to deliver them to any part of the city. At the Legislative Building, Aikins and his family gamely planted trees around the grounds, but many other Winnipeggers took advantage of the holiday to relax. Consequently, the first Arbor Day was a mixed success. Arbor Day continued in fits and starts through the 1890s but it never caught on as a major holiday. We do not know how many of the city's stately boulevard trees originate from those early planting efforts. Most of the trees today—the majority them American elm with fewer Manitoba maple and green ash—were planted in the 1920s and 1930s.

The period from 1928 through 1937 was one of extreme drought on the Canadian prairies. Farmers on the wind-swept prairies were encouraged to grow "shelter belts"— a fringe or ring of trees—around their farmyards. As Mines and Natural Resources Minister John McDiarmid noted in a 1938 publication:

> Every farm should have some trees. They add immeasurably to the appearance and to the value of the home. They can be planted and grown to form shelter belts for the protection of buildings, livestock and the farm garden. Their protective influence can be extended even to field crops. They can be made to take the place of

The overgrown building of the former Grainfields School No. 2186, August 2013. GORDON GOLDSBOROUGH

unsightly snow fences to assist in keeping open lanes and roadways. Extended to woodlots they will furnish a future fuel supply, fence posts, rails, and even materials for implement repair. Trees add greatly to the appearance of our schools, churches and other public buildings. They can forge an enduring link with the cherished memory of your childhood home.

At a practical level, shelterbelts provided at least six real benefits: 1) they reduced wind velocity and therefore reduced evaporation, conserving critical soil moisture in times of drought, 2) they reduced soil erosion by wind and improved air quality for humans and animals, 3) they held snow and rain in local areas, thereby reducing the extent of flooding after snow melt

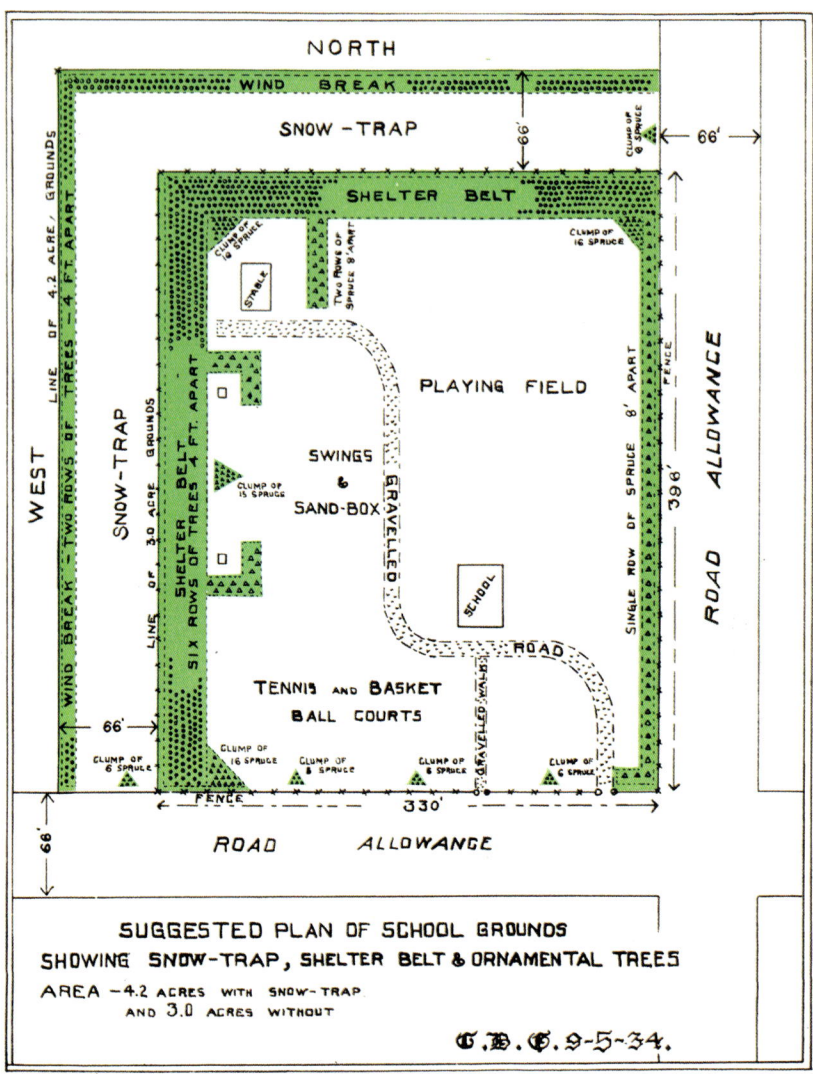

NORTH

WIND BREAK

SNOW-TRAP

SHELTER BELT

66'

66'

CLUMP OF 6 SPRUCE

CLUMP OF 16 SPRUCE

CLUMP OF 6 SPRUCE

STABLE

TWO ROWS OF SPRUCE 8' APART

PLAYING FIELD

SINGLE ROW OF SPRUCE 8' APART

396'

WEST

LINE OF 4.2 ACRE/ GROUNDS

WIND BREAK - TWO ROWS OF TREES - 4 FT. APART

SNOW-TRAP

LINE OF 3.0 ACRE GROUNDS

SHELTER BELT - 4 FT. APART

SIX ROWS OF TREES 4 FT. APART

SWINGS & SAND-BOX

CLUMP OF 16 SPRUCE

GRAVELLED

SCHOOL

GRAVELLED WALK

ROAD

FENCE

ROAD ALLOWANCE

TENNIS and BASKET BALL COURTS

66'

CLUMP OF 16 SPRUCE

CLUMP OF 6 SPRUCE

CLUMP OF 16 SPRUCE

CLUMP OF 6 SPRUCE

CLUMP OF 6 SPRUCE

FENCE

330'

66'

ROAD ALLOWANCE

SUGGESTED PLAN OF SCHOOL GROUNDS
SHOWING SNOW-TRAP, SHELTER BELT & ORNAMENTAL TREES

AREA — 4.2 ACRES WITH SNOW-TRAP
AND 3.0 ACRES WITHOUT

C.B.C. 9-5-34.

An ambitious plan for a rural school site in a 1934 pamphlet from the Manitoba Department of Education provided areas for various play activities surrounded by an extensive shelterbelt. I am fairly sure that no school in Manitoba followed this plan or, if one did, it was never developed as fully as the plan intended. MANITOBA LEGISLATIVE LIBRARY

and rainstorms, 4) they limited water erosion during the aforementioned runoff events, 5) they created habitat for beneficial birds and insects such as pollinators and predators of crop pests, and 6) they provided shade which, in the era before widely-available air conditioning, was a major plus during the sweltering heat of summer.

Returning to Grainfields School, which began operating in the early years of the prairie drought, it is likely the school trustees were encouraged by provincial officials to establish a shelterbelt. In fact, energy and water conservation might not have been the only motives for planting trees around schools. Through the 1930s and 1940s, teachers were urged to make tree planting and gardening a class activity that would teach the students about the world around them and give them useful life skills.

The Manitoba Department of Education distributed a thin pamphlet entitled "Tree Planting on School Grounds" to school districts around the province. It offered a detailed plan for a four-acre schoolyard with a wind break on the north and west sides—facing prevailing winds—of two rows of trees, four feet apart. Inside this wind break was a 50-foot-wide open area where snow would be trapped during the winter. Inside the snow trap was a shelterbelt of six rows of trees on the north and west sides, and a single row of trees on the east and south sides. In time, the schoolhouse and playground would be completely surrounded by stately, mature trees, with just a narrow opening where students could enter and leave the schoolyard. Within the yard, areas for different sports could be delimited with low caragana hedges. The pamphlet advised school trustees and teachers to prepare the ground for the trees in the fall of the year before planting would occur. Then, they would make a formal request to the local school inspector who, if he approved, would forward it to the federal tree nursery at Indian Head, Saskatchewan. The following spring, the trees would be delivered, ready for planting.

The trees to be planted around schools depended on the wetness and texture of the soil, with slow-, medium-, and fast-growing species recommended depending on the speed with which a shelterbelt was desired. The tree species recommended for shelterbelts included white or black spruce, Jack or lodgepole pine, tamarack, green ash, American elm, Manitoba maple, birch, bur oak, and poplar. In the first few years of tree planting, it was desirable to protect the young trees with a row of faster-growing shrubs. Among the species recommended were ones brought to Canada from areas of Russia having a similar climate and therefore tolerant of Canadian conditions. These included such species as caragana, Russian olive, and common lilac. These shrubs were typically grown from seed and were pruned in the first few years to make them branch more exuberantly to provide the best possible shelter.

What seems to have happened at Grainfields School was that hedges of caragana were planted as part of the shelterbelt. In the nearly six decades since the school closed, the entire schoolyard has been overgrown. This has taught me an important lesson that, when one is searching for abandoned sites, one should pay attention to trees. Often, when we see a straight row of plants in a place that otherwise has no evidence of human activity, we can be confident that, at one time, someone was there to plant them. Indeed, one of the most enduring signs of the early European settlement on the prairies are the numerous now-huge trees that grew from modest beginnings on the otherwise flat and seemingly featureless prairie. Unfortunately, many of Manitoba's finest shelterbelts have been lost over the past several decades, and many more are at risk. Some farmers view shelterbelts as an unnecessary impediment to their large farm machinery, that works best on expansive tracts, with the result that numerous mature trees are torn out long before their natural death. As we move into an uncertain future, where climate change may bring droughts like those in the 1930s, will we remember the lessons taught by the early conservationists and the people of Grainfields School, and maintain our shelterbelts?

ACKNOWLEDGEMENTS

I am indebted, as usual, to the librarians of the Manitoba Legislative Library for tracking down a pair of wonderful pamphlets from the 1930s that encouraged Manitobans to plant trees. John Morriss of the *Manitoba Co-operator* educated me on some of the benefits and risks of shelterbelts.

Conestoga
Campground

For over 100 years, Manitobans seeking summer recreation have headed off to "the cottage." As early as the 1890s, residential developments on the shores of Manitoba's large lakes began to spring up at places like Delta Beach on the south edge of Lake Manitoba, and around Lake Winnipeg at Winnipeg Beach, Grand Beach, Victoria Beach, and elsewhere. Railway companies, seeing an opportunity to make money transporting people to recreational destinations, built lines to the lakeshores that enabled these developments to flourish. Even those without the means to own (or rent) a cottage could take day- or weekend-long railway journeys to enjoy sun, refreshing breezes, and relaxation at the beach.

However, recreational options expanded greatly through the 20th century, and especially in the 1950s and 1960s. Improvements to the provincial road network, along with the increasing ubiquity of automobiles, made it possible for average Manitobans to choose their own travel itinerary and destination, not encumbered by those chosen by the railways. Today, we take for granted the ability to jump into our cars and head out on the road to adventure. An abandoned campground on Winnipeg's south edge reminds of a heady time when our travel options were beginning to blossom.

A map of southern Manitoba published in the 1920s by the Winnipeg Tourist and Convention Bureau

An unknown traveller mailed a promotional postcard for the Conestoga Campsites from Winnipeg to an address in Michigan, observing that there "sure are lots of trailer parks." The card touted the campground's amenities including "hook ups for travel trailers, large tent sites, 20 minutes downtown." GORDON GOLDSBOROUGH COLLECTION, 2017-0139

OPPOSITE All that remains of the former Conestoga Campsites in southern Winnipeg are a few campsite markers and a lone picnic table. Opened in 1966, the facility was ideally situated on the Perimeter Highway around Winnipeg to attract increasingly mobile travellers. GORDON GOLDSBOROUGH

Starting in the 1950s, travelling Manitobans began to flock to areas of the province that had once been remote and inaccessible. UNIVERSITY OF MANITOBA ARCHIVES & SPECIAL COLLECTIONS

who itched to go places not served by a railway. By the early 1920s, the City of Winnipeg, recognizing the opportunity to attract "motor tourists," had opened a public campground on a well-treed site at the Old Exhibition Grounds, at the western end of Dufferin Avenue. A building erected in 1922 provided "toilet facilities for both men and women, kitchen with large sink, cook-stove, electric light and an abundant supply of wood and water free of charge." The following year, the campground welcomed 1,475 tourists in 454 cars, nearly 80% of them Americans from as far away as California, Texas, and Washington DC.

Road building in Manitoba continued sporadically through the mid-20th century so that, by 1961, there were about 3,800 miles in the network. From the 1950s to 1970s, the provincial government made numerous highway improvements. When it started, barely 5% of the provincial highways were paved with concrete; the rest were asphalted (16 percent), covered with tarry mixtures referred to as "black

showed, in addition to the railway lines available to travellers, brightly-coloured red lines promoting the rapidly expanding network of municipal and provincial highways. These roads were made possible, in part, by the provincial government's ambitious program of bridge-building that began in

the 1910s and carried through the 1920s, along with financial support for roadway improvements from the newly-established Good Roads Board of Manitoba. Most of the roads were primitive by modern standards—the majority were neither gravelled nor paved—but they catered to adventurous motorists

top" (53 percent), or gravelled (26 percent). By the late 1970s, the proportion of gravelled provincial roads had plummeted to less than one percent. The Trans-Canada Highway was straightened between Winnipeg and Portage la Prairie, bypassing the winding route that it had traditionally followed along the Assiniboine River (today's highway #26). A paved highway between Winnipeg and Falcon Lake was built so travellers no longer had to take the circuitous route east of Beausejour (today's highway #44) to reach recreational areas in the Whiteshell. The Perimeter Highway was built around Winnipeg to handle greater volume of commercial and domestic traffic. It featured Manitoba's first cloverleaf intersection at its junction with the city's Pembina Highway.

In my experience, there are two kinds of Manitobans when it comes to summer recreation: those with summer cottages (or access to a rental) who are therefore sedentary, and those who travel from place to place, staying in tents, trailers, or hotels along the way. Either you are a bred-in-the-bone cottager, or you are not. As a kid in the 1960s, my family was in the latter group, among a growing number of Manitobans who took camping holidays throughout the summer, each time to a different destination. Dramatic improvements to the highway network were the incentive for "camping families" like mine to hit the road. In July 1965, the Manitoba government, recognizing the growing importance of provincial road infrastructure, split off responsibility for public roads from the Department of Public Works, creating a new Department of Highways.

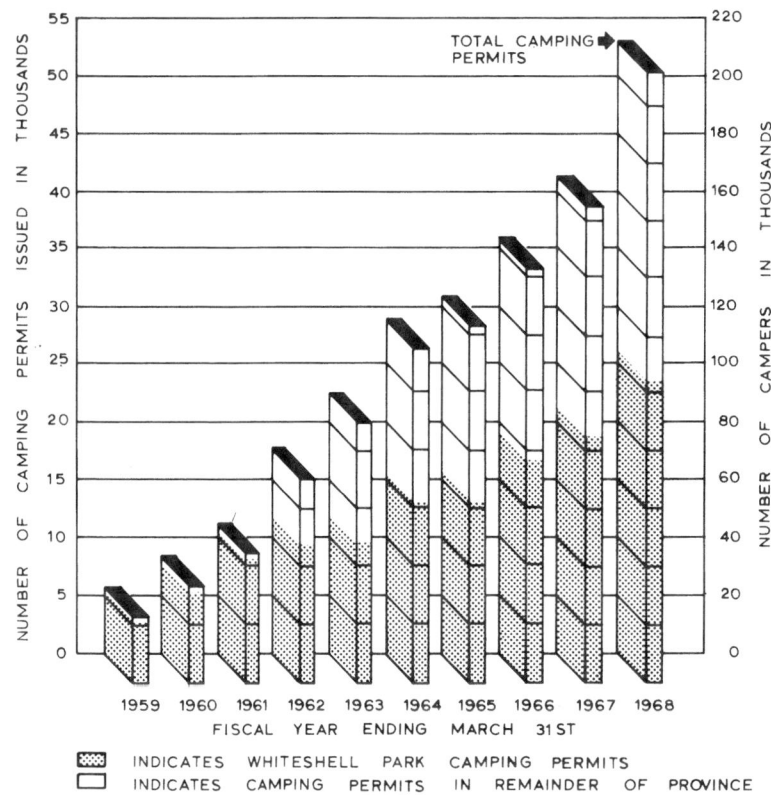

CAMPING GROWTH IN THE PARK SYSTEM

A chart from a government report shows the phenomenal growth in camping in the Whiteshell Provincial Park and elsewhere in Manitoba between 1959 and 1968. LEGISLATIVE LIBRARY OF MANITOBA, MANITOBA DEPARTMENT OF TOURISM AND RECREATION, ANNUAL REPORT: 1967-1968

Early in the following year, a new Department of Tourism and Recreation was created to focus on development of tourism that was taking advantage of the improved roads. Provincial spending on outdoor

Put Your Trash in Orbit

As Manitoba roads saw greater traffic volumes through the 1960s, the provincial government had to confront the greater quantities of litter discarded by passing motorists. In 1965, Peter Boychuk, a traffic-sign designer at the Manitoba Department of Highways, was asked to tackle the problem. He came up an innovative solution that drew on intense public interest in the Space Race that was occurring between the United States and the Soviet Union at that time. Space-inspired products were everywhere: new automobiles and buildings sported sweeping lines patterned after those on rocket ships while "The Jetsons" cartoon television program envisioned domestic life in the future with flying automobiles. Boychuk created a litter receptacle made from a four-foot-diameter white fiberglass sphere, with an upward-facing hole to its interior, sitting on black metal legs. Looking something like a cross between the Soviet Sputnik satellite and the American lunar landing module, the creation was named "Orbit" and a public advertising campaign encouraged motorists to "put their trash in orbit." In the first year of the program, ten Orbits were deployed along the Trans-Canada Highway. In keeping with the Space Age theme, road signs provided one-minute and ten-second countdown warnings

An old Orbit with its father, Peter Boychuk, June 2018. HOLLY THORNE

to motorists as they approached an Orbit. Public response to the Orbits was so favourable that 100 more were ordered, to be installed in late 1965 and early 1966. The following year, dispensers for small plastic bags—journalists dubbed them "launch bags"—were put alongside the Orbits. Hung from cigarette lighters, heater knobs, or window cranks, the bags collected litter until being deposited into an Orbit. (In the first year of use, the government gave away a half million bags, rising to 1.5 million bags annually by the mid-1970s.) The City of Winnipeg was so

enamoured with Orbits that it borrowed the idea and deployed smaller versions that designer Boychuk refers to as "Little Orbit Annies." Other municipalities around North America deluged the government with letters, asking for advice on how to create their own Orbit program. Manitoba's constellation peaked at more than 120 Orbits, deployed on major highways all over the province.

Orbits were intended for litter that would be otherwise thrown on roadsides. However, Department of Highways staff found them being

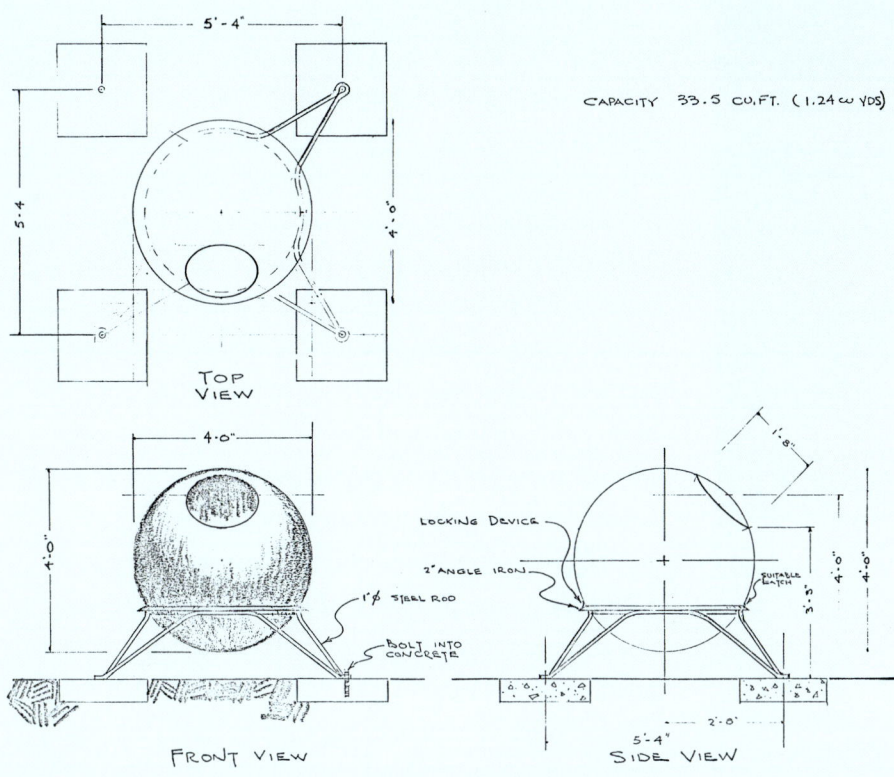

CAPACITY 33.5 CU.FT. (1.24 cu YDS)

TOP VIEW

FRONT VIEW

SIDE VIEW

LOCKING DEVICE

2" ANGLE IRON

1" ⌀ STEEL ROD

BOLT INTO CONCRETE

SUITABLE LATCH

Peter Boychuk's original drawing for the Orbit trash receptacle. PETER BOYCHUK

used for other purposes, including as impromptu overnight accommodations for bears and hitch-hiking hippies. Cottage owners on their way home frequently dumped large bags of household garbage next to an over-stuffed Orbit, causing road maintenance staff to complain that they were not in the garbage disposal business. Hunters dropped off messy bags of entrails from an animal kill. One of my friends recalls vomiting into an Orbit after a late-night drinking binge. Orbits were subject to

all sorts of vandalism, including fires and gun blasts. By the mid-1980s, the provincial government had had enough and quietly removed Orbits from service, having phased out the free litter bags a few years earlier. An Orbit was given to Peter Boychuk as a retirement gift and I hear occasionally from people who have seen an old Orbit here or there. Many Manitobans who grew up in the early days of the Space Age will remember fondly those whimsical, white spheres of Manitoba's provincial highways.

recreational facilities doubled between 1961 and 1965. A government report from 1959 estimated that about 5,000 families were camping in government-run facilities annually. Ten years later, that number had increased to 52,000 families. The three most popular destinations were, by far, the Whiteshell (43 percent), Grand Beach (16 percent), and the newly-opened Birds Hill Park (15 percent). A Manitoba tourist guide from 1967 listed 273 campgrounds, picnic sites, and trailer parks. The following year, a survey of highway traffic calculated that 431,350 tourists had visited Manitoba and that out-of-province traffic had increased by 20 percent between 1965 and 1968. A 1969 report noted that the number of vehicles coming into Manitoba from the United States increased by 85 percent between 1960 and 1966.

In 1966, 31-year-old Hardy Priess and his wife Alma must have seen the growing number of vehicles passing Winnipeg on the newly constructed Perimeter Highway at St. Anne's Road and decided to

Clear Lake in Riding Mountain National Park, seen here in 1957, became an increasingly popular tourist destination as provincial highways were improved and Manitobans were encouraged to "hit the road" in search of adventure. ARCHIVES OF MANITOBA

To facilitate high-speed traffic interchange between Winnipeg's Perimeter Highway and Provincial Trunk Highway No. 75 (Pembina Highway), the provincial government built Manitoba's first cloverleaf intersection between 1959 and 1960. Located just 4½ miles west of the Conestoga Campsites, the site was mostly agrarian when this aerial photo looking eastward was taken in 1962 but it has since exploded with residential and commercial development. ARCHIVES OF MANITOBA

open a campground in hopes of attracting recreational campers from among the hordes of traffic. Open from May through September, one of eleven campgrounds or trailer parks in the Greater Winnipeg area, their Conestoga Campsites offered one hundred campsites on six acres of land along the scenic Seine River, 60 unserviced sites with picnic table and fire pit ($2.50 per day) and 40 sites with electricity and water hookups ($3.00 per day). It boasted a small store with groceries, propane and souvenirs; a potable water supply and sewage disposal area; a washroom and laundry building; and the obligatory playground and swimming pool for kids cranky after a day of driving. There are no indications of how successfully the Priess business venture may have fared but, in any case, Hardy Priess saw little of it, dying only five years after his campground opened. The property changed hands several times and, by the 1980s, it was described by one camper—whose family from rural Manitoba stayed at Conestoga while on shopping trips to Winnipeg—as a "broken down roadside attraction from a bygone era" run by "an affable if somewhat grizzled guy." The reason for the campground's decline was probably the change in the style of camping. Whereas tents and small trailers were the norm in the 1960s when Conestoga was

All that remains of the former Conestoga Campsites in southern Winnipeg are a few campsite markers and a lone picnic table. Opened in 1966, the facility was ideally situated on the Perimeter Highway around Winnipeg to attract increasingly mobile travellers. GORDON GOLDSBOROUGH

through the former campground. When I visited the site in late 2016, it would have been easy to overlook that a campground had ever been there. It is mostly overgrown. My guide pointed out a few weathered campsite numbers nailed to trees, along with a sad, moss-covered picnic table, and some plumbing fixtures. My first impression was to regard the site as a short-lived business venture of little consequence, until I began to think about my own childhood camping trips. I came to realize that the Conestoga Campsites is a visual reminder of a time when Manitobans began to explore the province in ways that did not entail living at a cottage.

established, through the 1980s and 1990s, trailers and RVs were becoming larger with all the conveniences of home: air conditioning, hot and cold running water, microwave ovens, satellite television. In short, people wanted all the comforts, not the "roughing it" of former days. There may not have been enough room at Conestoga to build the "drive through" spots needed by modern RVs and behemoth-campers.

The last reference that I could find to Conestoga was from 2002 when the owner was tied up by an unknown assailant, beaten, and robbed. Sometime between then and now, the site was converted into residences and mini-storage. A local group has established a walking trail

ACKNOWLEDGEMENTS

I thank Bob Van Aertselaer who first made me aware of the Conestoga site and the late Jerry Gosselin who gave me an enthusiastic tour of its remains. Tom Dobson shared reminiscences of his childhood stays at the campground. An enjoyable afternoon with the inimitable Peter Boychuk—the "Father of Orbit" and numerous other inventions—provided useful insight into the development of Manitoba's highways in the early 1960s. Stuart Hay and his helpful staff at the Legislative Library of Manitoba provided a wealth of material on the provincial road network, especially from the 1950s and 1960s when dramatic improvements were taking place.

Davidson Dairy Farm

Former dairy barn "A,"
January 2018. ERNEST BRAUN

An historical postcard shows a "walking dredge," similar in design to the one used near Marchand, and a newly dredged channel through the Whitemud River from Big Grass Marsh on the west side of Lake Manitoba, 1906. Machinery was housed in what looks like a building that moved along with the dredge. GORDON GOLDSBOROUGH, 2013-0052; *GOLDEN MEMORIES*

When Manitoba joined Confederation in 1870, one could scarcely imagine a region more poorly suited to agriculture than the southeastern corner of the "Postage Stamp Province." Most of the land there was densely forested or covered in vast expanses of wetlands. How things have changed in nearly 150 years. The area around Marchand, about 40 miles southeast of Winnipeg on the western edge of the Sandilands Provincial Forest, is no longer so wet. Through the actions of an eager American entrepreneur, the region was converted from what were perceived as worthless wetlands into one of the largest dairy farms in Canada, if not all of North America.

This was one of the last parts of Manitoba to become developed as agricultural land, largely because it was poorly drained. In 1909, businessman Watson P. "Wat" Davidson came to Manitoba from St. Paul, Minnesota and bought 100,000 acres of land. He approached the La Broquerie municipal council, asking them to build roads in his vicinity, but was told the municipality had no power to undertake the drainage needed to do so. Consequently, in 1910, an Act of the provincial legislature was passed that permitted Davidson to construct, at his own expense, "roads, drains, ditches, and bridges and other improvements upon public road allowances." In return, Davidson's land would be subject to little or no municipal taxation for twenty years. He bought three "walking dredges" and, over a period of 15 years, used them to dig 121 miles of ditches. Powered by wood, and later by gasoline, each dredge had gigantic arms protruding from its sides. They could be lifted and lowered, just like a person's arms, to anchor the dredge while it was digging, then lifted so it could inch forward (hence, the "walking" part of its name) to continue the work. A dredge, operated by a crew of seven men, was capable of moving 1½ cubic yards of soil per minute and could dig a mile-long, sixteen-foot wide, six-foot deep ditch in a week. They started in low-lying areas and moved to progressively higher ground, following the edge of surveyed land sections, so that water in the saturated soil would naturally drain away by gravity. The excavated soil—consisting mostly of highly organic muck ranging in depth from one to six feet—was piled on one side of the new ditch to become a roadbed. Small dams at strategic spots maintained adequate soil moisture for crop production on the adjoining lands. It is estimated that,

Davidson Dairy Farm   79

American land developer Watson Pogue Davidson (1871–1954). ARCHIVES OF MANITOBA

Former dairy barn "A" at the Manitoba Dairy Farms in the 1920s. ARCHIVES OF MANITOBA

between 1909 and 1939, Davidson spent some $3,000,000 (over $50 million in today's dollars) for drainage and road-building.

Davidson frequently spent summers at his property in Manitoba although he maintained a residence in St. Paul and also had large land holdings in Oregon. Day-to-day oversight of the Manitoba operation was provided by a live-in manager. In 1920, six 230-foot dairy barns were built—each emblazoned with Manitoba Dairy Farms Limited on its roof—where workers milked more than 800 purebred Holstein cows (from a total herd of 1,000 to 1,500 animals) each day. Electric power to run the milking machines was generated in an on-site powerhouse. A second ranch about twelve miles to the southwest, called Meadowlawn, was connected to the main facility by a private telephone system. Davidson employed more than 150 workers during the spring, summer, and fall. Each man received a daily salary of fifty cents as well as a tobacco ration and meals (served in a communal dining hall, called by a bell said to have been salvaged from a wrecked Missouri River steamboat). The labour force was drawn from the surrounding communities but also included newly-arrived immigrants from Poland and Hungary. The work was hard and the workday was long so turnover was high. By 1960, long-time manager Bill Davenport joked that "I think almost everybody in Manitoba worked here at some time or other." Yet, the operation was efficient. A 1934 newspaper story reported that:

The barns are scrupulously clean. The udders and flanks of the cows are washed before each milking. The men who do the milking wear white linen suits and the milk is not at any time exposed in open containers. At every point the utmost care and latest scientific methods are employed to keep the animals in prime condition and to make sure that the precious and super-sensitive fluid reaches the consumer as sweet and clean as it leaves the cow.

Milking typically began at 3:00 AM in the winter and earlier in the summer, and continued over a period of about four hours. A second milking period started about twelve hours later. Eight-gallon metal cans full of milk—130 of them each day in the late 1920s—were shipped by CN rail from Marchand to the Modern Dairy Limited in St. Boniface. Cows were continually tested for disease, as well as milk and butterfat production, with under-producing cows sent to slaughter. In addition to the dairy herd, Davidson had 3,000 to 5,000 sheep on his ranch, along with 200 to 350 horses. The sheep provided an additional source of income, sold for meat at the Union Stockyards in St. Boniface. For the first 15 years of the farm's existence, haying and cropping was done by horsepower. Later, the work of clearing, breaking, and seeding the land was taken over by a fleet of gasoline-powered tractors.

As Manitoba's largest dairy farm, it was inevitable that Davidson's operation would draw the interest of provincial politicians, especially ones like Premier John Bracken whose power base was in rural Manitoba. In 1933, Lord Bessborough, the Governor General of Canada, paid a visit to Manitoba and was shepherded by Bracken and Lieutenant Governor John McDiarmid on a tour of the Marchand dairy and land drainage work in the surrounding area. A large tent was duly set up and a photo taken that day shows a bevy of assorted politicos enjoying a fancy catered luncheon on white linen tablecloths, fine china, and silver cutlery. Davidson's operation also drew attention of a negative kind. Two years before

Cans of milk being loaded on a train at Marchand, bound for the Modern Dairies facility in St. Boniface, date unknown. ARCHIVES OF MANITOBA

the Governor General's visit, Davidson had been the victim of a blackmail attempt. The farm had received a note with atrociously bad grammar, in which the blackmailer described himself as "a leader among the other two bandits which are in company with me. And we became heartless and fearless." He demanded one thousand dollars in ransom or "your bodies will be burned in the ashes of your buildings." Rather than cave to the blackmailer, the farm manager sent the note to the Manitoba Provincial Police in Winnipeg. A token payment of $25 was left at the designated spot in the Sandilands, along

A view of Benjamin Carter's "package farm," circa 1924. ARCHIVES OF MANITOBA

A view of the "package farm" bought by Amos Schau and his family, taken by Winnipeg photographer Lewis Foote around 1924. The barn was destroyed by a "spontaneous combustion" fire in September 1931 but its two concrete silos have stood the test of time. When I visited the site in June 2017, the silos were riddled with depressions made by bullets shot at them. ARCHIVES OF MANITOBA

with reply explaining that Davidson was "travelling in the south and we have been unable to get in touch with him." After several exchanges of messages with the blackmailer over a period of several months, he was caught in May 1931, charged with extortion, found guilty, and sentenced to ten years in Stony Mountain Penitentiary. The felon turned out to have worked at the farm at one time and, although Davidson sought clemency on his behalf, he apparently served the full sentence.

Davidson did not confine his plans solely to the area that he and his employees farmed. He intended for a portion of the land to be subdivided and sold to other dairy farmers. Unlike unscrupulous land developers, however, he did not sell unproductive, wet farmland to unsuspecting settlers from abroad. Not only was the land drained and ready for livestock grazing and cultivation, Davidson offered "package farms" that were turnkey operations. Farms bought under his "Davidson Plan" consisted of 160, 320, or 640 acres of drained land, of which 20, 40, or 100 acres were planted to alfalfa, clover, or timothy for use by dairy cattle. The remaining land could be planted to such crops as wheat, oats, barley, rye, potatoes, sunflowers, and corn. (Promotional literature that I found at the provincial archives did not admit the soil was poorly suited to some of them.) There was a white, four-room "cottage" house (or a two-storey model for larger families) and a red barn with white trim on a solid concrete foundation. Attached to the barn were one or two silos for storing livestock feed made from corn

An aerial view of the former Carter "package farm," June 2017. The concrete silo standing to the right of the barn floor lost a large chunk when a tornado torn off the barn's roof. GOLDSBOROUGH

and, inside, there were ten, twenty, or forty prime dairy cows (larger farms also included a stud bull) and a team of horses with a wagon. Not surprisingly, water was plentiful in the area, and each homestead site had a well with a hand-pump. Wild hay, wild fruit, and wild game teemed nearby. Buyers benefitted from Davidson's sweet deal on taxation, paying no property tax until 1939, but they had to share the upkeep of the nearby Cedar Grove School No. 2152 and contribute up to $20 per year for

The Modern Dairies Building, constructed in 1929 by pioneering dairyman Alfred De Cruyenaere, seen in June 1965. Vacant as of 2017, it is slated to be demolished to make way for residential development. CITY OF WINNIPEG, HISTORICAL BUILDINGS AND RESOURCES COLLECTION

road maintenance costs (in cash, or equivalent manual labour on road repair crews). A buyer need only move into the house and start farming immediately. In 1929, the package prices ranged from $6,500 to $22,000 (or $95,000 to $315,000 in modern dollars) with one-tenth due immediately in cash. After three years, Davidson would begin to receive half of the farm's milk shipments and half of its crops until the remaining balance was paid. Farmers were at liberty to construct horse barns, pigpens, chicken coops, and other buildings as desired. More adventurous souls could buy unimproved land, and do all the work that Davidson had done, for $15 per acre. Starting in 1924, advertisements and pamphlets for Davidson's "package farms" were sent all over the United States and Europe. In time, more than 20 families were enticed to take up farms in the area. The first, in 1924, was Benjamin Carter, his wife, and sister on a 160-acre farm. Ten more families followed in 1925, and a handful in subsequent years.

Unfortunately, the Great Depression weighed heavily on the Davidson dairy operation and a labour shortage during the Second World War had an even more severe impact. The sale of "package farms" ended during the war, not having met Davidson's lofty expectations, and henceforth only undeveloped 160-acre land parcels were sold. In 1942, the dairy herd was sold and the headquarters farm was rented out, marking the end of Davidson's tenure as Manitoba's largest dairyman. Through the late 1940s and early 1950s, his company did little work other than to rent out hay meadows and sell vacant farms and farmland.

After Davidson's death in January 1954, his sons held the land until 1960 when they sold 54,000 acres to a consortium led by a man from South Dakota intending to turn them into rangeland for cattle. Later, the land was flipped to a doctor from Kansas who also had visions of establishing a large ranch. The Davidson family still owned 3,000 acres as of 1970. Ten years later, after Davidson's namesake son died, they sold the remaining land and retreated to St. Paul, along with the steamboat bell from the dining hall. Some artifacts went to museums at La Broquerie, Dugald, St. Claude, and Winnipeg, and a collection of family photos and documents were donated to the Minnesota Historical Society. Today, the main "headquarters" farm on the west side of Marchand is owned by a local farmer. The dairy is no longer in operation but the land is still dominated by corporate farming; the landscape is dotted liberally with high-capacity hog barns.

Most of the "package farms" are abandoned although remnants remain. I visited a couple of them in June 2017. A few miles south of Marchand, we found two abandoned concrete silos from a package farm bought by Amos Schau and his family in 1926. Although prosperous-looking when Winnipeg photographer Lewis Foote visited around 1924, the farm's barn was destroyed by fire in September 1931. Two miles to the north was the former Carter farm, abandoned within a decade of its purchase. There, a single concrete silo and the concrete foundations of outbuildings were still readily visible, although the silo had a huge chunk missing from its northern side. The present landowner told me this happened when a passing tornado ripped the roof from the nearby barn and threw it against the silo.

There are other visible reminders of Wat Davidson's legacy in Manitoba. In addition to the miles of roads throughout the Marchand area, many flanked by large soil berms where his walking dredges piled excavated soil, there is a 9½-square-mile area where provincial land managers sought to foster endangered wildlife. Before he died, Davidson donated this land to the Manitoba government, which in 1961 established the Watson P. Davidson Wildlife Management Area, the first of its kind in Manitoba. (Since then, 83 other WMAs have been created around the province.) So, let us raise a glass (of milk) to the memory of this pioneering dairyman of southeastern Manitoba.

A bottle of the former Modern Dairies Limited had its well-known slogan molded into the glass: "You can whip our cream but you can't beat our milk". STEFANIE GOLDSBOROUGH

ACKNOWLEDGEMENTS

I thank Ernie Braun and Glen Klassen of the EastMenn Historical Society for taking me on a tour of the Marchand area last summer, and Alvin Wiens, Eric Wiens, Tim Wiens, and Tyler Wiens for giving me access to their properties that were once the Davidson "Package Farms." The Dairy Museum at St. Claude has an exhibit on the Davidson Dairy Farm and also sells copies of Cynthia Faryon's book about it.

If you ever visit Churchill, you will be struck by how much abandonment is visible in the area. We can see a stone fortress from the 1700s, a large ship that ran aground in a storm, an airplane that crash-landed on the open tundra, the remains of an Indigenous village whose inhabitants were forcibly resettled there by the federal government, a rocket launching facility, and, most recently, a grain-handling terminal that stands idle while the railway line that supplies it awaits repair. The present-day airport was, from 1942 to 1980, an active military base known as Fort Churchill. Alongside the main road between the Fort and the town, about two miles southeast of Churchill, is an eerie grey metal building on stilts. Many of its windows are now covered with plywood. It harkens back to the tense days of the Cold War when Canadians and Americans worried about nuclear missiles coming over the North Pole from the Soviet Union, and took measures to develop an early-warning capability. Known as HMCS Churchill, this building was the centre for a clandestine listening post of the Royal Canadian Navy.

In late 1950, the Navy began building a communication centre at Churchill to be known as HMCS (His Majesty's Canadian Station) Churchill. As far as the general public was concerned, its purpose would be to

Aerial view of the Fort Churchill military base looking inland, 1958. GORDON GOLDSBOROUGH PHOTO COLLECTION, 2017-0141

conduct research on the atmosphere and to make measurements of the intensity and duration of northern lights and their effect on radio transmissions. As with many military facilities, its specific purpose and activities were not fully disclosed. In addition to monitoring routine military communications in Canada's northern region, it also intercepted Soviet radio signals in hopes of hearing incoming bomb-carrying aircraft and other hostile actions. Due to the nature of this place, information on it is hard to find, so what we know about the building comes from the recollections of people who worked there, and what we can deduce from a tour of its disheveled remains.

OPPOSITE An aerial view of the naval building in June 2018 shows the accommodations wing in foreground, the service wing in right background, and the surveillance wing attached at the rear. It acquired a new paint job in 2017 as part of a public art project. GORDON GOLDSBOROUGH

The complex consisted of 6½ acres of land containing an array of radio antennas, three buildings, and a water tower. The most notable of those buildings was a T-shaped, metal-clad, two-storey structure. The land in this region is mostly frozen year-round, but shifting and melting permafrost presents unique challenges for the construction of buildings on top of it. This building featured, at that time, innovative technology to keep it true and level, and the soil below it cold; it is perched atop numerous concrete piles driven deep into the ground and sits about six feet above ground level. Consequently, it appeared to be sitting on stilts. This was one of the first applications of this design, and the idea would later be copied widely in other parts of the world subject to permafrost, including the Soviet Union. The facility had its own sewer and water systems and, although it received electricity from nearby Fort Churchill, it also had a diesel-powered generator as a backup. The public area of the building included offices (among them Churchill's only dental office, staffed by a naval officer), dormitories, eating and recreational space for Navy personnel. There were engineering and storage rooms and, at the back, a high-security locked area where the communications equipment was located.

HMCS Churchill went into operation in late 1950 and continued to June 1965 when most of its personnel were transferred to Ottawa or Inuvik. In July 1966, the complex was renamed CFS (Canadian Forces Station) Churchill and it closed fully in mid-1968 with a closing ceremony on 4 June 1968. Control transferred from the Navy to Public Works Canada. In 1971, Churchill MLA Gordon Beard and port commissioner John Kristiansen toured the vacant building and, hoping to preempt a sale to two developers from Alberta, they proposed the complex as a site for a new Canadian university based at Churchill. They conferred with Premier Ed Schreyer, who asked federal minister James Richardson to delay the sale pending provincial discussion of what role it would play in establishing a university in northern Manitoba. Nothing came of those plans but, later that year, the provincial government purchased the site from the federal Crown Assets Corporation for $20,000. In 1972, renewed plans called for the facility to become a "job training, higher educational, and research centre." The public offered such other possible uses as "a consumers' co-op store, a fish and fur buying co-op, a trucking, bus and taxi service, a wholesale supply centre for northern co-ops which would

HMCS Churchill at the height of its operations, date unknown. The water tower behind it was removed sometime in the 1980s. *CHURCHILL, NORTH OF 58° ... THROUGH THE YEARS* BY CHURCHILL LADIES CLUB, 2002

include purchasing of boats and the handling of their own deliveries, a handicraft production and sales industry, a nursing home for old people, and a hotel bar and catering service."

Unfortunately, none of these plans came to fruition, but the building still remains a provincial government asset. In 1984, my wife and I wandered around inside it during a summer spent in Churchill. I remember the thoroughness with which the building was stripped of most contents. Three huge boilers that had once provided heat, and the diesel power generator, were still inside mechanical rooms on the main floor. Otherwise, the building consisted of little more than empty rooms, painted in the sort of pastel shades that we associate with the 1950s and 1960s. Graffiti was splattered here and there, and most of the glass in the windows was broken, but otherwise the building was remarkably intact. The government later covered the windows with plywood (and thieves subsequently stole much of it) and, in June 2017, the exterior was painted in a large black-and-white mural as part of a public art project around Churchill.

I visited the building for a second time in the summer of 2018. Since my first visit, 34 years earlier, the water tower had been dismantled and removed. A close look at the exterior showed the lengths to which the builders had gone to shield the walls and bottom of the building against the prevailing cold. Below its main floor were air chambers about one foot in height, below which were two layers of dense styrofoam, presumably intended as

An innovative system of piles and insulated floors allowed the main building of HMCS Churchill to stand on shifting or melting permafrost, June 2018. GORDON GOLDSBOROUGH

insulation. The foam was protected on the exterior side by a layer of cement board. The outside walls of the building, and many of the inside walls too, were filled with paper-backed batts of brown, fluffy material that looked like today's fiberglass insulation. Later, I learned that the durable, fireproof, pest-proof stuff first appeared in western Canada in 1936, made in Winnipeg by Gypsum Lime and Alabastine Canada Limited using gypsum quarried at Gypsumville. Moving inside through an open rear doorway, I found that damage from vandalism was more extensive than when I was here years ago, with holes punched in many of the walls. Missing window boards made it easy to see, and I found that I could guess the functions for most of the rooms from labels on the few remaining doors or from room layouts. A person entering the building via its front entrance would encounter a small lobby leading to each of the three main wings. To the left was the "accommodations wing." On each of its two storeys, on either side of a central corridor running the entire length, were dormitory-style rooms for up to six men each, a few single rooms probably reserved for officers, and several communal washrooms containing toilets, sinks, shower stalls, and bathtubs. To the right of the lobby, the "service wing" had a storeroom, laundry, and boiler room on its main level and a spacious kitchen, dining hall, and recreation hall on its second level. Straight ahead from the lobby, at the back of the building, was the "surveillance wing." On its main floor were offices and workshops and, on the second floor was the guarded, high-security area. Most of the window boards were still intact here so, using my cellphone as a makeshift flashlight, I cautiously climbed the steel stairs to the upper level. There was a heavy metal door at the top

A hallway on the second floor in the accommodations wing of the former HMCS Churchill, June 2018.
GORDON GOLDSBOROUGH

leading into a central corridor, with several small rooms on either side and a larger, open room at one end. I suspected that was the "command centre" where the surveillance work was done. Curiously, most rooms had a trough in the floor, at least a foot deep and up to three feet wide, running through them. Having seen something similar in modern rooms containing computer hardware, I guessed they were intended for cables connecting the electrical equipment in the various rooms. It was exciting to think that I could walk readily through rooms where, if I had visited during the building's heyday in the early 1960s, the security guards would have kept me out.

Given the general level of disarray that I witnessed during my recent visit, it seems doubtful the former military building will ever return to any direct, useful purpose. However, it will continue to serve an indirect purpose as a reminder of a tense period in the mid-20th century when the Cold War and "mutually assured destruction" (whose acronym, appropriately enough, was MAD) was a topic of widespread concern. With that in mind, when visiting Churchill, I encourage you to stop by this old building for some introspective "naval-gazing."

The main electronics room on the second floor in the high-security surveillance wing, June 2018. GORDON GOLDSBOROUGH

ACKNOWLEDGEMENTS

I am indebted to Jerry Proc whose website provided a wealth of information. He also answered my questions patiently and informatively, and provided feedback on an early draft of this chapter. My 2018 visit to Churchill, during which I spent several hours exploring the old naval building, was made possible by the Manitoba Heritage Grants Program.

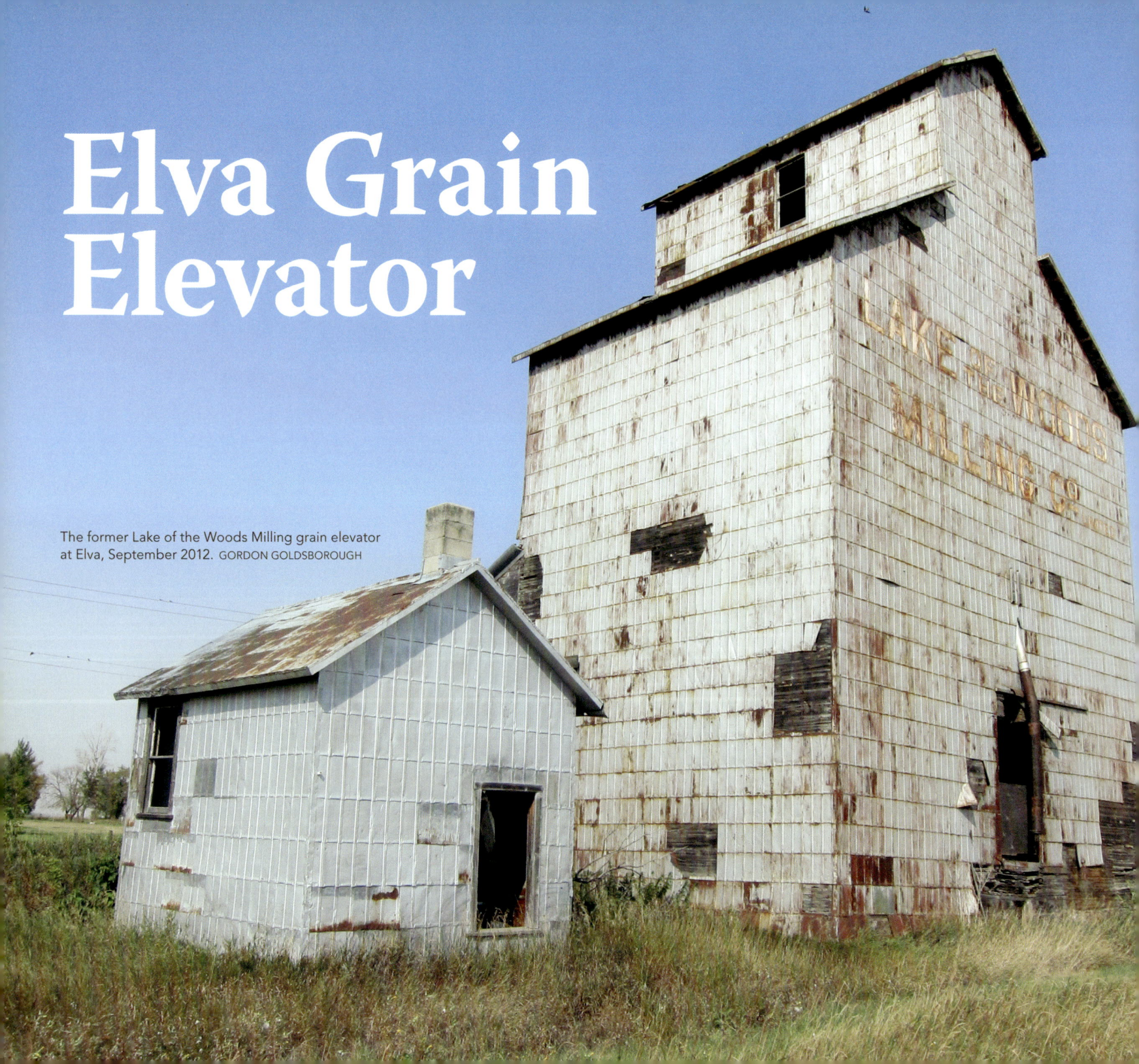

Elva Grain Elevator

The former Lake of the Woods Milling grain elevator at Elva, September 2012. GORDON GOLDSBOROUGH

In 2010, a wooden grain elevator at Fleming, Saskatchewan, three miles west of the Manitoba border, was due to be designated as a national historic site. Built in 1895, it was Canada's oldest "standard-plan" grain elevator on its original site. Unfortunately, in the wee hours of 9 February 2010, the elevator was set on fire and destroyed. A Manitoba man was arrested, convicted of arson, and sentenced to two years in jail with a fine of $30,000. The former second-oldest grain elevator in the nation now became the oldest. That elevator, built in 1897 by the same company that owned the one at Fleming, stands vacant in the village of Elva, in the southwestern corner of Manitoba. It is too bad that nobody seems interested in recognizing its historical significance.

In 1887, a group of Montreal investors affiliated with the Canadian Pacific Railway established a large mill at Keewatin, Ontario (now Kenora) to process prairie wheat into what became known as the Five Roses brand of flour. Operating as The Lake of the Woods Milling Company, they also built mills at Portage la Prairie, Medicine Hat (Alberta), and Brantford (Ontario), an extensive network of elevators across the prairies to purchase grain from farmers, and a regional administrative office in Winnipeg. The company operated until November 1954, when its assets were purchased by another Montreal-based firm, the Ogilvie Flour Mills Company. In 1959, their grain elevators in Manitoba were re-sold to Winnipeg-based Manitoba Pool Elevators. The Lake of the Woods mill

at Keewatin was destroyed by fire in the 1960s and not rebuilt. The nice little administrative office in Winnipeg's Exchange District is now occupied by a private art gallery. Four of the former Lake of the Woods elevators remain standing in Manitoba, at Cameron, Elva, Harmsworth, and Tilston.

German-born businessman William Hespeler holds the distinction of building the first grain storage structure in Manitoba. Constructed in 1879 using a distinctive circular design, the wooden structure looked remarkably like the steel granaries used on most Manitoba farms today. The next generation of buildings used to store grain was the flat warehouse (see sidebar), which saw their peak in the 1880s through early 1900s. The standard-plan elevator

In 2002, when this photo was taken, Canada's oldest surviving grain elevator stood at Fleming, Saskatchewan. JOHN FRIESEN

This historically-significant photo of Niverville was taken in 1910, when three generations of grain-handling facilities were standing together. On the right was the first elevator in western Canada, a round 25,000-bushel facility built in 1879 by William Hespeler of Winnipeg. It received grain from newly-arrived Mennonite farmers and was used until 1904. On the left is a flat warehouse that, after its usefulness for storing grain ended, was used as a community hall from 1929 to 1963. In the centre is a 27,000-bushel standard-plan elevator built in 1904 by Ogilvie Flour Mills and dismantled in 1938 to make way for a new 35,000-bushel elevator. MANITOBA POOL COLLECTION, S. J. MCKEE ARCHIVES, BRANDON UNIVERSITY

with which we are familiar—so called because it was built according to a standard set of specifications—appeared first at Gretna in 1881 and was predominant throughout the 20th century. In 1925, a document entitled "Standard 32,000 Bushel Wood Clad Elevator" was given to elevator builders by one of the grain companies, United Grain Growers (UGG). It described in complete detail how an elevator was to be built using 90,000 board-feet of lumber, 5,000 pounds of nails, 42 gallons of paint, and an assortment of pulleys, buckets, and other metal hardware.

To make the 54-foot-tall "crib" that was the main body of an elevator, carpenters stacked 2-inch by 6-inch boards (or 2-inch by 4-inch boards nearer the top) on top of each other and fastened them all together with copious nails. Inside the crib were a dozen or more separate bins where various types of grain—32,000 bushels in total—could be stored. The crib was topped with a roof covered in cedar shingles and a wooden cupola where a metal manifold, sometimes called a "gerber," was housed. A driveshed (also called a driveway) on the ground alongside the crib provided the passageway for grain-delivery wagons (or, later, trucks). Below the driveshed, partly buried in the ground, was an inverted metal pyramid called the "pit." A long wooden box from the bottom of the pit to the top of the gerber enclosed a looped reinforced-rubber belt to which were riveted numerous metal buckets. This was the "leg." Next to the leg was a "manlift," a hand-operated dumbwaiter on which its single occupant could pull themselves by rope up to the gerber.

Standing some distance from the elevator (to minimize the risk of fire) was the elevator office and engine room. In the early days, the engine room held a steam- or kerosene-powered engine that moved the belt in the leg. (Electrically-powered legs did not exist until well into the 20th century, when transmission lines were installed around southern Manitoba.) The office was the only part of the elevator to be heated, usually with a wood-burning stove, so it was the only place habitable during the winter. Sometimes, when more grain capacity was needed than the elevator bins provided, a secondary storage structure—an annex—was built beside the crib. Ideally, this annex was built with the same stacked-lumber method as the crib. A more economical form was the "balloon annex" made with vertical wooden studs with boards on their inner side—so called because it was not nearly as strong as a crib-type annex and would tend to balloon out under the weight of grain inside them. Most busy elevators had at least one annex, and some had several. Balloon annexes were built as temporary storage facilities, usually during periods of excess supply, or when grain could not be readily transported to market, such as during the Second World War, when German submarines disrupted Allied grain shipments to Europe.

The way that an elevator operated was straightforward. A wagonload of grain entered the driveshed and stopped over a metal grate above the pit. The grain was poured into the pit. The moving buckets of the leg picked up scoops of grain and carried them to the top of the elevator

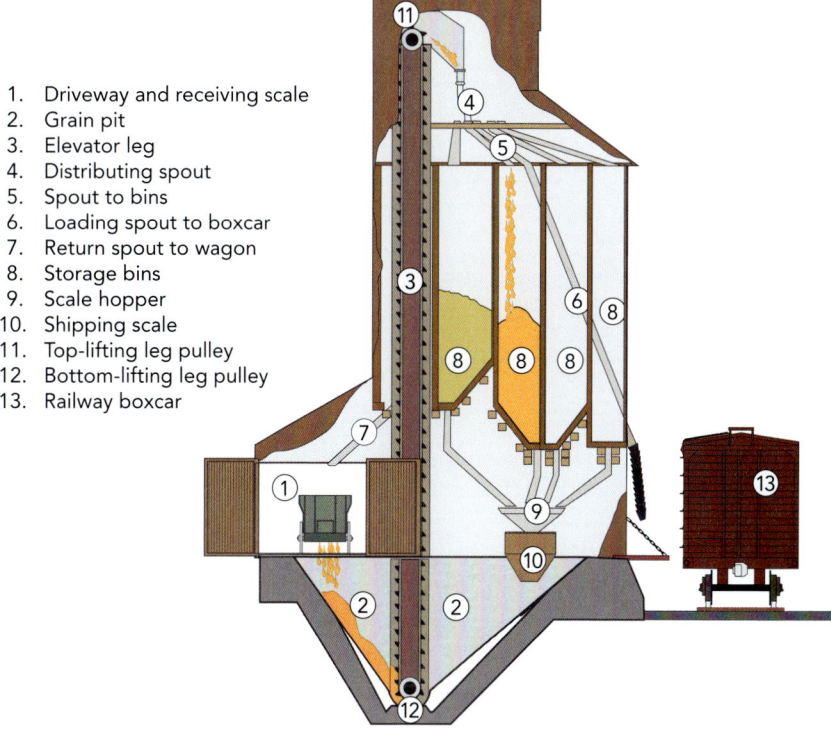

1. Driveway and receiving scale
2. Grain pit
3. Elevator leg
4. Distributing spout
5. Spout to bins
6. Loading spout to boxcar
7. Return spout to wagon
8. Storage bins
9. Scale hopper
10. Shipping scale
11. Top-lifting leg pulley
12. Bottom-lifting leg pulley
13. Railway boxcar

This cutaway diagram of a grain elevator from the early 20th century shows how grain delivered in a horse-drawn wagon at left (1) is transferred to the storage bins (8) and eventually to a railway boxcar (13). JIM A. PEARSON

where the gerber routed the grain into a spout leading to one of the bins, depending on the setting of a large wheel on the leg down in the driveshed. When grain was to be taken out of a bin, a hatch in its bottom was opened and the grain poured into the pit where the leg took it back to the top, then the gerber shunted it into a spout leading to a railway boxcar or to an empty wagon in the driveshed.

In the vast majority of cases, elevators were built by large companies which had the resources needed to build and operate them. In the 1890s, some of the major

In an aerial view of Elva, probably taken in the 1940s, we see the town's two grain elevators, United Grain Growers in the foreground and Lake of the Woods Milling in the back. BETTY MINSHULL

firms were the Canadian Northwest Elevator Company, Dominion Elevator Company, Manitoba Grain Company, and Northern Elevator Company. However, these would all change in the 20th century. A few private entrepreneurs built elevators in their immediate vicinity, including Alfred Arnold at Shoal Lake, Andy Forsythe at Portage la Prairie, John McConnell at Hamiota, and Finlay Young at Killarney. The "Golden Age of Elevators" was from the 1920s to the 1950s when the number peaked at 745 elevators (in 1928), and a growing proportion were operated by farmer-owned cooperatives—UGG (founded in 1917) and Manitoba Pool Elevators (1925). Any town of note in southern Manitoba had at least one elevator, and sometimes several. In 1950, for example, there were six elevators at Dauphin. The decline in number of elevators began with railway abandonment in the early 1960s then accelerated rapidly in the mid-1970s. Today, there are just 84 licensed commercial elevators in Manitoba. Other elevators are used for private purposes but the total number is less than 200. A map of all the places in Manitoba that have ever had an elevator, with black symbols denoting elevators that are now gone and white symbols for survivors, is overwhelming dominated by blackness.

As the number of elevators declined in the 1970s, the size of elevators increased. In 1960, the average elevator held 68,500 bushels of grain, over twice the capacity of UGG's 1925 specification. Today, the average is almost exactly ten times bigger: 697,600 bushels. The largest elevator in Manitoba is 4,440,700 bushels: 65 times the 1960 size and 178 times the average size in the 1920s. Now, the grain industry is dominated by a

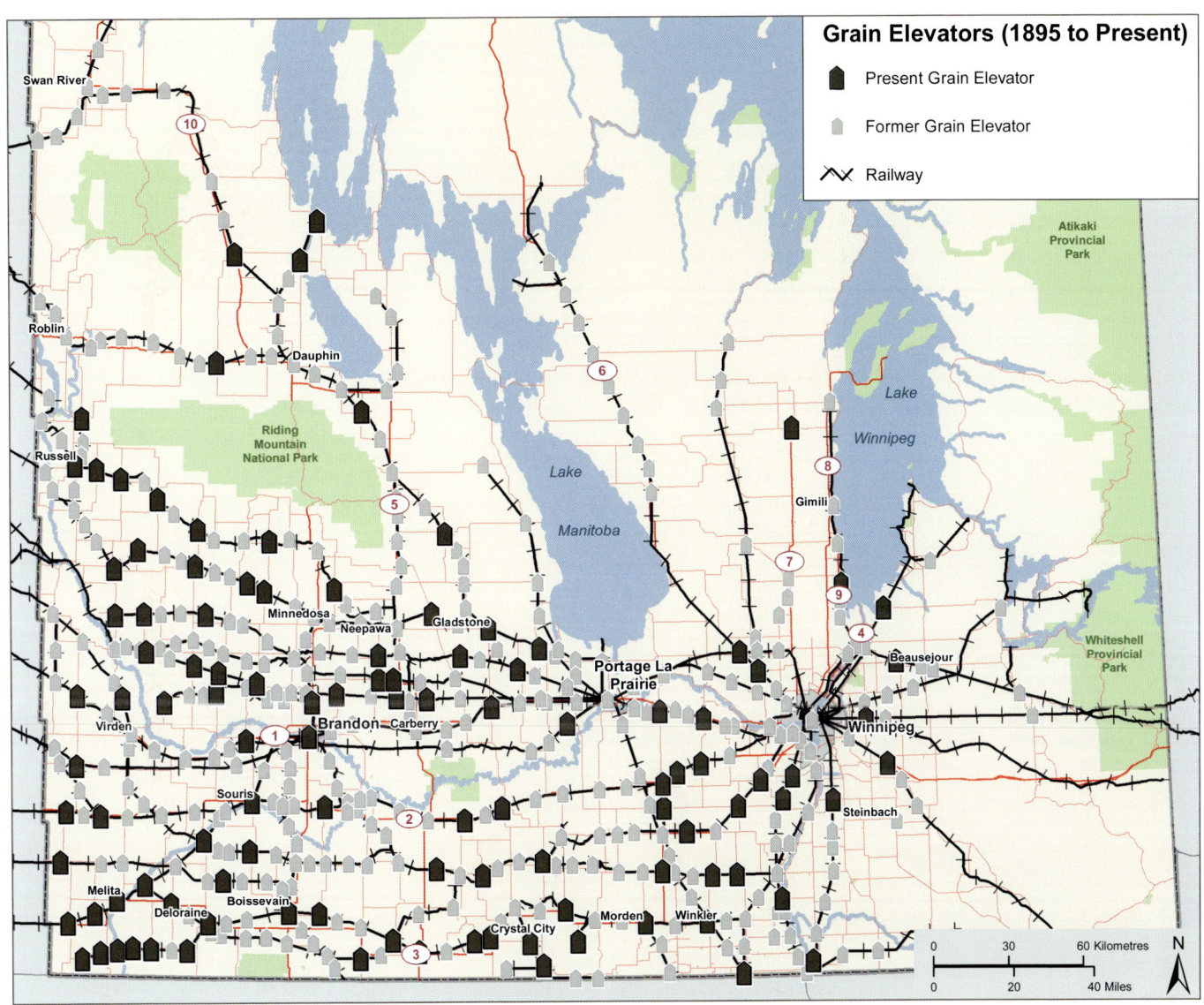

Grain Elevators (1895 to Present)

- **■ Present Grain Elevator**
- **■ Former Grain Elevator**
- **⋀⋁ Railway**

Swan River
Roblin
Dauphin
Russell
Riding Mountain National Park
Minnedosa
Neepawa
Gladstone
Virden
Brandon
Carberry
Souris
Melita
Deloraine
Boissevain
Crystal City
Morden
Winkler
Portage La Prairie
Steinbach
Winnipeg
Beausejour
Gimili
Lake Manitoba
Lake Winnipeg
Atikaki Provincial Park
Whiteshell Provincial Park

0   30   60 Kilometres
0   20   40 Miles
N

This map shows the locations of grain elevators that have operated in southern Manitoba since 1895. The dark grey symbols are elevators that still stand; light grey symbols are elevators that are gone. MAP BY JENNIFER LIDGETT USING DATA FROM GORDON GOLDSBOROUGH

Brookdale Flat Warehouse

From the 1880s through early 1900s, many Manitoba farmers delivered their grain to a "flat warehouse," so called because it was horizontal, as opposed to elevators, which were vertical. A flat warehouse was a one-storey rectangular building with a ramp on one side for horse-drawn wagons, and rails on the other side for loading grain into boxcars. Farmers would fill large, cloth sacks with their grain then load the sacks into their wagon. (Sometimes, they would carry loose grain in their wagon box.) Arriving at the warehouse,

Manitoba's last surviving flat warehouse, built in 1902 at Brookdale, was occupied only by pigeons when I visited in June 2016. GORDON GOLDSBOROUGH

the farmer drove up the ramp, stopping beside a large door. The grain sacks were loaded onto a trolley and hauled inside. There, they were weighed and stacked, or emptied into a bin, from which sacks could be later filled and sold. To ship grain farther afield, the sacks were loaded back onto a trolley and wheeled into a railway car sitting on the opposite side of the warehouse. The process was labour-intensive so it could take an entire day to load a single boxcar. The first standard-plan elevator was built in 1881, at Gretna. Through the next two decades, flat warehouses and elevators were both popular but, because elevators moved grain without need of manual labour, they quickly began to displace the flat warehouses. In 1901, Manitoba had 76 licensed flat warehouses; by 1917, it had none.

The last remaining flat warehouse in Manitoba is in Brookdale, in the Municipality of North Cypress-Langford, about 30 miles by road northeast of Brandon. The building is rectangular with a gable roof. Made of wood covered on the outside by overlapping tin panels painted bright red, there is a large door in the centre of the south side, and another large door on the railway side. Its main floor contains one large room, although there was once a small office (indicated by windows and a brick chimney) in the southeast corner.

A ladder inside the warehouse leads up to a second floor where there was additional storage space. This flat warehouse was constructed in 1902, in the waning days of the style's popularity, by local businessman David McNaughton. Two years later, it was sold to John P. Lawrie (who would later serve three terms as an MLA) and used for buying grain and selling farm supplies. In 1919, Lawrie bought a hardware store in Brookdale and used the warehouse to store farm supplies and fertilizer. The warehouse was subsequently owned by his son Angus, and later by non-family members.

The warehouse used to sit alongside two standard elevators, one owned by Manitoba Pool and the other by UGG. The Pool elevator still stands, but is no longer used actively, and the UGG elevator was torn down in 2013. The flat warehouse is presently unoccupied and open to the elements. Its windows are broken out and pigeons have deposited mounds of poop everywhere. The wooden posts on which the warehouse stands are tilting severely on front so it won't be long before this last vestige of early grain shipping technology collapses.

few huge elevators, typically made of concrete or steel, sparsely distributed across the landscape. Curiously, the trend toward fewer, larger elevators has not meant a change in the total storage capacity for grain. In fact, the total capacity is greater now than at any time in the past. The important change is that farmers must drive farther to deliver their grain. This means larger trucks to haul it. Such trucks require better municipal and provincial roads. The net result of improved roads and greater traffic is rural depopulation. Communities decline as rail lines are abandoned; small rural businesses close along with schools, churches, and post offices. These days, when an elevator is closed by a grain company, it is demolished. Why is a perfectly good building, often only 20 or 30 years old, demolished rather than being offered for sale? At one time, grain companies that were closing a rural elevator were willing to sell to farmers for their own personal use. Today, most companies refuse to do so, either because they do not want their former asset to become competition or because the railway on whose land the elevator stands will not allow the lease to be transferred. I am told the railway companies are concerned about the risk of having deteriorating elevators adjacent to their lines if maintenance is neglected by small, private owners.

In the summer of 2014, Winnipeg nurse Jean McManus resolved to photograph all the surviving elevators in Manitoba as a retirement project. She and her husband Tighe drove all over the province and she later shared her photos with me. I was struck at how quickly we were losing what was once considered to be a symbol of the prairies. I decided that we needed to capture information on the disappearing wooden grain elevators. Since January 2016, I have collaborated with the *Manitoba Co-operator*, a weekly agricultural newspaper, in a feature called "This Old Elevator." Each week, we feature a photo of an elevator somewhere in Manitoba— either surviving or gone—and provide a brief sketch of its history. I have heard from many *Co-operator* readers who faithfully clip the weekly story for their scrapbooks. Clearly, there is a lot of emotion about the disappearing elevators. The website of the Manitoba Historical Society, which I administer, now has an interactive map called the "Manitoba Elevator Countdown." It shows all the remaining wooden elevators (we do not map the concrete and steel ones, which are not at risk) and the count decreases every time an elevator is lost. At the time that I write this, the count stands at 133 survivors. Of this total, my rough tally suggests about half are used for private grain storage. Another one-third are clearly abandoned and falling into ruin. I am uncertain about the rest because I cannot ascertain if they are being used. (I usually check if the ramp leading into the driveshed is covered with grass and if there is any evidence of trampling from vehicle traffic.) In the past year, six elevators were lost, all but one to demolition, the other to accidental fire. The act

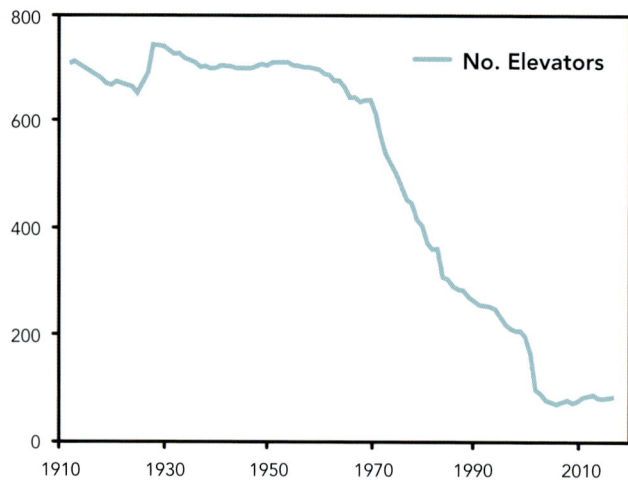

800

600

400

200

0

1910   1930   1950   1970   1990   2010

— No. Elevators

The number of licensed grain elevators in Manitoba has changed dramatically over the past 106 years, decreasing from a high of 745 (in 1928) to 84 in use today. DRAWN FROM GRAIN ELEVATORS IN CANADA, COMPILED BY BOARD OF GRAIN COMMISSIONERS FOR CANADA, WINNIPEG, 1912–1930, 1930–1953, 1953–1998 [PEEL'S PRAIRIE PROVINCES, UNIVERSITY OF ALBERTA LIBRARIES], 1998–2016 [CANADIAN GRAIN COMMISSION]

of demolition should be considered carefully because, once the elevator is gone, no amount of nostalgia will bring it back. An important task is keeping the elevator dry by ensuring its roof shingles and wall sheathing are intact. However, it is not merely a matter of keeping the elevator for its own sake; fundamentally, a use must be found that preserves it as a useful structure, if not for grain storage, then for something else.

The best example of elevator preservation in Manitoba is undoubtedly the row of five magnificent elevators at Inglis. Owned at one time by four companies, four of the elevators were built in the early 1920s and the fifth went up in 1940. By the early 1990s, the number of owners

had dwindled to two—Paterson Grain and UGG. In 1992, John Everitt, a geographer at Brandon University with a long-standing interest in the prairie grain industry, had completed a major study of Manitoba elevators on behalf of the provincial government's Historic Resources Branch. The project had collected information on most of the elevators in the province and it had specifically identified the five elevators at Inglis as the cream of the crop. However, Everitt predicted that:

> Paterson is building an inland terminal at Binscarth which it hopes will be operational by 1995. As soon as this is completed, Paterson will close its operations in Inglis. With Paterson gone the railway may decide to pull the line out, forcing UGG to close, or UGG may just decide to consolidate its operations in Russell and Roblin, leaving no reason for the line to exist. Either way, the last traditional row of elevators left in Manitoba will almost certainly cease to exist within three to five years.

The new concrete elevator opened at Binscarth in 1995 and, as Everitt had predicted, the railway line to Inglis and all five elevators closed the following year. However, local attention had been drawn to a potential new life for the elevators. In 1994, using Everitt's report and their own research, Historic Resources Branch staff had ranked the historical and architectural significance of elevators around Manitoba on a scale from 0 to 200. Those receiving a high score would ideally be 1) built between 1880 and 1900, 2) in a rural setting among other elevators, 3) have a building largely unaltered with original equipment in functional condition, 4) have other "support" buildings such as annexes and coal storage sheds surviving, 5) be in very good structural condition, and 6) be located on an easy-to-locate site near a major highway. Of course, no single elevator met all these criteria so the highest score achieved by any elevator was 150. It was one of the elevators at Inglis, all of which ranked highly.

In October 1994, Historic Resources Branch staff gave a presentation to the Russell Chamber of Commerce. They mentioned the potential benefits to tourism of preserving the Inglis elevators as a local museum, seeing as there were few, if any, intact "rows" in western Canada. Local resident Marcia Rowat was at the presentation and went away impressed by the possibility. Within weeks, she and other concerned citizens formed and later incorporated a charitable organization called the Inglis Area Heritage Committee. They began negotiating with the grain companies to delay tearing down their elevators, donate money that would otherwise pay for the demolition, and transfer ownership to the group. They developed a business plan and invited the general public to become supporters. People were aroused but not always favourably. When residents were told at a meeting that the elevators were likely to survive, John Everitt recalls that "about half the room loved me and about half hated me for wasting their taxes." Those people saw the old elevators as eyesores, rat magnets, fire hazards, or worse. Ultimately, the Committee prevailed. The elevator row was recognized

as a national (1996) and provincial (1999) historic site. The elevators received new coats of paint and considerable restoration work to return them to their former glory. Now that the Inglis elevators are preserved for the benefit of future generations who otherwise may never see a wooden grain elevator, perhaps we can consider others for similar protection? The point, it seems to me, is not trying to save all of the old elevators but to identify a few especially noteworthy ones. How about the oldest elevator in the province and the nation?

Is the elevator at Elva, about seven miles southwest of Melita, truly the oldest in Manitoba? There are three lines of supporting evidence. First, its architecture is consistent with elevators built in the 1890s. The general outline follows the standard-plan architecture common throughout the 20th century but its squat design is especially consistent with elevators built between 1881 and 1910. Unfortunately, design details do not provide a tight estimate of construction date. Second, I found a Canadian Pacific Railway map of Elva at the provincial archives. It showed the locations of four elevators there in the early 20th century. A label beside the Lake of the Woods elevator said "Sept. '97." Was this the elevator's date of construction? Maybe, but maybe not. Third, and most definitively, I found a "smoking gun" among Lake of the Woods Milling Company documents at the University of Manitoba Archives. Dated in January 1933, the document listed all elevators operated by the company at that time, noting about the one at Elva:

This is a very old elevator, having been built in 1897, and as far as our records show no major repairs have ever been made since that time. At the present time the equipment is obsolete and the plant should be carried on the Company's books at the very lowest possible figure. It has a wrecking value of the salvage from the building only as all of the machine is obsolete.

The report further claimed that "this is an elevator that for the past 10 or 12 years has contributed nothing in the way of an earning for the Company" so that repairs should be done only "sufficient to keep the plant in operation." Some historians have speculated that parts of the structure were replaced in 1950, specifically its foundation and weigh scale, but the vehemence with which the 1933 report argued against an upgrade makes me wonder. Purchased by Manitoba Pool in 1959 and closed in late 1967 or early 1968, the building was sold to a private owner. I have not been inside the elevator, but it appears not to have been used for many years and is becoming quite badly deteriorated. Beside it is another old decrepit elevator. The second elevator is about 20 years newer than its neighbour, built by the Manitoba Elevator Commission (an agency of the provincial government) in 1916. Later leased to UGG, it was purchased by the firm in 1926 and used until July 1967 then sold into private ownership. In its assessment of the Elva elevators in 1994, the Historic Resources Branch concluded that both were in poor condition and not especially good candidates for

designation as historic buildings because of their out-of-the-way location and "minimal level of site context."

Stating that Elva is the oldest elevator in Manitoba leads naturally to a question about which elevator is the second-oldest, third-oldest, and so on. I have spent several years researching grain elevators around Manitoba, yet I cannot provide a definitive list because there are few surviving records from the turn-of-the-20th century. A table in this chapter lists what I believe are the ten oldest commercial elevators remaining in Manitoba. By my reckoning, the second-oldest elevator is the one at the Manitoba Agricultural Museum south of Austin. Built in 1901 at Austin for the Western Canada Flour Mills, the structure is not completely original, its driveshed having been rebuilt (according to the original specs) when it was moved to the museum in 1976. My list includes only the ones built by companies, excluding ones built by farmers for their own needs. However, a pair of outstanding examples of old private elevators are the Dobbin family elevator in the Municipality of Norfolk Treherne, built in 1901, and the Durston family elevator near Dauphin, built in 1917.

I am confident is saying that Elva is the oldest grain elevator in Manitoba. Is it the oldest in Canada? It depends on the definition of an elevator. An elevator at Port Perry, Ontario was built in 1874, but it is quite different in appearance from the standard plan that is our modern stereotype. When research was done by federal historians twenty-five years ago, the oldest standard-plan elevator in Saskatchewan was the one at Fleming, and it

Present Location (Original Location)	Municipality	Builder	Built
Elva	Two Borders	Lake of the Woods Milling	1897
Manitoba Agricultural Museum (Austin)	North Norfolk	Western Canada Flour Mills	1901
Cameron	Two Borders	Lake of the Woods Milling	1902
Napinka	Brenda-Waskada	Ogilvie Milling	1902
Kaleida	Pembina	Ogilvie Milling	1905
Harmsworth	Wallace-Woodworth	Lake of the Woods Milling	1910
Isabella	Prairie View	Western Canada Flour Mills	1910
Purves	Louise	Maple Leaf Milling	1910 (est.)
Woodland Hutterite Colony (Grosse Isle)	Woodlands (Rockwood)	Manitoba Elevator Commission	1911
McConnell	Hamiota	Alfred S. Arnold	1913

The ten oldest commercial standard-plan grain elevators in Manitoba.

is now gone. The oldest one in Alberta was the "Ritchie Mill Elevator" in downtown Edmonton, built in 1892, and still standing … after a fashion. That elevator has been heavily renovated into fancy office space. So much of the original structure is gone that I would scarcely consider it an elevator at all. With an assumption that standard-plan elevators of Elva's general vintage exist only in the three prairie provinces, I contend that Elva is the oldest *intact* grain elevator in Canada. The gauntlet is down and I challenge some reader to prove me wrong.

In 2012, British Columbia-based artist Christopher Walker offered half the proceeds from sales of signed, limited-edition art prints for the preservation of historic grain elevators in Manitoba. His print was a winter scene of the Elva elevator with a diesel locomotive passing by. It was a great gesture of support but, unfortunately, it did nothing to ignite widespread public enthusiasm for preserving the Elva elevator. I worry that, someday soon, Elva will meet the same fate as its slightly older brethren at Fleming.

ACKNOWLEDGEMENTS

I am grateful to Betty Minshull for sharing her photo of Elva in its glory days, and John Friesen for sharing his photo of the late elevator at Fleming, Saskatchewan. Bernice Still helped to clarify the age of the grain elevators at Isabella. Susan Angie, now retired from Parks Canada, generously gave me her files on grain elevators, including a copy of the 1925 specification for standard-plans elevators. I encourage anyone wanting to know more about the wooden grain elevators of Manitoba to pick up a copy of Jim Pearson's excellent, thoroughly illustrated 2017 book *Vanishing Sentinels Volume 4: The Remaining Grain Elevators of Manitoba*, from which the cutaway diagram shown here was taken (with Jim's kind permission). Finally, I must acknowledge the wonderful resources on grain elevators at the University of Manitoba Archives & Special Collections and the S. J. McKee Archives at Brandon University. Collectively, they provided a wealth of information, some of which I used in this chapter, and much that will end up in another book someday.

Brookeville
Granite Quarry

I love cemeteries. I know that a lot of people find them scary or creepy, but I think they offer a treasure trove of information on the community in which they are situated. They reveal family genealogy, population demographics, and noteworthy events such as epidemics that carried off community residents. Often, one of the most interesting attributes of a cemetery is the material from which the grave marker for a deceased loved one is made. If the means of the family were modest, the marker might be correspondingly modest, made from concrete or possibly even short-lived wood. Sometimes, the marker is incredibly elaborate and ornate, using stone brought from great distances at enormous cost. If you ever see a pink-coloured gravestone, it might have an interesting origin. It might date from the early 20th century, cut from a now-abandoned quarry nestled in the boreal forest of eastern Manitoba.

OPPOSITE Concrete mount for a millhouse machine at the Brookeville Quarry, September 2016. GORDON GOLDSBOROUGH

Our story starts with the Greater Winnipeg Water District (GWWD) railway, built to assist in construction of the aqueduct between Shoal Lake and Winnipeg from 1913 to 1919. Not only did this railway facilitate aqueduct construction and maintenance, it also provided transportation for people living in a relatively undeveloped part of the province. (The Manitoba Prison Farm described in a later chapter also made use of the GWWD railway line.)

British-born John Brooke came to Canada in 1905 and worked for a marble and granite dealer in Winnipeg. Six years later, Brooke founded his own company, taking his two sons into the business four years later as "J. H. Brooke & Sons." The firm specialized in "granite and marble monuments, statuary, fonts (baptismal bowls in churches), memorials, tablets, vaults, etc." Some of its products were made from grey- or pink-coloured granite obtained from local sources. This is interesting because, up to that time, most granite was brought into Manitoba

The office of the Brookeville Quarry and a sign advertising its red and grey granite, circa 1920. OSCAR BERGENSTEIN

from elsewhere, sometimes from as far away as Scotland. Granite is a described by geologists as an igneous (volcanic) rock containing a mixture of silicon, aluminum, and other elements. It is a hard, tough stone, well-suited for construction projects going back to antiquity. Polished granite slabs often have attractive colourful patterns and are the materials of choice for decorative floors and countertops in offices and homes. Its strength and durability makes it useful for marking graves.

Men use a derrick at right to move large blocks of granite from the quarry up to a narrow-gauge railway to convey them into the millhouse for processing, circa 1920. OSCAR BERGENSTEIN

However, carving granite with hand tools is difficult, at least until the 1830s when a Scottish stonemason, inspired by ancient Egyptian granite carvings on exhibit at the British Museum, invented a steam-powered machine to polish granite with relative ease. His granite slabs became highly desirable for gravestones and monuments all over the world.

In theory, Manitoba has an abundance of granite, contained in the Precambrian Shield that underlies much of the eastern part of our province. However, commercial development of the granite deposits has been hampered by the difficulty of accessing this relatively remote, heavily forested area. In 1917, John Brooke learned that, during the course of constructing the GWWD railway, granite had been discovered near Mile 79, about one-third mile north of the tracks. The close proximity of transportation could make a granite quarry commercially feasible.

Brooke staked a homestead claim on the land beside the future quarry site. He also bought the former railway construction camp at Mile 79, consisting of a bunk-house, cookhouse, and equipment, as well as cranes, narrow-gauge railway, and steam engine, and began quarrying granite at the site in late 1918 or early 1919. A large L-shaped millhouse measuring 5,800 square feet, where the rough rock was cut and polished, was constructed between 1918 and 1919. Cost of developing the quarry was said to be $125,000, about $1,750,000 in today's dollars. Advertised in Winnipeg newspapers as the "Brookeville Red and Grey Granite Quarries," Brooke apparently based the quarry's name on the community that he expected to develop nearby. Unfortunately, his grand plans for Brookeville were quashed when the local postmaster instead chose Braintree after a town in Massachusetts where he had once lived. (The prefix "East" was added later by postal officials.)

One of Brooke's first hires for his new quarry was Swedish-born Gustav Bergenstein, an experienced quarry-man who had previously worked at the Garson limestone quarry. Bergenstein and his family took up residence in a house built for the GWWD's engineer. He supervised the drilling and blasting of granite blocks weighing up to 135 tons from deposits near the quarry buildings. Chunks of up to twenty tons were lifted by a steam-powered crane onto a horse-drawn railcar, and moved about one-quarter mile on narrow-gauge rails into the millhouse. There, the rock was cut into regular shapes and polished or sand-blasted. Electricity to power lights and run the polishing machines was provided by an engine standing beside the millhouse. Workers were initially accommodated in the GWWD construction camp but the company announced plans to build cottages for married workers next to the Birch River. There was a house to store ice for refrigeration during the summer. Midwinter School (named for Charles Midwinter, Chair of the GWWD) stood nearby for the children of workers, and there was telephone service to the outside world. Brooke predicted confidently that the area was primed for development and

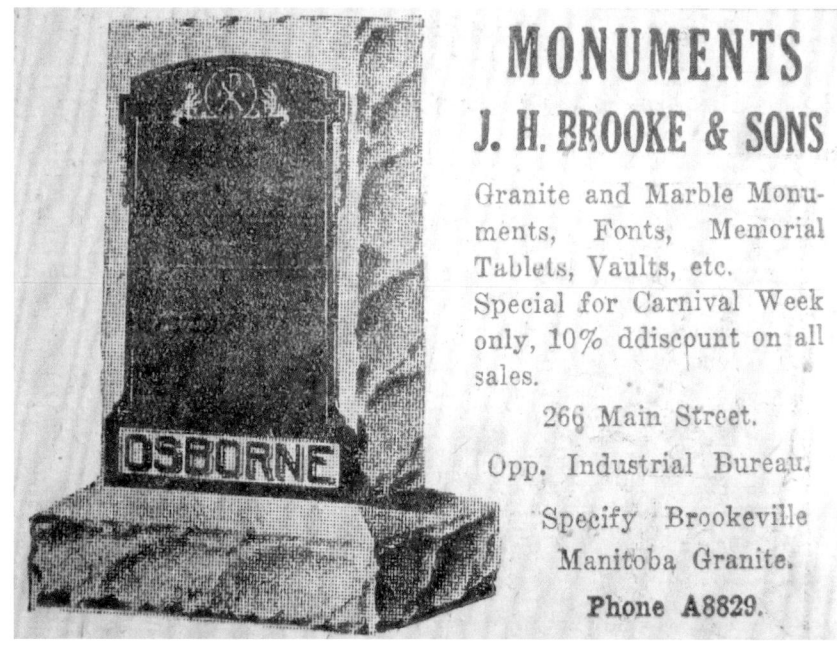

By the time this ad was published in the *Winnipeg Tribune*, in February 1922, the Brookeville granite quarry near East Braintree had been closed for over a year. John Brooke was probably drawing on his supply of quarried stone.

Former rock-processing millhouse at the Brookeville Quarry, September 2016. GORDON GOLDSBOROUGH

Sample of the red granite from the Brookeville Quarry. GORDON GOLDSBOROUGH

would eventually support a population of 18,000 people. He claimed the area had "more granite in this neighbourhood than in all Scotland" and it was the "only granite quarry under development west of the Great Lakes." The future for the quarrying of high-quality granite in eastern Manitoba looked rosy, with Brooke boasting to local reporters that:

> We are now in a position to supply our granites for any purpose as we can quarry blocks of any size. We do not intend to use any foreign granite in future as our own granite outrivals any imported granite. In showing customers our samples they prefer the Manitoba stone to any other. There are several large buildings going up in the near future and the architects are specifying our granite. Our expert [presumably, Brooke himself] has had forty-two years in the marble and granite business and he has not yet handled a better granite.

In November 1920, a regular-gauge spur line to the GWWD line (built by the GWWD but paid for by Brooke) replaced the original narrow-gauge tracks, allowing finished stone to be moved directly from the millhouse to market. Just days after it was completed, the quarry closed for the winter. By early January 1921, Brooke had completed the incorporation of his company as the Brookeville Granite Quarries Limited, with four Winnipeg-based shareholders in addition to himself: manager George John Seale, lawyer Alexander Shirriff Morrison, financial agent John Crichton, and undertaker Arinbjorn Sigurgeirsson Bardal. Brooke had, by far, the largest number of shares in the new venture but, of the other shareholders, Bardal probably had the more direct interest in the quarry: to obtain low-cost, high-profit granite for gravestones to sell to his customers.

Unfortunately, the quarry had already reached the pinnacle of its activity and did not reopen in 1921. Bardal's descendants speculate the cause might have been a flu pandemic that swept the globe from 1918 to 1920, killing between 50 and 100 million people. Numerous Manitobans were among the casualties and cash flow to the granite quarry might have been restricted when one of its major shareholders could not collect on bills for a large number of burials for impoverished families. Despite the setback to its plans for global supremacy in the granite industry, J. H. Brooke & Sons remained in business until 1950, later operating as Brooks [sic] Memorials under different ownership. However, the quarry was abandoned after a mere two years of operation. Brooke continued to advertise "Brookeville Manitoba Granite" in his newspaper advertisements through 1922 but he might have been merely selling the backlog of previously quarried stone. In October 1922, in what may have been a final attempt to resuscitate the quarry, Brooke led a tour of prominent citizens on a visit to the site, including "ladies interested in work in connection with war memorials." In the aftermath of the First World War, numerous war cenotaphs were being constructed around the province and Brooke probably hoped to cash in on that business. Although I have visited numerous stone war memorials in communities large and small around Manitoba, I have found no evidence that any of them was made from Brookeville stone, nor I have I uncovered records, despite Brooke's bold claims to newspaper reporters, that any buildings erected in Manitoba around this time contained granite from Brooke's quarry. The Brookeville quarry never reopened. A resident caretaker looked after the site into the late 1920s. The property fell into tax arrears in 1927 and

the narrow-gauge rails between quarry and millhouse were removed in 1929. Locals scavenged the site for building materials and equipment. During the 1930s, granite would be quarried at nearby McMunn and used to face a GWWD building in St. Boniface. That quarry never developed to its full potential either.

I visited the former Brookeville Quarry in the autumn of 2016. The concrete foundation of its millhouse is still readily visible, as is a small concrete stand beside the foundation that once held a tank used in the facility. Large trees inside the building attest to the long period of time for which the facility has been abandoned. Stout brick walls that had once stood on the foundation were mostly gone except for a few broken discards. The bricks had been scavenged for use in building projects all over the region, including for the buildings at the aforementioned Prison Farm.

Thievery of building materials to construct other structures is a time-honoured practice going back centuries. My grandfather, who grew up in the English region of Northumberland, lived in a house made of stone scavenged from a wall built by the Roman emperor Hadrian. This past winter, my family and I vacationed at a resort on Mexico's Yucatan Peninsula near the magnificent Mayan temple at Chichen Itza, two sides of which are mostly intact but one side was cannibalized to build, among other things, the first Roman Catholic church in Mexico.

Returning to Brookeville, I also found, a short walk from the former millhouse, the quarry itself, where large

More Abandoned Manitoba: Rivers, Rails, and Ruins

granite boulders, presumably deemed unsuitable for processing, had been abandoned. The rugged, unpolished chunks of rocks lacked the lustre and colour of the finished product, the supply of which is now strictly limited due to the short period of time in which it was produced. So, if you ever visit a cemetery around Manitoba, or admire a monument, and are struck by its pink colour, it is possible that you are seeing local granite from the short-lived Brookeville Quarry near East Braintree.

ACKNOWLEDGEMENTS

I would know nothing about the Brookeville Quarry were it not for the indefatigable Lorna Annell. She first drew my attention to it and was my enthusiastic guide on a visit there in September 2016. She put me in touch with Walter Loewen who has done exhaustive research on the site, rescuing it from obscurity. He generously shared with me a rare collection of historical photos from Oscar Bergenstein, son of the Brookeville quarryman, and provided feedback on an early draft of this chapter.

Cutting slabs of Tyndall Stone at the Gillis Quarries of Garson, July 2017. GORDON GOLDSBOROUGH

OPPOSITE Abandoned blocks of granite at the Brookeville Quarry. GORDON GOLDSBOROUGH

Grand Rapids
Tramway

In 1877, the Governor General of Canada, the 51-year-old Lord Dufferin, visited the country's newly acquired province of Manitoba. He was accompanied by his wife, the 34-year-old Marchioness of Dufferin and Ava. During their seven-week visit, the couple got a good taste of the transportation options available to Manitobans at that time. They travelled by steamboat on rivers and lakes. By horse-drawn wagon, they crossed virgin prairie and a rough corduroy road. They paddled in a canoe and crashed through raging rapids aboard a York boat. Perhaps most significantly, they rode on a small, wooden cart whose wheels rolled on a pair of parallel steel rails. Completed shortly after the vice-regal party returned home to eastern Canada, the Grand Rapids Tramway is now largely forgotten and mostly under water.

OPPOSITE A restored section of the Grand Rapids Tramway with one of its tramcars, July 2017. GORDON GOLDSBOROUGH

Some people think the famous photo of a "last spike" being hammered in at Craigellachie, British Columbia in November 1885 marked the completion of the first railway in western Canada. It was not. Almost seven years earlier, in December 1878, a last spike was driven for a railway from the United States to St. Boniface, along the east side of the Red River in Manitoba. However, this railway was also not the first one in western Canada. The Grand Rapids Tramway holds this distinction … by several months. Its story goes back to the days of the fur trade when voyageurs for the Hudson's Bay Company (HBC) used the Saskatchewan River to transport goods destined for western trading posts, farm implements for the few settlers in the region, and supplies for the federal government's Indian Department. They faced a daunting set of rapids—the Grand Rapids that dropped 70 feet over the course of four miles—as they paddled up the river from Lake Winnipeg on their way to points west. Rather than risk

The Hudson's Bay Company ship *Colvile*, named for HBC Governor Eden Colvile, was built in 1875 for operation on the Red River and around Lake Winnipeg. It transported men and materiel to build the Grand Rapid Tramway and it brought Lord and Lady Dufferin to Grand Rapids during their 1877 visit to Manitoba. This photo of the *Colvile* at Norway House was taken in mid-1881 by American photographer Jay Haynes. It was destroyed by fire on 15 July 1894 while moored at Grand Rapids. GORDON GOLDSBOROUGH

losing their valuable cargo, the men carried everything around the rapids but that, too, was a challenge because the portage was several miles long. In 1876, the HBC hired English-born

This illustration of travellers aboard the Grand Rapids Tramway was contained in a slim 1883 booklet entitled "Manitoba and the Northwest," published in Toronto by James Campbell & Sons. GORDON GOLDSBOROUGH PHOTO COLLECTION

engineer Walter Moberly to replace the labour-intensive portage with a mechanized means of conveyance. He bought 24-foot-long steel rails from a foundry at Cleveland, Ohio and had them shipped to Winnipeg by Red River steamboat. The construction started in the spring of 1877. The HBC ship *Colvile* unloaded the materials, work crews, construction equipment, and camping gear at the mouth of the Saskatchewan River, near the downstream end of the rapids. As Moberly surveyed a right-of-way on land leased from the federal government, some of his men cleared and graded it while others sought suitably-sized trees to be cut with axes into squared wooden ties. These were laid on the cleared ground over a total distance of 3¾ miles. It was a narrow gauge line where the rails were spiked to the ties 3½ feet apart, closer together than the 4⅔-foot gauge used by railways in eastern Canada and the United States. They used lightweight 18-pound-per-yard rails, compared to the 56-pound-per-yard

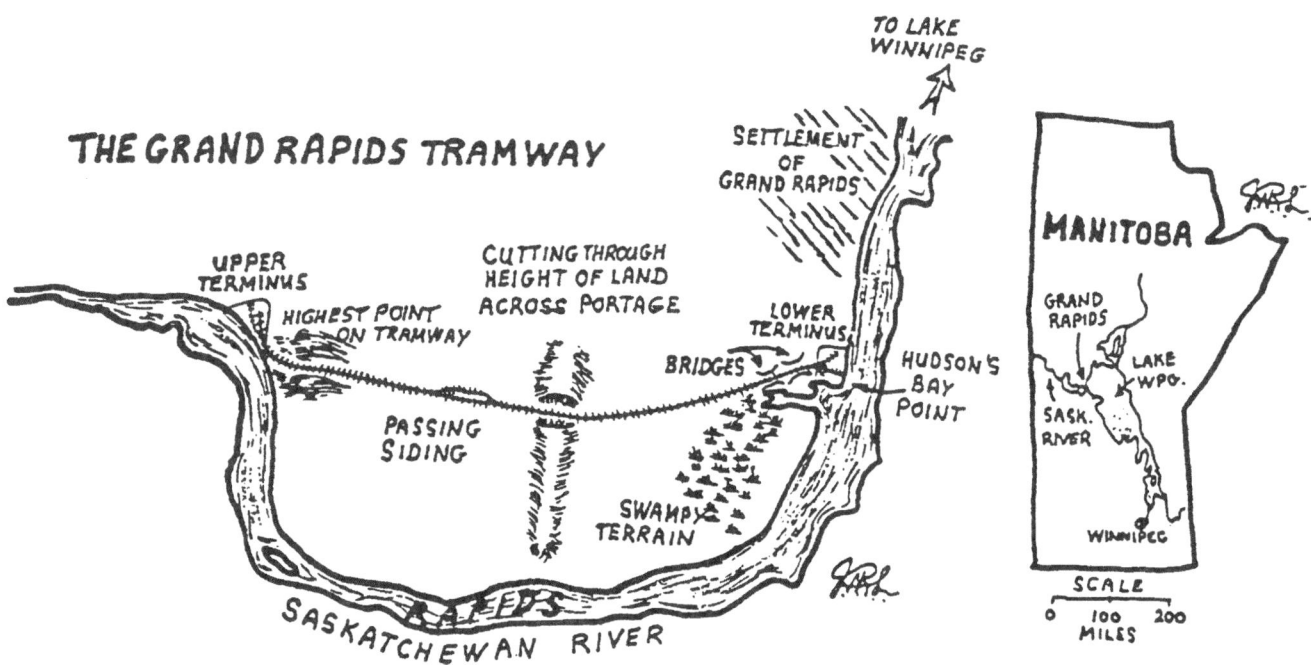

A sketch of the Grand Rapids Tramway while in operation. RODGER LETOURNEAU, *MHS TRANSACTIONS*, SERIES 3, NUMBER 32, 1975-1976 SEASON

rails in common railway use at the time, so the resulting "tramway" could support only small vehicles capable of carrying few passengers and light freight. Six tramcars, each five feet wide and six feet long, made of oak and iron brought by the *Colvile*, capable of carrying up to three tons, would be pulled not by a steam-powered locomotive, but by a horse or mule. Cargo from boats arriving at either side of the rapids would be unloaded, piled onto the tramcars, and pulled past the rapids, then loaded on another boat for transportation to its final destination.

On 11 September 1877, Lord and Lady Dufferin arrived aboard the *Colvile* at the lake-ward terminus of the new tramway. Moberly and his workers had been working feverishly to complete the new tramway on schedule and the two vice-regal visitors became its first official passengers to the upper terminus, although some of the rails had not yet been laid. Lady Dufferin would observe in her memoir *My Canadian Journal*, published 14 years later, that:

> Mr. McTavish, one of the Hudson's Bay Company, came to meet us, and took us two miles across the portage on a tramway laid down since July, and the first railway in

The Second "First Railway"

On the morning of Tuesday, 3 December 1878, the first steam locomotive in western Canada stood hissing softly at the station in St. Boniface. Three flat cars and a caboose were linked behind it. Slightly before 9:00 AM, a group of men and women climbed aboard, the women heading into the caboose and the men onto the flat cars. Among them were numerous luminaries of Winnipeg society. With a bellow of its whistle, the train slowly pulled out of the station, heading south, chuffing happily as it picked up steam until it was cruising along at 25 miles per hour. The train passed the village of St. Norbert, then Niverville before stopping briefly at Otterburne to replenish its supply of firewood and water. Then, it continued on through Dufrost and Arnaud, arriving at the siding of Penza beside the Roseau River, the site of today's Dominion City, at noon.

Here the train stopped, for it had reached a 750-foot-long section of roadbed without rails. Beyond, a second locomotive was waiting, newly arrived from the south. The passengers disembarked to watch as two crews of workmen busily completed the missing section of rails, fastening them to wooden ties with metal spikes, but leaving a dozen spikes undone. Customs official George Spencer invited the women to come forward and drive home the remaining spikes. So far as we know, unlike a famous later ceremony in British Columbia, no photographer was on hand to record the event for posterity. Everyone re-boarded the train to return to a railway construction camp ten miles north where they enjoyed a catered luncheon of oysters and chicken, washed down with champagne and other beverages. Music was played, songs were sung, and toasts were made to Queen Victoria, US President Rutherford Hayes, and Mr. Willis, their host and the railway's contractor. After further socializing, the little train headed for home, arriving back in St. Boniface before nightfall. Everyone aboard must have been jubilant in realizing that Manitoba was now connected by rail to the outside world. Previously, the only routes in and out of the province were fraught with adventure. Henceforth, trips to and from Manitoba would be faster, more comfortable, and relatively inexpensive aboard the 63-mile Pembina Branch, connecting to American railways and thence to the wider world. It was technically the second railway in western Canada, but it was the first one to carry substantial quantities of cargo and passengers, more than any canoe, York boat, Red River cart, steamboat, or tramcar. The West was about to change.

the North-West. The car was most gorgeously lined with coloured blankets, and when we got out of it we jumped into spring-carts, in which we did the unfinished part of the railway. During the drive we saw some views of the river, and went to the Hudson's Bay Company's store. We then inspected a new steel steamer, and lunched; and I put in a rivet in the last bit of the railway, and was presented with the hammer.

After Lady Dufferin drove the ceremonial "last spike" for the tramway, they were taken down the rapids in a York boat before heading back south on Lake Winnipeg aboard the *Colvile*, stopping for a visit with Icelandic settlers at Gimli along the way. After two weeks as guests of business magnate Donald Smith at Silver Heights, west of Winnipeg, and shooting and eating wild birds with MLA James McKay at his cottage on Lake Manitoba, they performed one more official duty before leaving the province. In the morning of 29 September, they arrived at a newly constructed railway station in St. Boniface to be met by Lieutenant Governor Alexander Morris, Archbishop Alexandre-Antonin Taché, Bishop Vital Grandin, and other dignitaries. Conspicuously absent was contractor Joseph Whitehead, who was in the United States picking up a steam locomotive for the railway that he was building. The Governor General and Lady Dufferin were given silver-plated hammers and they proceeded to drive in silver spikes (not gold ones, as is popularly imagined) on rails adjacent to the railway station. Then, work crews took over the work, completing "in an exceedingly short time a long piece of the road." It was the beginning of construction of the Pembina Branch of the Canadian Pacific Railway (CPR), the first true railway in western Canada— as opposed to Moberly's lighter gauge tramway that was nearing completion up at Grand Rapids. Later that day, the royal guests boarded the steamboat *Minnesota* to begin their return trip to Ottawa. Eleven days later, Joseph Whitehead arrived in Winnipeg with a shiny, new steam locomotive aboard a barge towed by the steamboat *Selkirk*, to be used to construct the Pembina Branch.

The Grand Rapids Tramway helped to make the Saskatchewan River a viable northern transportation route to western Canada. Indigenous men living in the area worked as teamsters to transport tons of material around the rapids over a period of about twenty years. Meanwhile, in southern Manitoba, the Pembina Branch was completed a little more than a year after the Governor

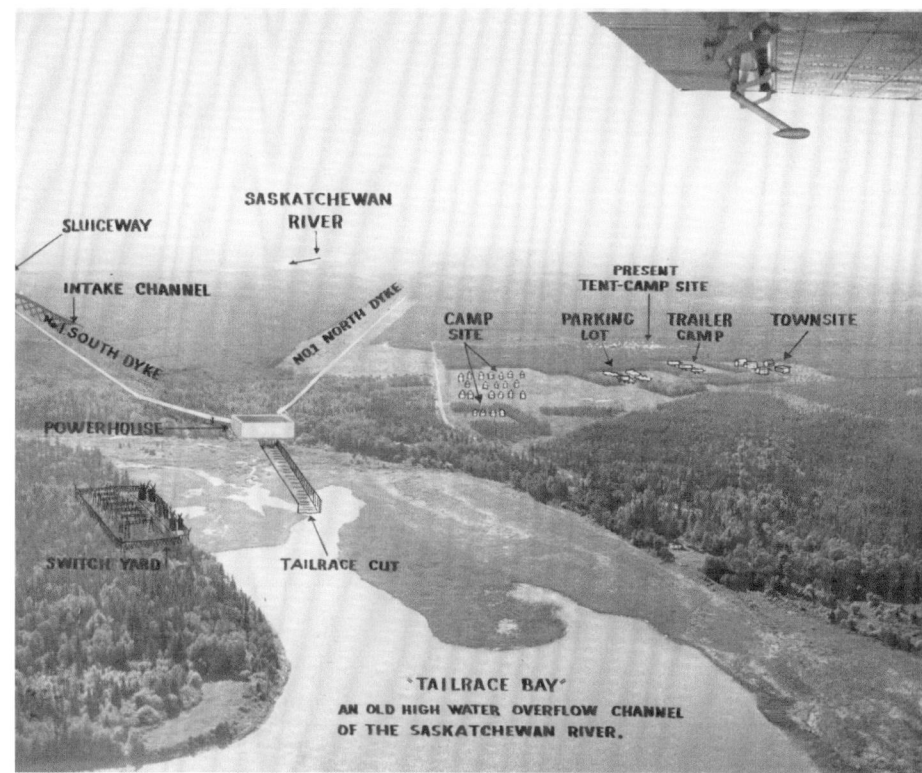

An aerial view of the Saskatchewan River in the early 1960s before construction of the Grand Rapids Generating Station, with the future positions of various structures drawn on it. The Grand Rapids Tramway would be at the right side of the photo. MANITOBA HYDRO

A section of the original Grand Rapids Tramway, probably taken prior to its removal during construction of the Grand Rapids Generating Station in the early 1960s. MANITOBA HYDRO

General's departure. By 1883, the CPR had built another line through inhospitable territory north of the Great Lakes to establish an all-Canadian route to the west. Together, these two railways would bring thousands of people from around the world into Manitoba and start an agricultural revolution that would transform the prairies. Through the 1890s, as the CPR gradually made shipping on the Saskatchewan River less attractive economically, the little tramway around the Grand Rapids fell into disrepair and the HBC lease of the right-of-way was surrendered to the federal government. In 1932, a group of tourists at Grand Rapids walked "by foot over the mossy, flower-strewn right-of-way, among rusty rails, and crumbling ties, enveloped as in a corridor by the forest growth looming on either side to the very foot of the roadbed. The once-sturdy, little team cars lay mildewed and forlorn."

In 1960, Manitoba Hydro began constructing its Grand Rapids Generating Station, the first hydro dam in northern Manitoba after the water resources of the Winnipeg River had been fully exploited. A massive concrete and earthen dam was built to impound the Saskatchewan River and enlarge Cedar Lake. One of the early tasks in the project was to remove about two-thirds of the former tramway in an area due to be flooded. As the water behind the dam started to rise, the former right-of-way, along with the once-daunting rapids on the Saskatchewan River, disappeared into Cedar Lake. By the mid-1970s, about one-third of the original rails were still present but "badly deteriorated and vandalized." A section of rails were moved to a Hydro building near the new station and a replica tramcar was set on them. Between 1983 and 1984, students from the Grand Rapids school restored a short section of the original tramway, along with two of its original tramcars.

In July 2017, I visited Grand Rapids with a group of engineers. We read commemorative plaques installed beside the restored section of the tramway in 1987 by the Canadian Society for Civil Engineering and, in 2001, by the Manitoba Heritage Council. We walked along the old tracks, climbed on one of the restored tramcars—now looking somewhat disheveled—and inspected a crumbling wooden bridge nearby. As we paid our respects at this inconspicuous spot near the mighty Grand Rapids Generating System, whose reservoir eliminated the navigational obstacle that had motivated construction of the tramway, I wondered if Lady Dufferin ever considered her place in the transportation history of western Canada? She and her husband arrived at a pivotal time in our history, as the canoes, York boats, and steamboats of the past were giving way to steel rails. She ushered in the future when she drove the last spike of the Grand Rapids Tramway and the first spike of the Canadian Pacific Railway. Her name has become synonymous with the history of railways in western Canada. In a nod to the royal guests that he had missed, Joseph Whitehead named his new locomotive—the first in the west— the *Countess of Dufferin*. It still sits proudly on display at Winnipeg's Railway Museum.

ACKNOWLEDGEMENTS

I learned details about the Governor General's visit to Manitoba, not from digitized historical newspapers that are my usual to-go source, but from a bound volume of the original *Manitoba Free Press* from 1877 and 1878. I find the experience of reading news from the pages of a fragile, old newspaper profoundly more engaging than peering at a computer screen.

McKenzie
Seeds Building

My late father Len was what you might call an "extreme gardener." What dad's garden lacked in diversity, it made up in abundance. His garden was several acres in area and it produced far more than he would ever need to feed his family. His obsession with gardening probably had something to do with growing up during the Great Depression when self-reliance became ingrained in the personality of many Manitobans. In later years, the wealth of dad's garden mostly went to Winnipeg Harvest but, I admit, a lot of it ended up on my table too. Nothing reminds me of him more than a trip through the produce aisle at the grocery store or seeing displays of colourful seed packages at the garden centre. I am not certain where dad obtained his seeds, but I suspect a lot of them came from the McKenzie Seeds Building on Brandon's Ninth Street. This building was once the centre of Canada's seed industry and it was the city's tallest building for 63 years. Now, it stands empty and disintegrating.

In 1882, 12-year-old Albert McKenzie moved with his family from Ontario to the newly founded city of Brandon, where his father Francis McKenzie established a seed and grain business. In time, Albert joined his father in the business and, when his father died suddenly in late 1896, he took it over and, along with a staff of three or four people, shifted its emphasis to the retail selling of garden seeds bought from growers. Three years later,

A dour Albert McKenzie sits with his business managers in the centre of this undated photo. He had the same stern facial expression in every one of the archival photos that I found of him. S. J. MCKEE ARCHIVES, BRANDON UNIVERSITY

his Brandon Seed House produced, for the first time, a 28-page illustrated catalogue—one of the first in western Canada—and mailed it far and wide. Gardeners all over the prairies could browse its pages and fantasize about the plants they could grow in their gardens with help from Albert McKenzie. By 1905, the firm had 50,000 catalogue customers and that number had blossomed to nearly 82,000 within two years. In March 1906, McKenzie incorporated the firm, becoming A. E. McKenzie & Company, with himself as President. He enticed Spencer Bedford, a well-known agriculturalist who had been founding superintendent of the Brandon Experimental Farm, to become general manager of the firm. Horticulturist Henry

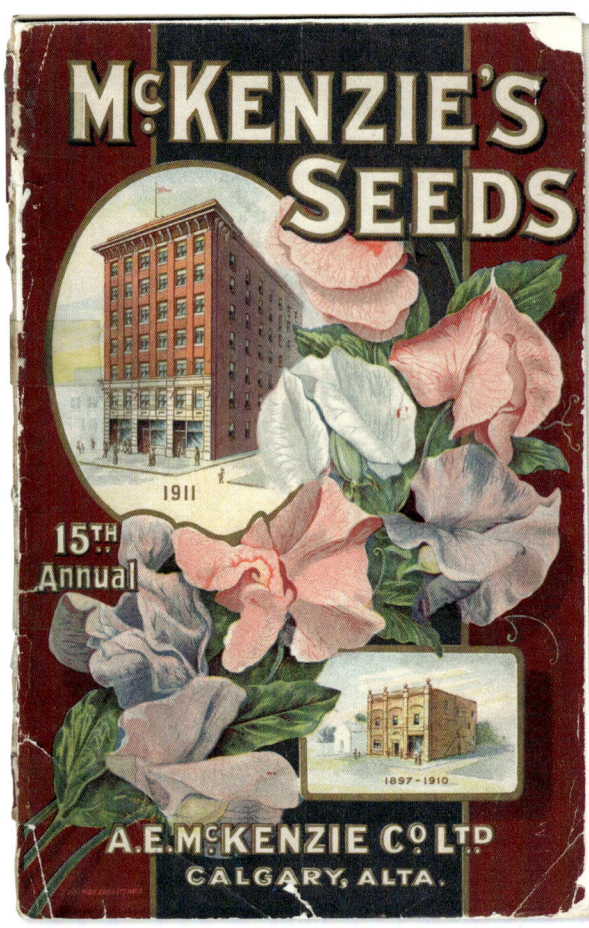

The cover of Albert McKenzie's 1911 seed catalogue featured images of his first store, operated from 1897 to 1910, and the newly constructed seven-storey structure that still stands on Ninth Street in Brandon. S. J. MCKEE ARCHIVES, BRANDON UNIVERSITY

Patmore became its vice-president, with responsibility for nursery and greenhouse operations, and William McCracken was put in charge of the warehousing, shipping, and mail order functions.

In 1910, the company and its thirty employees moved into a grand, seven-storey concrete and red brick building—later known as the South Building—designed by Brandon architect Thomas Sinclair, and constructed for $100,000 (or $2.5 million in today's dollars) by the Brandon Construction Company. It was the first reinforced concrete building in Brandon (the nearby Clements Block came second, in 1911) and it held the record as Brandon's tallest building until 1973, when it was surpassed by the eleven-storey Scotia Towers. It was a huge building, with 7,200 square feet of floor space on each level, including a full basement, over an acre in total area, with twelve-foot ceilings. Company offices were located on the ground level, equipped with the most modern equipment, including a letter opening machine for incoming mail, a letter sealing machine for outgoing mail, and a bookkeeping machine for maintaining ledgers and monthly statements. The shipping and receiving department, and seed laboratory, were also at ground level. The second floor was dedicated to storing over one thousand varieties of vegetable and flower seeds, while the seed packing and shipment departments were on the third floor along with a testing section where seed germination and vitality were monitored. Two seed packing machines were capable of filling up to 25,000 packets daily, while a bulk packing machine could fill 12,000 one-pound packages per day. The upper levels had bulk storage and cleaning facilities for seed grain. Two elevators allowed freight and people to be transported between floors. As a protective measure against fire that could destroy its valuable seed stock, water sprinklers were installed throughout the building. Heat was provided not by a fired source like a boiler or furnace, but by a central plant operated by the

Women filled bags and packets with seeds in this undated photo in the warehouse of the McKenzie Seeds Building. S. J. MCKEE ARCHIVES, BRANDON UNIVERSITY

Brandon Electric Light Company. Adjacent to the building was a railway spur where two boxcars could be loaded or unloaded simultaneously. Between 1918 and 1919, to expand the firm's seed-cleaning capability, and expand its livestock and poultry feed department, large concrete storage tanks were built at the rear of the South Building. A 47-foot steel spiral staircase from the seventh floor of the original building to the top of the new storage tanks led to the "twelfth floor," an observation deck 183 feet above the ground from which workers and visitors could get a panoramic view

of Brandon, the Assiniboine River valley, and rural areas to the south. Between 1944 and 1946, the five-storey, 70,000-square-foot "North Building" was built alongside the South Building, with overhead bridges providing a pedestrian connection between them, bringing the size of the total facility to nearly 3½ acres of floor space.

Albert McKenzie was a cool, principled man, married with two daughters, known for his scrupulous honesty, loyalty to his employees, and hard-driving business acumen. In the course of researching this chapter, I

Colourful packages for some of the seeds sold by Albert McKenzie, for ten or fifteen cents each, are retained in archival collections at Brandon University. S. J. MCKEE ARCHIVES, BRANDON UNIVERSITY

found several photos of him, and in every single one, he was scowling. However, he did laugh occasionally. Long-time employee Lasby Lowes recorded in his memoirs an anecdote told to him by a travelling hardware salesman who had once shared a seat with McKenzie on a crowded train. McKenzie introduced himself as being "A representative of A. E. McKenzie Seed Company in Brandon" to which the salesman responded "Don't tell me you work for that old bugger?" Lowes explained that:

> Mr. McKenzie very seldom ever said who he was. He was always "A representative of …" I didn't think to ask him what Mr. McKenzie then said to him about his remark but he did tell me they had lunch together and it was then that A. E. told him who he was. The Ashdown's man said he apologized and felt like crawling under the table. He said Mr. McKenzie laughed and laughed about it and thought it was a great joke.

Whatever his personal shortcomings, McKenzie was a zealous philanthropist, at least when it came to supporting the local institution of higher learning, Brandon College, the predecessor of today's Brandon University. Founded at Brandon in 1899 and long affiliated with the Baptist faith, during the Great Depression the College could not pay its bills and came close to closing. Despite not being a Baptist, McKenzie helped college administrators to lobby the provincial government for financial aid and rallied local support to keep it open. In 1939, he established the A. E. McKenzie Endowment Fund to financially assist the college. Six years later, McKenzie transferred 90% of his personal shares in his company, valued at one million dollars (about $18 million today), to the provincial government on the condition that dividends would go to Brandon College, in perpetuity, via the newly created A. E. McKenzie Foundation. For the next 49 years, the company was owned primarily by the provincial government, though McKenzie continued to manage it until his death in 1964.

Over time, A. E. McKenzie & Company grew into the largest of its kind in western Canada and employed up to 150 people, most of them in Brandon. Its expansion across the country was gradual. In 1908, it opened a branch office at Calgary to serve Alberta and British Columbia, and later another at Edmonton (1922). Two offices focused on the Saskatchewan market opened in 1923, at Moose Jaw and Saskatoon. The opening of a Toronto office in 1934 enabled the firm to grow its

Exterior of the McKenzie Seeds Building, October 2012. GORDON GOLDSBOROUGH

Boarded-over entrance to the McKenzie Seeds Building, alongside a provincial plaque commemorating its historical significance, June 2016. GORDON GOLDSBOROUGH

business throughout eastern Canada so it could become a truly national enterprise, eventually with branches at Vancouver and Quebec City. In August 1941, it purchased the McFayden Seed Company in Winnipeg's Exchange District, at that time the largest mail order seller of garden, vegetable, and flower seeds in Canada, along with its 91-acre nursery on Henderson Highway north of the city. Operated initially as a subsidiary, the operation was merged into the Brandon head office in 1962. Albert McKenzie died on 25 September 1964 and was replaced as president and general manager by Lasby Lowes. McKenzie would not witness the transformation of his company over the next decade, as it grew progressively larger through a series of corporate acquisitions after it rejected a 1966 takeover offer from Toronto-based Maple Leaf Mills. For a brief time in 1969, it stopped selling seed to farmers to focus its business solely on gardeners, marketing seeds directly through to consumers, though not by catalogue—its last edition appeared in 1966—and via a network of some 20,000 retail merchants.

Expansion began in 1969 when it returned to the field seed market by buying Winnipeg's Brett-Young Seeds Limited for $1.3 million. In November 1971, it spent another $2 million to swallow its largest competitor—Steele-Briggs Seed Company of Toronto, and began trading under the name of McKenzie Steele-Briggs Seeds, though it retained the corporate name of A. E. McKenzie Seeds Company. In March 1972, it ventured for the first time beyond the Canadian borders when it purchased one-third interest in the Mexico City-based Bon Jardin SA so it could gain access to the Latin American seed market. In 1975, the remaining 10% of Albert McKenzie's personal shares were transferred to the provincial government so the company became a wholly-owned provincial Crown Corporation. By the 1980s, it was Canada's only national seed-packing plant and its largest distributor of garden seed. The company returned to the private sector when, in December 1994, it was sold to Regal Greetings & Gift, the largest non-retail, mail-order company in Canada. In 2002, the managers at the time bought the company back from Regal. In 2006, it was sold to a Norwegian company, Jiffy International.

In December 2008, the company moved out of the building it had occupied for nearly a century, into a new, single-storey building a quarter-mile north, on the valley flats close to the Assiniboine River. The original building, which had become a provincially-designated historic site in 1996, was sold to real estate developers from British Columbia. In 2009 and 2010, it was used as a Halloween Haunted House by the Big Brothers and Big Sisters of Brandon. By 2011, there was a plan to renovate the building, to be called McKenzie Towers, into 93 condo units with one, two, or three bedrooms.

In early 2013, Brandon filmmakers Nate Bower, Shaun Cameron, and Graham Street schlepped 45 sheets of plywood up the stairs to the building's seventh floor to film a performance in the vacant building by ballet students from the Brandon School of Dance. The plywood was to provide flooring on which the dancers could dance. Their purpose was to film a beautiful performance in an unfamiliar, deteriorated space—and the vacant McKenzie Building fit the bill.

Shortly after they and the dancers departed, it became clear the condo project was in trouble. The plan changed into development of rental apartments. In late 2013, a website touting the project disappeared. Meanwhile, the building continues to deteriorate. In August 2017, a piece of the decorative cornice from its seventh floor exterior detached and crashed to ground. The street was closed for a time. The owners submitted an engineering report and schedule of work but, nearly a year later, the redevelopment project is not mentioned anywhere on their company website. As it nears ten years of vacancy, a building that for over a century was prominent on Brandon's skyline and in the lives of numerous Canadian gardeners, seems no closer to receiving a new life.

ACKNOWLEDGEMENTS

Long-time McKenzie Seeds employee Lasby Lowes compiled a large archive of information about the firm that is now held at Brandon University. Hopefully, someday, an historian will use his archive to produce a more comprehensive history of this important company than my brief summary here. I thank Shaun Cameron for sharing video and photos from his 2013 project inside the McKenzie Seeds Building.

In 2013, dancers from the Brandon School of Dance performed on a makeshift dance floor in the vacant McKenzie Seeds Building. MATTHEW DUBOFF

Fort Whyte
Clay Quarries

An aerial view of the former clay quarries that are now lakes at FortWhyte Alive with the Canada Cement facility in the background, June 2015.
GORDON GOLDSBOROUGH

One of the many reasons that people visit FortWhyte Alive in southwest Winnipeg is to see the huge flocks of ducks and geese that spend a few weeks each spring and fall relaxing on the small lakes there. It may surprise you to learn that these lakes are not natural; they are abandoned quarries. They were excavated, some of them over a century ago, to obtain raw materials for the manufacture of Portland cement at a nearby plant that is now mostly gone. Together, the lakes and the plant underpin the origins of one of Canada's leading environmental education facilities.

Cement is one of the ingredients used in making concrete. It is the adhesive that binds together sand and gravel to make a stone-like building material whose origins date back to the Egyptians, Greeks, and Romans. In Manitoba, the earliest record of cement manufacturing dates to 1900, at a shale quarry at Deerwood, northwest of Miami, and from 1907 to 1924 at Babcock, not far from the former Leary Brickworks near Roseisle. (I wrote about the Leary Brickworks in this book's predecessor.) Both of these facilities made "natural cement" using a mixture of clay or shale and burned limestone in a process that dates back to Roman times. Portland cement, invented in Britain around 1820 and named for its resemblance to Portland stone, took a mixture of limestone, gypsum, clay, sand, and iron oxide, heated it to temperatures over 1,200 °C to create a solid material called "clinker." Then, the clinker was ground into a caustic, grey powder. When combined with water and the other

The Canada Cement Company plant at Fort Whyte, 1956. ARCHIVES OF MANITOBA

ingredients, Portland cement produces a harder, stronger concrete than natural cement.

By the early 20th century, there were several companies across Canada making Portland cement. In 1909, ten companies from Quebec, Ontario, and Alberta merged to form the Canada Cement Company. In an offering to prospective shareholders, the company argued that, by consolidating cement manufacturing across the country into a near-monopoly, the "elimination of competitive salesmen, middlemen, and brokers is … expected to effect a considerable saving in the costs of the Sales Department

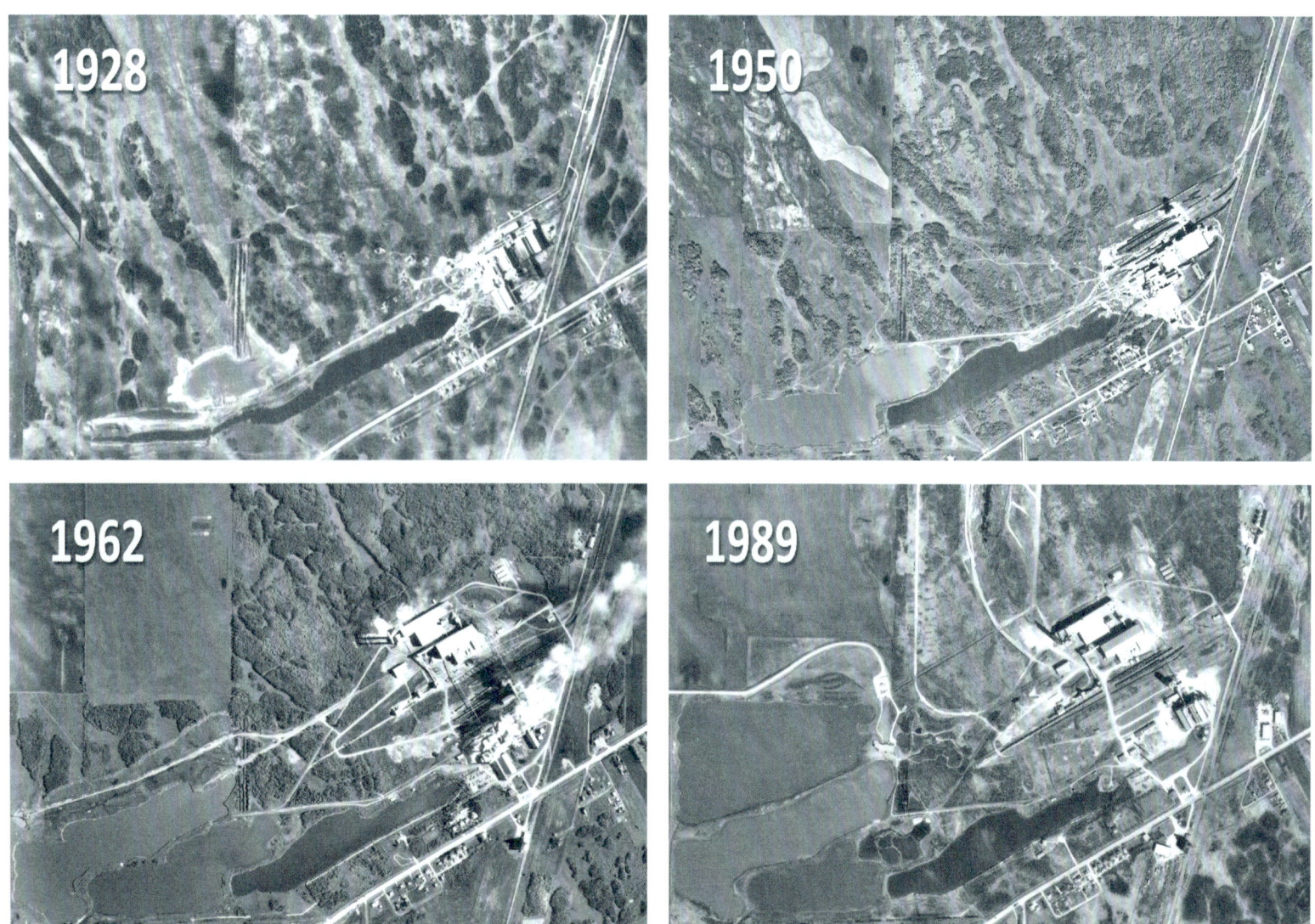

A sequence of air photos taken in 1928, 1950, 1962, and 1989 show the gradual development of lakes from the pits excavated as sources of clay and water by the Canada Cement plant. MANITOBA AIR PHOTO LIBRARY

under the new management." Canadian engineers were beginning to use concrete reinforced with embedded steel rods as an alternative to all-steel construction. Between 1904 and 1908, the production of Portland cement in Canada increased four-fold. With a booming economy that stimulated demand for new buildings, bridges, roads, piers, and other concrete structures, the future looked rosy for Canada Cement.

In early 1911, Canada Cement announced its intention to build a clinker-grinding and storage plant at Winnipeg. The plan was to make clinker at the company's facility at Belleville, Ontario then transport it by ship to Fort William (now Thunder Bay) and by rail to Winnipeg. Here, the clinker would be ground into 3,000 barrels of finished cement (each barrel representing 350 pounds) per day, then stored in a 150,000-barrel warehouse prior to shipment throughout Manitoba and Saskatchewan. General manager Frank Jones was cagey when asked where the plant would be constructed. It turned out the company's plans changed before construction got under-way. The high cost of transporting clinker from Ontario, combined with surging demand for cement in western Canada, convinced Canada Cement that it made sense to manufacture cement locally. Consequently, it purchased land in the Interlake, on the shore of Lake Manitoba, for development of a limestone quarry. On a 90-acre parcel of land a few miles southwest of Winnipeg, at a spot described by a newspaper reporter as "not an easy place to locate," the company constructed the previously announced clinker grinding mill, along with storage warehouses for raw materials, machine shops, cement bagging building, three-storey office, superintendent's residence, and warehouse with space to store up to 500,000 barrels of the finished product. The final cost was $3 million, or $80 million in today's dollars. A substation of the Winnipeg Electric Railway Company provided electricity to run the machinery, while powdered coal provided the heat for its cement kiln. The out-of-the-way site beside a CPR railway siding (later named Fort Whyte for a corporate "battle" in 1888 that had pitted the railway against the provincial government) was chosen because it had deposits up to 40 feet deep of clay dumped there by glacial Lake Agassiz. The clay was ideal for providing the alumina and silica needed to make Portland cement. Construction of the plant began in late 1911 and was completed in early 1913.

The new cement plant employed a dry process—it did not use water—which was an important considera-tion given that the nearest river or lake was miles away. Limestone quarried in the Interlake was delivered to the site by rail while sand arrived from a pit at Beausejour. Horse-drawn scrapers dug into the ground southwest of the mill, scooping out mounds of clay-rich soil, gradually excavating a trench that grew longer and deeper over time. By 1928, when the plant underwent a major refit to convert it to a wet manufacturing process, the clay pit was almost a half-mile long and 200 feet wide, dug to a depth of six to eight feet. Seepage of groundwater into the pit, along with

Concrete Forest of Sturgeon Road

Before the Centre Port development on the northwest corner of Winnipeg was built, cutting Sturgeon Road into two unconnected pieces, northbound drivers along the road would pass an unusual concrete forest. There were four large mounds standing at least eight feet high, in two pairs, with numerous concrete pillars protruding from each mound. If you looked from above, you saw that each mound was almost perfectly circular and the pillars were generally oriented in a regular grid of rows and columns. The two mounds nearest Sturgeon Road were the largest, each being about 70 feet in diameter, while two farther from the road were smaller, about 50 feet in diameter. The site was near the Inkster Junction station that is home to the Prairie Dog Central Railway. I recall, as a kid, driving past this place with my family on the way to the Prairie Dog and wondering about it, being told by my dad that it was a site for quality-testing concrete piles used in the construction industry. It turns out that dad was completely wrong.

In fact, the site was developed between late 1963 and early 1964 by BACM Limited (which stood for British-American Construction and Materials Limited), founded by four brothers, the Simkins, to amalgamate 31 companies into one large entity, based in Winnipeg. The company was involved in three major businesses: building supplies, land and property development, and construction. BACM was involved in such construction projects as the Red River Floodway, several airports, hydroelectric developments in Manitoba, Alberta, British Columbia, and James Bay, and the Athabasca Tar Sands Development at Fort McMurray, Alberta. BACM's building supplies division made concrete products such as precast beams, piles, girders and other structural members; concrete sewer pipe; concrete blocks and brick;

An aerial view from July 2017 of what remains from a game of "corporate chicken" in the 1960s, where local businessmen threatened to establish the British American Cement Plant on the northeast edge of Winnipeg. A grid of concrete piles protruding from the ground would have supported cement kilns at the site. GORDON GOLDSBOROUGH

and ready-mix concrete. Perhaps most significant, from the standpoint of our story here, were its concrete piles.

In May 1963, BACM announced plans to build an $8.5 million manufacturing plant, using limestone quarried at Steeprock with locally-dug clay, to make Portland cement. This was just a month after Inland Cement had announced similar plans for a $8 million plant near the existing Canada Cement plant at Fort Whyte. Industry analysts observed that, if two new plants were built, they would produce almost triple the amount of cement required by Manitoba's entire construction industry. Two new cement plants were definitely not needed.

People that I have spoken to about the site suggest the BACM plant was a ploy in a high-stakes game of "corporate chicken" that was never intended to become an actual facility, and that BACM was paid not to build an unnecessary plant that would increase competition and drive down prices. If this view is correct, pile driving started at the site to convince the Canada Cement and Inland Cement that BACM was serious in its intentions to build the plant, but never proceeded past this phase. In June 1964, Inland Cement announced it had purchased the site from BACM. The deal came on the heels of an April 1964 decision by the Winnipeg city council to give all of the city's cement business to Inland, whose plant at this time was located in Saskatchewan, despite howls of protests from the local Canada Cement that they deserved some of the deal.

Each of the piles in the mounds had a series of numbers written into the wet concrete. My engineering friends tell me the numbers represent the date on which the pile was made (so they will know when it has sufficient strength to withstand the stress of being pounded into the ground) and its length (in feet). If this is correct, the piles at this site are 50, 55, and 60 feet in length. An minor engineering mystery surrounds the mounds amongst the piles. Some have said the mounds were caused by the upward shifting of the earth caused by the annual freezing and thawing of the ground. However, my engineering friends tell me there is no basis for this, especially if a hole was augured for the pile before driving began (there would be limited soil for the pile to displace). They propose two explanations: either the mound were platforms purposely built to support the pile-driving equipment and would have been removed at some point, or the top of the mound was intended to be the final ground level at the site.

surface water runoff, soon turned it into a lake (called Pit No. 1 by the company) that provided the water needed to feed the cement manufacturing process. The horse-drawn scrapers were replaced by a dragline that sat on the lakeshore and brought up buckets of clay from the bottom, dumping them into a row of small railcars towed by a locomotive. Eventually, four pits were created, side by side, as a result of clay excavation to supply the plant.

Meanwhile, in 1913, Canada Cement opened a quarry in what is now the Rural Municipality of Grahamdale, at present-day Steeprock, to obtain high-calcium limestone for the plant at Fort Whyte. Large chunks of the sedimentary rock were excavated year-round, crushed into small pieces, and shipped by rail. By 1971, the quarry was about 2,600 feet wide and 3,000 feet in length, and ranged from 35 to 40 deep, producing some 550,000 tons of crushed limestone annually. Gypsum came from a surface quarry at Gypsumville, from

Canada Cement employee Don Muir, along with others, established a waterfowl sanctuary at the lakes beside the plant, seen here in June 1958. FORTWHYTE ALIVE

underground mines at Amaranth or Silver Plains (south of Winnipeg), or a quarry at Harcus on the west side of Lake Manitoba. Iron oxide came from Ontario.

The wet process for making Portland cement worked like this. The clay railcars arrived from Pit No. 1 and their contents were dumped into a wash mill, essentially a massive blender to which water was added. The resulting mixture of clay and water was a grey-green colour with the consistency of a

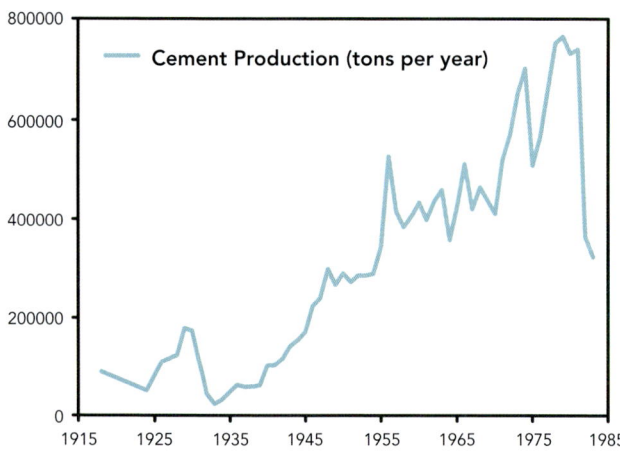

Production of Portland cement in Manitoba between 1918 and 1983. DRAWN FROM ANNUAL REPORT, MANITOBA DEPARTMENT OF MINES, RESOURCES AND ENVIRONMENTAL MANAGEMENT, MANITOBA LEGISLATIVE LIBRARY & INDUSTRIAL SURVEY OF THE RESOURCES OF THE PROVINCE OF MANITOBA, INDUSTRIAL DEVELOPMENT BOARD OF MANITOBA, 1947

thin milkshake. The milkshake was added to a grinding mill containing ¾-inch limestone chunks, iron cinders, sand, and varyingly-sized steel balls to provide grinding action. The output from this mill was a thicker version of the milkshake, now barely pourable, containing about 36 percent water. This mixture was transferred into the 1,500 °C kiln—a sloped, rotating pipe ten feet in diameter and 287 feet long—where the water was driven off, and about 30 percent of the solids were converted into gaseous carbon dioxide. (Hence, the wet Portland process is a major producer of greenhouse gases.) The remaining solid material was clinker consisting of 74.8% limestone and gypsum, 20% clay, 4.6% sand, and 0.6% iron oxide.

The cement plant was operated by a crew of 85 to 100 men. The remoteness of the plant site meant that most of them lived in its immediate vicinity and a small community started to coalesce. In January 1914, the Tuxedo School District No. 1709 was established and a two-classroom brick schoolhouse was constructed northeast of the plant, in what is now the Linden Woods suburb of Winnipeg. (The district also operated a second school, a couple of miles to the northwest, and it still operates today as Tuxedo Park School.) In their free time during lunch breaks and after school or work, schoolchildren and cement plant workers enjoyed swimming in Pit No. 1 and some of the men stocked the lake with fish

The artificial lake created in a former limestone quarry near Steeprock that was operated by Canada Cement, June 2018. STEFANIE GOLDSBOROUGH

for a sport fishery. The lake had excellent water quality, so much so that, from 1936 to 1938, the Arctic Ice Company abandoned its ice-cutting operation on the Red River and began cutting winter ice from the surface of Pit No. 1, selling it to Winnipeggers during the summer as a source of home refrigeration. Ducks and geese would stop at the lake while migrating through the area, which may have given plant engineer Don Muir the idea to establish a waterfowl sanctuary. In 1957, he and several other employees formed the Lucky 13 Rod and Gun Club to support recreational outings and nature conservation projects. They bought six Canada Geese, whose wings had been pinned so they were unable to fly, and built them a home beside Pit No. 1. They added a flock of mallard ducks obtained from a hatchery at Delta Marsh and, the following year, forty more geese from a source

at Morris. The new facility had pens for the birds in the summer and winter, along with a small building to store feed and rear young birds. In 1966, Muir and local lawyer Alan Scarth incorporated the Wildlife Foundation of Manitoba to operate the new wildlife sanctuary and carry out other conservation projects around the province. An expanded role for the sanctuary soon began to evolve when six school principals from the greater Winnipeg area approached the provincial government's conservation education section. They wanted to establish a nature trail for their students. After examining several possible sites, Fort Whyte was chosen due to its close proximity to Winnipeg, its intact woodlands, and the several lakes on the property. Starting in September 1966, busloads of children began visiting the site to commune with nature.

In one last belch, a vestige of the Canada Cement plant came down during the summer of 2001 when its two massive kiln smokestacks, built in 1955 and 1964, were demolished. KEN ROSS

In 1948, the Canada Cement plant made 1,686,345 barrels (roughly 295,000 tons) of cement and demand for its product continued to grow. Seven years later, the plant was expanded with a new 450-foot long, twelve-foot diameter kiln, followed by a second, identical kiln in 1964. Between 1957 and 1972, the facility produced an annual average of 445,000 tons of cement. In 1963, as the demand for Portland cement continued to grow, the British Columbia-based Inland Cement Company announced plans to build a second manufacturing plant about a mile north of the Canada Cement site, capitalizing on the abundance of clay deposits there by excavating a lake in addition to the five dug by Canada Cement, and using limestone from Canada Cement's quarry in the Interlake.

In May 1970, Canada Cement became Canada Cement Lafarge Limited after its purchase by the French firm Lafarge Coppee. Two years later, the company leased for ten years (for $1) the land around Pit No. 1 to the Wildlife Foundation, allowing it to expand its modest sanctuary with a new two-storey reception centre overlooking the lake, supported by the local Kiwanis. A grant from The Winnipeg Foundation enabled the Wildlife Foundation to build a new waterfowl building and pens, and the facility opened with a broad mandate as the Fort Whyte Nature Centre. Before the lease was due to end in 1982, Alan Scarth began negotiating an arrangement between the company and the provincial government, in which 80 acres of provincially-owned land would be swapped for the company's 200 acres of exhausted quarries, then the government would extend Fort Whyte's lease (for a second dollar). Future Premier Gary Filmon, a minister in the Progressive Conservative government of Sterling Lyon, played a key role in the deal, which was finally consummated by a newly-elected New Democratic government of Howard Pawley.

The heady days of the 1960s, when the demand for Portland cement seemed limitless, were bound to end. In the early 1980s, Manitoba's construction industry began a long slump. By 1982, when the land swap at Fort Whyte was finalized, Lafarge found that it could supply its customers across the prairies from a newer, more modern plant at Exshaw, Alberta where shale replaced the high energy costs of de-watering the clay milkshake. Cement manufacturing at its Winnipeg facility ended in September 1982, after which local demand was met with cement stored in two large warehouses at the site. The unneeded buildings were demolished between 1995 and 2001, including two massive kiln smokestacks that fell in a demolition during the summer of 2001, leaving just a building for unloading cement from railcars and a storage warehouse. Today, in addition to selling raw cement, Lafarge makes an array of precast concrete products including road curbs, traffic barriers, beam, piles, pipes, culverts, and girders. The company's quarry at Steeprock, closed around 1989, was eventually transferred to the Rural Municipality of Grahamdale. One of its giant scoop shovels and a locomotive used to haul limestone are still on display near the abandoned, water-filled pit. The Inland plant continued to operate after a temporary closure in 1982, but on a limited scale, the equivalent of only 85 days a year by the early 1990s. Finally, it closed in 1992 and its kiln was removed through a large hole cut in the roof, and sold to a company in Central America. For two more years, Inland's mill ground clinker shipped from other plants. In 1994, it was closed entirely. Cement manufacturing was consolidated at the company's facility at Edmonton. The plant and its elegant two-storey office building, made entirely with concrete,

A machine once used at the Canada Cement limestone quarry near Steeprock, now on display as a museum piece, July 2017 GORDON GOLDSBOROUGH

sat abandoned. Vandals broke most of the windows and festooned it liberally with graffiti. Both were being demolished as I wrote this chapter in mid-2018.

In 1982, with a long-term lease secured for the former Canada Cement quarries, Alan Scarth and the other trustees of the Wildlife Foundation began planning to expand the Fort Whyte Nature Centre. A new interpretive centre was built in 1983 on the shore of Lake No. 4 (later renamed Devonian Lake). Two new staff were hired to oversee the expanded operation: Bill Elliott as Chief Executive Officer and Ken Cudmore as Site Manager. Under their management, the property was expanded with additional land to the north, gaining a fifth lake from the Canada Cement site. This provided space to develop a resident bison herd, a social enterprise farm for using sustainable growing practices to build life skills in underserved youth, and a field station for expanded educational opportunities. A new reception centre, funded in part by The Winnipeg Foundation, was built in 2000. On the cusp of its 40th anniversary, in 2005, the facility was rebranded as FortWhyte Alive.

Unfortunately, Don Muir would not see the transformation of his modest wildlife sanctuary at an industrial site into a world-class environmental education facility. He died in 1990. However, he is commemorated by Muir Lake, the renamed Pit No. 1. The lake, and the

OPPOSITE Interior view of the abandoned Inland Cement plant in Winnipeg, August 2016. GORDON GOLDSBOROUGH

An aerial view of the former Inland Cement plant in Winnipeg that was being demolished as I wrote this chapter in mid-2018. Unlike the Canada Cement plant nearby, Inland used an internal kiln system so, when the facility was decommissioned, most its machinery was removed through a large hole in its roof. GORDON GOLDSBOROUGH

area around it, preserves visible signs of its industrial heritage. A small pumphouse that once supplied water to the cement plant stands quietly on its north shore. Rails that were used by the plant's clay railcars can be seen criss-crossing the FortWhyte Alive site. Thousands of ducks and geese—some of them descendants of Muir's original flocks—still visit the lakes every spring and fall.

ACKNOWLEDGEMENTS

I thank geologist Jim Bamburak for educating me about industrial minerals in Manitoba, Dawn Fraser of Lafarge Canada for providing information on her firm's industrial heritage at Fort Whyte, and retired Lafarge manager Ken Ross for providing a wealth of details on how Portland cement is made. I should note, in the interest of full disclosure, that I serve proudly on the (unpaid) Board of Trustees for FortWhyte Alive. It is a truly exceptional facility as a result of the dedicated service over 52 years by fine people like Don Muir, Alan Scarth, Bill Elliott, Ken Cudmore, and others too numerous to name.

Gilbert Plains Beef Ring Building

Most people have never heard of a "beef ring." They wonder if it refers to a gang of cattle rustlers or a bunch of people who complain a lot. Few people—and none without roots in rural Manitoba—know that it was the primary means by which farm families were assured a supply of fresh meat in the days before refrigeration. As far as I know, there is only one place in Manitoba that reminds us of this once-common practice: a small building south of Gilbert Plains is a former beef ring slaughterhouse.

Generations of Indigenous peoples have made pemmican using dried meat (traditionally, bison) mixed with melted fat, sometimes with dried berries, that would keep for long periods of time. Pork, beef, and fish can be cured with smoke or salt. However, preventing fresh meat from spoiling is a problem.

Manitoba's cold winters provide a natural means of preservation but the warmer temperatures of summer have always posed a challenge. In the old days, refrigeration was difficult or impossible. Some people stored blocks of ice, cut from rivers and lakes during the winter, and used them to keep items cool, but not frozen, in an "ice chest" during the summer. In the early 20th century, long-term freezing of food was next to impossible for most Manitobans.

In cities such as Winnipeg, the population was large enough that butchers supplied by meat processors near the Union Stock Yards could sell fresh meat to their customers year-round. In less-populated rural areas, farm families had live animals that, as the need arose, could be slaughtered for their meat. Smaller animals such as chickens, turkeys, sheep, and hogs could be used up quickly, especially if the family was large, so the need for refrigeration was minimal. But larger animals such as cattle provided more meat than a single family could use before

The Gilbert Plains Beef Ring slaughterhouse before it was restored between 2007 and 2008. LORNE SMITH

it spoiled. So the concept of "beef clubs" or "beef rings" was a natural solution that became popular in farming communities.

Beef rings were formal organizations that elected officers—usually a president, secretary, and treasurer—to ensure that its operation was done fairly and efficiently. They had rules and regulations. People had to apply for membership and new members were only accepted if there was room for them. Once each week, a beef ring member would contribute a live cow—a

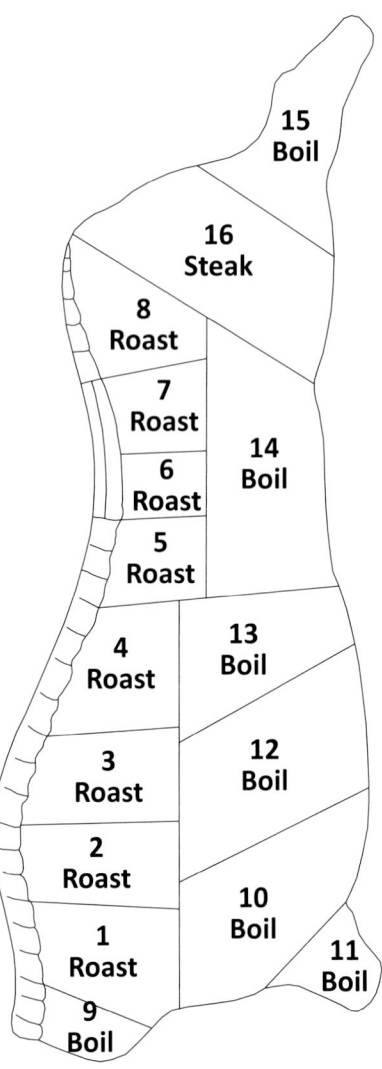

15 Boil

16 Steak

8 Roast

7 Roast

6 Roast

14 Boil

5 Roast

4 Roast

13 Boil

3 Roast

12 Boil

2 Roast

1 Roast

10 Boil

11 Boil

9 Boil

Members of a beef ring shared portions of meat in each of three categories. The choicest cuts were designated "steak." Less desirable cuts were "roast" and the poorest ones were only thought to be edible after boiling. *NOR'WEST FARMER, 20 FEBRUARY 1905*

heifer (female) or steer (castrated male)—from their herd when it was their turn, as determined by the beef ring's officers, and that animal would be slaughtered and cut into a portion for each member. The number of weeks during the "warm months" of the year, usually late April through mid-October, determined how many members could participate in a beef ring, unless a member chose to receive a half-portion, in which case more members could be admitted. The number of members typically ranged between 16 and 40 families, averaging at 20, and each member was expected to contribute money to build a small slaughterhouse (in a central location to all members), and buy knives, weigh scale, and other equipment needed to cut and apportion the animal carcass. The slaughterhouse often had a small building on its side, or a small paddock, where the animal was kept prior to slaughter, and where the animal was killed. The order of animal delivery to the slaughterhouse was usually selected by

drawing names from a hat to prepare a delivery list. In this way, beef rings served two important functions. The obvious one was to provide families with a regular, reliable supply of fresh meat during the summer when there were few other options for families living far from a butcher shop. Another, less obvious function was to provide social cohesion. Public good will and cooperation were fostered among families who were dependent on each other for food.

The beef ring's butcher, who may or may not be a member, would carry out the killing, cutting, weighing, and distribution of meat, supervised by a member who served as inspector to ensure the quality and weight of the animal that had been delivered. The butcher was usually paid for their service. Some men supported themselves and their families by serving as the butcher for several beef rings in a region. Around Darlingford, for example, five beef rings were served by one butcher, Oliver Law. For his efforts, each slaughterhouse paid Law $4 to $5, depending on the distance that he travelled. Some rings allowed the butcher to keep the animal's hide, heart and other internal organs, and any parts the members did not want. (Considering that Oliver Law had a family of 13, the extras were probably much appreciated.) Other beef rings required the butcher to sell the hide and provide the proceeds to the ring.

Animals were typically delivered to the slaughter-house at least 12 hours before being killed. They were slaughtered on Thursdays so the carcasses could cool overnight then cutting and meat distribution took place on Fridays. In this way, families would have a nice roast or steak for the big weekend meal. Beef rings were encouraged to build an ice house or cold storage plant so they could store the meat at 35-40 °F for periods ranging from five days to two weeks but this was not feasible for all beef rings. The cold storage improved the quality and flavour of the meat compared to freshly-killed meat.

The dressed carcass would typically weigh between 400 and 650 pounds, providing between 15 and 30 pounds of meat per family. One week's share (or, for a smaller family, a half-share) would be a steak, roast, or boiling piece—a poor meat cut deemed unsuitable for anything but boiling. However, variations did occur. In the Regent Beef Ring northwest of Boissevain, for instance, members received a roast and steak one week, and a boiling piece and steak the following week. Each member's share would be weighed to ensure fair distribution then placed into a clean, bleached flour sack that had been boiled in lye

An abandoned beef ring slaughterhouse near the railway siding of Smart, August 1979. LAWRENCE STUCKEY COLLECTION, S. J. MCKEE ARCHIVES, BRANDON UNIVERSITY

to keep it white from week to week, with a social stigma on those who brought stained sacks to collect their meat. Meat sacks were hung on a hook labeled with the family's name inside the slaughterhouse. In the morning after the cutting, a family member would arrive to pick up their sack and leave a clean sack for the next week. Sometimes, people would pick up sacks on behalf of their neighbours and deliver them to reduce the need for travel. Each fall, there was an accounting of how much meat a particular family's animal had produced versus how much meat they had received throughout the period of beef ring operation. Those who had received more meat than they had contributed had to pay for the extra meat to those whose animals had provided more meat than they had received back. During the Second World War, beef was rationed but farmers were allowed to continue operating their beef rings. To ensure the rings did not become a source of "illicit beef," the rings had to register with the government and membership was restricted to farmers obtaining meat for their own consumption on their own premises.

Beef rings seem to have begun in Manitoba during the early 20th century. I scoured local history books for mentions of beef rings, and found the earliest one to be at Image Creek, a small community northwest of Portage la Prairie. It started in 1905. An information circular published by the Manitoba Agricultural College in 1911, entitled "The Farmers' Beef Ring, Or, How Fresh Beef

May Be Obtained for the Farmers' Table in Summer," seems to have stimulated the formation of many others around Manitoba. I calculated that the average founding year of the beef rings mentioned in history books was 1918 and the latest started in 1930. A 1923 farm bulletin stated that 125 beef rings were operating in Manitoba that year. Statistics for subsequent years were hard to find because the beef rings were mostly unregulated, at least until 1930 when they were required to obtain a license from the provincial government. Between 1930 and 1947, the number ranged between 39 and 60. License records also document the demise of beef rings, for they show how, after 1947, the number dropped year-by-year until 1952, when responsibility for licensing was turned over to municipalities. By that time, there were only 24 licensed beef rings.

My informal survey of beef rings showed that, while some ended in the 1930s, the majority closed in the late 1940s or through the 1950s. One of the last to disappear was the Image Creek Beef Ring, after 61 continuous years of operation, following a celebratory supper—featuring, of course, beef—for its 60th anniversary in 1966. At the end, it had only five members, down from a high of 31 in the 1930s. The reason for the end was electricity. In 1944, the provincial government had begun licensing "frozen food lockers." Typically, these were buildings in local towns that had been connected to the province's expanding electrical transmission system, which started with a modest 60-mile line between Winnipeg and Portage la Prairie in

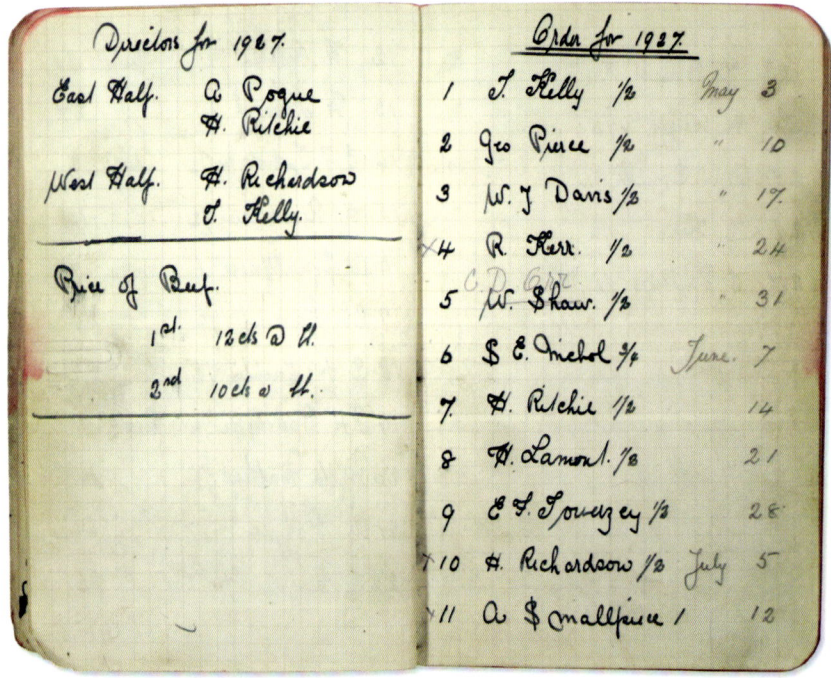

A sample page from a record book for the Image Creek Beef Ring recorded its directors in 1927, the price charged for beef, and part of the schedule by which members would contribute animals to the beef ring. ARCHIVES OF MANITOBA

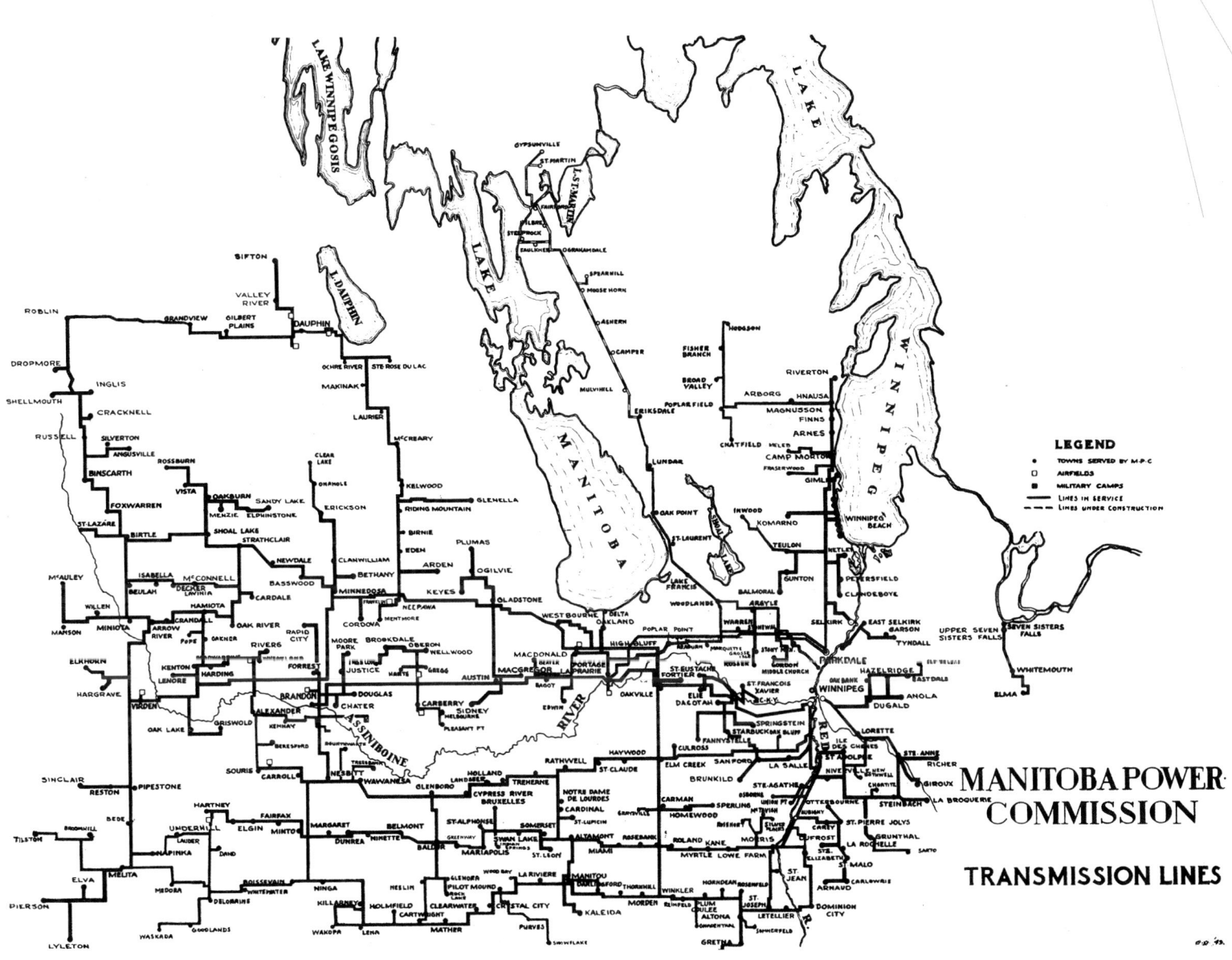

MANITOBA POWER COMMISSION
TRANSMISSION LINES

LEGEND

• TOWNS SERVED BY M.P.C
□ AIRFIELDS
■ MILITARY CAMPS
—— LINES IN SERVICE
- - - LINES UNDER CONSTRUCTION

The town of Gilbert Plains had been previously served with electricity generated at Dauphin, but by the time this Manitoba Power Commission map was drawn in 1949, it had hydro-electrically generated power from the Winnipeg River. Widespread rural electrification during the 1950s spelled the end to the region's beef rings. MANITOBA POWER COMMISSION, 1949 ANNUAL REPORT, MANITOBA LEGISLATIVE LIBRARY

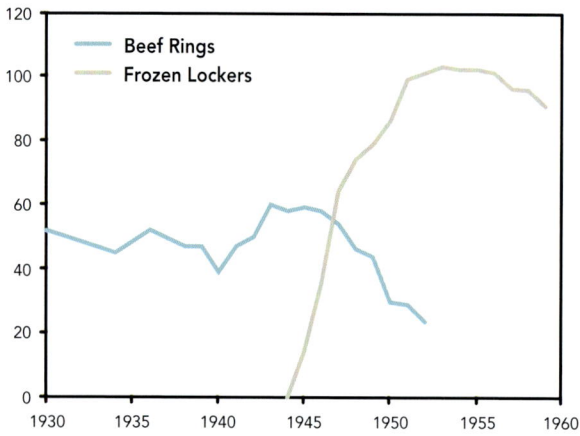

As the number of beef rings in Manitoba waned through the 1950s, frozen meat lockers became more common but began to give way to home-based freezers in the late 1950s. These trends were all driven by rural electrification. DRAWN FROM BUREAU OF FOOD CONTROL, MANITOBA DEPARTMENT OF HEALTH AND PUBLIC WELFARE, 1930-1959. MANITOBA LEGISLATIVE LIBRARY

In April 1966, members of the Image Creek Beef Ring northwest of Portage la Prairie, one of the earliest and longest-running beef rings in Manitoba, held a beef supper to commemorate their sixtieth year of operation. ARCHIVES OF MANITOBA

1919. Electrification made it possible for local businesses, usually the butcher, to have a walk-in freezer that kept large quantities of food frozen. These plants, essentially a communal freezer, had partitioned lockers that could be rented by individual families for their own needs. My dad's family, for example, rented a meat locker from the butcher at Starbuck. I recall, as a child, accompanying my grandfather to get a large roast from his locker when my aunts and their families were all coming home for a weekend meal. These food lockers eliminated the need for beef rings so their numbers increased as beef rings diminished. The lockers peaked at 103 in 1953.

Interestingly, the lockers were a transitory technology. By the late 1950s, their number already started to diminish as rural electrification began to put a freezer in many farm homes. Having a personal freezer meant that one did not have to rent a locker from the local butcher. Now, we take for granted that homes routinely have freezers so we can take advantage of sales at the grocery store and keep a frozen cache handy in case of unexpected guests. Instead of consuming meat that was produced within a few miles of our homes, we buy meat in stores that may come from another province or country. It is no wonder that people today are usually unaware of the source for their meat. Yet, to some, having a personal relationship with the farmer who produced their meat is important. With such things as the 100-mile diet becoming popular, some Manitoba farmers are interested in marketing their products directly to consumers via "meat shares."

However, concerns about the safety of meat obtained from local sources go way back. I found reports as early as 1920 on concerns that meat not subject to government inspection could jeopardize public health. This issue still resonates. Over the past couple of years, there have been a handful of high-profile cases where farmers were charged for selling uninspected meat. In February 2017, for instance, a farm near Winnipeg was fined $7,500 for "operating a slaughterhouse and meat-processing establishment without a permit" and "operating without a valid permit and selling un-inspected meat."

In 1923, a beef ring slaughterhouse was built 3½ miles south of Gilbert Plains, on one-tenth of an acre leased from farmer Selby Smith. It operated until 1951, two years after the Manitoba Power Commission had begun installing power lines throughout the Gilbert Plains region. The little slaughterhouse fell into ruin after it was abandoned. By the early 2000s, it was near to falling down. Fortunately, its uniqueness

was recognized. Local farmer Lorne Smith, grandson of Selby, advocated to have it designated as a municipal heritage site by the Rural Municipality of Gilbert Plains in late 2006. He led its restoration between 2007 and 2008 using small government and community grants, donated materials, and volunteer labour. On a new concrete foundation and sporting a spiffy coat of red paint, the slaughterhouse is believed to be the last of its kind still standing in Manitoba. I visited the little slaughterhouse a few times and was able to see inside during a visit in July 2017. A metal hook hanging from a large spool near the roofline was where animal carcasses were hung during butchering. A neat row of nails along one wall once held flour sacks for the family portions of meat. It was a wonderful illustration of the resourcefulness with which Manitobans fed their families in the days before refrigeration, and an important lesson on how our food supply chain has changed over the past several decades.

Some of the tools used in the Gilbert Plains Beef Ring, and a chart of what each member received in 1960, were on display when I visited the restored slaughterhouse in July 2017
GORDON GOLDSBOROUGH

ACKNOWLEDGEMENTS

I thank Julie Russell, the Community Development Officer for the Municipality of Gilbert Plains, for allowing me to see inside the beef ring slaughterhouse there. As I have found for most places discussed in this book, the Manitoba Legislative Library and the Archives of Manitoba were invaluable sources of information, the latter having one of the only surviving sets of records for a Manitoba beef ring. Archivist Chris Kotecki made me aware of this rare collection. I commend Lorne Smith for the foresight to restore the rare little slaughterhouse for the benefit of future generations.

East Braintree Prison Farm

A Holiday at The Prison Farm

Six leaders of the Winnipeg General Strike of 1919 took a "holiday at the prison farm" in August 1920, according to this photo in the labour newspaper, *One Big Union Bulletin*. Shown in prison garb, left to right, are William Ivens, George Armstrong, William Pritchard, Roger Bray, John Queen, and Richard Johns, with their respective wives standing behind them and two of their children. ARCHIVES OF MANITOBA

These days, it seems all too common for someone to be elected to public office then to be imprisoned for criminal behaviour during their term. The reverse, when an incarcerated person is elected to public office, is highly unusual. So imagine how unusual it would be if several prisoners were elected at the same time, all while still in prison. This happened in Manitoba, in 1921. Before their one-year sentences were up, three prisoners were elected to the Manitoba Legislature, while two others who had also run were defeated. The prison to which they were sent was a facility like no other in the province, a place where few would escape, not because the walls were so high but, just the opposite, because there were no walls at all. This was the now abandoned Provincial Industrial Farm—referred to at the time as the Prison Farm—in eastern Manitoba.

We might think of society as a complex collection of rules for human behaviour. Over millennia, society has developed measures to deal with those who chose to break the rules. Today, we like to think that our penal system is based on rehabilitation, turning criminals into productive members of society. This was not always the case. In 1870, Englishman Samuel Bedson was dispatched by the Canadian government to the newly established province of Manitoba as a member of the Wolseley Expedition to confront Louis Riel and his supporters. Afterward, when most of Wolseley's soldiers returned home, Bedson stayed behind and, in 1871, was appointed Warden of the Manitoba Penitentiary. Initially based at Lower Fort Garry, five years later Bedson and his criminal charges were transferred to a new facility built atop a hill with a commanding view of the surrounding territory, at Stony Mountain. The objective was punishment, not rehabilitation.

In the early 20th century, the administration of justice in Manitoba was organized around six judicial districts with courts at Brandon, Dauphin, Morden, Portage la Prairie, The Pas, and Winnipeg. Those convicted of serious crimes were sent to Stony Mountain Penitentiary. Otherwise, they went to gaol—an old English word that has been replaced by "jail." Between 1914 and 1921, the six gaols of the provincial system held an average of 1,315 prisoners annually (about one-quarter of one percent of the provincial population at that time), with the majority (about 70 percent) going to the Eastern Judicial District Gaol on Vaughan Street in downtown Winnipeg.

In 1913, Manitoba judge John P. Curran was asked to "make an investigation into the management and supervision of the Gaol ... of the Eastern Judicial District of Manitoba." Curran reported on the job that prisoners were given, noting that female prisoners typically performed domestic tasks such as laundering and mending prison clothes and bedding. The male prisoners were sent to the newly built Agricultural College (today's University of Manitoba) where they occupied dormitories that had previously housed construction workers and were put to work building roads, weeding the gardens, digging drainage ditches, caring for poultry, tending the boilers, and helping to maintain the experimental crop plots at the site. As part of his fact-finding for a more suitable prison farm location, Judge Curran sought advice from the superintendent of the Ontario Reformatory at Guelph, who recommended that:

> The farm should be sufficiently far from a large city that the hobos and tramps will not visit it to "plant" contraband and be a source of annoyance to the management. ... The temptation to escape is greater in proportion to the nearness to a city.

In February 1916, the government announced it would establish a prison farm modelled on the one at Guelph. The objectives of the new facility would be:

> (a) To provide open air employment, with moral and physical reformatory methods, for persons who would otherwise have been kept in idleness in the common gaols of the province of Manitoba; (b) To lessen the expenditure hitherto made for gaol maintenance by making the industrial farm as nearly self-sustaining as possible; (c) To permit the earnings of a person sentenced to the industrial farm to be applied towards his own maintenance, the maintenance of his wife, children or other members of his family dependent upon him, and to pay any necessary travelling expenses of any person to any place where employment has been secured on his parole or discharge.

Once the necessary legislation for creating a prison farm was passed, the next task was finding a suitable spot for it. Forty to fifty sites in the Eastern Judicial District were offered to the government but it would take another two years before a site was chosen. It met the remoteness criterion perfectly, being about 65 miles east of Winnipeg, south of the present-day Trans-Canada Highway, between the communities of McMunn and East Braintree. The region was mostly covered in dense forest, but "the farm experts of the Provincial Government … unanimously recommend the land as ideal for an industrial farm site." Today, the site is easily accessible via the Trans-Canada Highway but before it was constructed in 1953, the only reliable way to get there (the nearby Dawson Road being passable only when dry) was by railway aboard the Greater Winnipeg Water District (GWWD) train that ran to the water intake structure on Shoal Lake. Communication with the outside world was made possible, in 1919, by the installation of a long-distance telephone line.

To develop a farm at the site, the government bought 2,350 acres of land from local homesteaders. The initial site where the farm staff and prisoners were to be accommodated had been used, between 1914 and 1918, as Camp No. 4 for construction workers building the GWWD aqueduct. The construction company, having no further use for the camp, sold its eleven buildings and land for the princely sum of $800. An additional $1,000 was spent in making them "comfortable for the winter." In time, a site several hundred feet from the GWWD railway line, south of the Birch River, was developed as a more permanent facility.

The former prison farm superintendent's residence, before being completed by its occupants, 1960. ARCHIVES OF MANITOBA

The former prison farm barn, 1960. ARCHIVES OF MANITOBA

The farm buildings, most made out of locally cut logs, included three prisoner bunkhouses, farm implement shed, blacksmith shop, kitchen and dining room, root cellar, and administrative offices. Three other buildings were built more robustly from an eclectic mixture of stone, bricks, and wooden timbers: a large barn for hogs and cattle, four-cell jailhouse, and residence for the farm's superintendent that featured 26-inch-thick stone walls. Blacksmith August Anderson was hired to manufacture metal bars and doors for the jailhouse. Gustav Bergenstein, the former quarryman from the Brookeville Quarry (see a chapter on it elsewhere in this book), was hired to obtain stone for the buildings. "Old bricks" used to build the jailhouse were scavenged from the Brookeville Quarry. Both men would continue as "turnkeys" (guards) at the Prison Farm, with Anderson as Assistant Superintendent under Superintendent William "Bill" Murray. In total, the farm would have from 8 to 13 guards.

The inmate population of the farm typically ranged between 40 and 55 men—as far as I have determined, no female prisoners were sent there—who were transported to the farm aboard the GWWD train. The first cohort from the Vaughan Street Gaol arrived in the fall of 1918 and the cordwood they cut while clearing

When the Brookeville Quarry was fully abandoned in the late 1920s, the bricks from its rock-processing building were scavenged to build structures all around the region. Among them may have been a small brick building at a minimum-security prison farm built by the provincial government about 2½ miles away. It housed low-risk inmates between 1918 and 1930 when it was replaced by the Headingley Gaol. The building, seen here in September 2016, is nicely maintained by the family who purchased the former prison. GORDON GOLDSBOROUGH

A barn at the Prison Farm was made from various materials, including what may be locally quarried stone (perhaps from the Brookeville Quarry) and bricks scavenged from the quarry's millhouse. Its roof is not original, as can be seen by comparing this photo with the one on the previous page. GORDON GOLDSBOROUGH

the forested land for farming was shipped to Winnipeg to heat government buildings during the winter. The original plan had been to use the farm from spring through autumn then return the men to the Vaughan Street Gaol for the winter. However, I have found work reports in the provincial archives dating from mid-November to the end of December, describing the work being done, so it seems likely the Prison Farm was used year-round. The plan to select those sent to the farm from the best-behaved members of the general prison population was occasionally superseded by the extreme level of crowding in Winnipeg. A prison inspector in late 1921 noted that:

> As the Jail in Winnipeg is packed, Mr. Downie [Chief Turnkey at the Vaughan Street Gaol] proposes sending out another 10 to 12 prisoners to the Farm, but as it is only possible to accommodate 3 more men in the Bunk Houses and every seat in the Dining Room is taken up, the Guards Bunk House is also packed.

It seems doubtful that the Prison Farm ever achieved its goal of self-sufficiency. An annual accounting provided by the provincial government listed numerous expenses for what sound like food-related purchases, and the cost of running the farm during the 1920s typically ran around $30,000 a year (about $420,000 in today's currency). However, the farm did provide tangible products for the government. During the winter of 1919-1920, for example, it delivered over 760 cords of firewood to Winnipeg. In addition to clearing land and growing crops, the farm had cows and hogs to tend, along with horses used in land clearing and farming. The life of a prisoner mostly entailed daily hard work, but it was occasionally alleviated with a concert where the prisoners themselves provided the entertainment. There are reports that moonshine was made, some of the prisoners having been convicted for bootlegging. In one case, the farm's own cook was found to be making the stuff. He was promptly fired.

The farm was remote and the only way out was via the railway line, as much of the land was otherwise boggy and hard to traverse. If the lack of food and water did not dissuade a potential escapee in his long walk to civilization, hordes of marauding insects would. But they did try. Between 1922 and 1925, seven prisoners attempted to escape from the farm (out of 117 escapees from all gaols) of which five were not recaptured. Those who were recaptured were given additional prison time. For example, James Durham was serving a six-month sentence for bicycle theft. He walked away from the farm but, nine hours later, was found five miles away. Taken to the police court in Winnipeg, he was sentenced to an additional year of hard labour. George Bagan hated the Prison Farm enough that, after he was caught and a judge added six months to his original three-month sentence, he pleaded to be sent to a regular gaol. Prisoners guilty of lesser offences than attempting to escape were sent to the on-farm jailhouse, usually for periods of a few days. Some of the jailed prisoners spent their free time inscribing the brick walls in their cells with their names, sentences, and other details. When I visited the jailhouse in September 2016, I saw a beaver and at least two Masonic symbols among the inscriptions. There was a man aiming a pistol, with the phrase "Hands up" beside him. It seemed like this fellow had not learned his lesson.

Unquestionably, the most famous prisoners at the farm were six leaders of the 1919 Winnipeg General Strike. On 27 March 1920, George Armstrong, Roger Bray, William Ivens, Richard Johns, William Pritchard, and John Queen were convicted of "seditious conspiracy." Each was sentenced to one year of incarceration and, contrary to widespread belief, they were not sent to the Stony Mountain Penitentiary. They were first sent to the Vaughan Street Gaol, where a famous photo of them (supposedly at Stony Mountain) was taken, and in late April 1920, they were transferred to the Prison Farm. There, they were put in positions of responsibility. Ivens was in charge of the garden. Bray looked after the prison's flock of chickens and

Someone with time on their hands in one of the Prison Farm's four jail cells carved a warning into its brick walls. Numerous other carvings adorn the walls, including names, lengths of sentences, and the Masonic symbol. GORDON GOLDSBOROUGH

Armstrong built chicken coops as the head carpenter. Queen put in fence posts. The rest of the strike leaders, along with the other prisoners, worked in the prison's fields. Although labour newspapers joked that the men were "on holiday," and enjoyed visits from their wives and children, two of them suffered personal tragedies while incarcerated. Two-year-old Louis Ivens died a week before his father was sent to the farm, and three-year-old Gordon Bray died 2½ months later. The grieving fathers were treated compassionately; Bray was given a one-week reprieve to attend his son's funeral.

The imprisoned men were definitely not forgotten by the people of Winnipeg. All but Bray were nominated as Labour candidates in the provincial general election in June 1920 and, given their fame (or notoriety, depending on your perspective) and despite their inability to participate in any campaigning, all of them received substantial numbers of votes. In the end, three of the five (Armstrong, Ivens, and Queen) were elected to seats for the Winnipeg constituency, under a new proportional voting system. The farm's long-distance telephone advised them of their wins. Labour leaders in Winnipeg predicted confidently that the men would soon be released from their prison terms. However, this did not turn out to be the case. The strike leaders were released from prison in late February 1921, eleven months after their conviction, fulfilling nearly their full one-year sentence. They immediately took their seats in the Legislature where Ivens would comment, in relation to the Prison Farm, that "as a farm, it is an absolute failure." He was clearly speaking from experience. Despite the early glowing accounts of "experts" about the suitability of the land for agriculture, a more realistic assessment was likely one provided to the government in 1917 that:

> [T]he land we saw in this district, that is not settled, is very low, mossy muskeg. Some sections of it could be drained by putting in dredge channel, and if the land was left lying for years and cattle turned in to tramp it, it might become fair land for certain purposes.

I suspect it was the dubious agricultural value of the land that doomed the Prison Farm experiment. It closed in October 1930. The guards, prisoners, livestock, and farm equipment were transferred to the newly constructed Headingley Gaol west of Winnipeg. The old Prison Farm land and buildings stood vacant until 1945 when they were sold to Haakon and Lena Feilberg whose son Carl still owns them. No vestiges of the wooden buildings remain at the site but the jailhouse, barn, and superintendent's residence are there. The superintendent's residence stood without a roof or interior walls for over thirty years and had a large tree growing from its basement. In 1967, Carl Feilberg built walls and a roof and he and his family are still living in it today. The jailhouse doors are mostly rusted open, but the owner has taken steps to preserve it by putting plastic over the barred windows to keep out nesting birds, and built a peaked roof to shed rainwater.

History makes us think. We think about the ways that things used to be done in the past. We think about how we do things differently today. We think about how things might have gone differently if circumstances had changed. When I think about the prisoners at the former Prison Farm, I think about the 1919 Winnipeg General Strike and what it has meant to the development of Canadian society in general and labour relations in particular. Was it appropriate for the police, political leaders, and judges to treat leaders of the Strike in the ways they did? What did it mean to send someone to prison for advocating on behalf of better working conditions? Even in 1920, when the leaders were convicted, it was not clear what their crime of "seditious conspiracy" meant. The fact that three of them were elected to the Legislature, and went on to distinguished careers in public service, speaks volumes. All three men elected in 1920 ran again in the general election of 1922. Two of them, Ivens and Queen, were re-elected. Bill Ivens was an MLA until being defeated in 1936. John Queen remained an MLA until 1941 and also served for seven years (1935–1936, 1938–1942) as Mayor of Winnipeg, at a time when a person could hold provincial and municipal offices simultaneously.

The Prison Farm itself makes me think about the treatment of prisoners and the purpose of incarceration. Should a prison be merely a place to keep rule-breakers to prevent them from re-offending? Should prison be a place where we strive to turn them into law-abiding, productive citizens? Is a low-security Prison Farm, where people are made to work to support themselves and minimize their impact on the public purse, a better way to deal with prisoners than putting them in a room with bars? We may not all have the same answers to these questions. I am glad, though, that we have places like this that lead us to consider those questions in the first place.

ACKNOWLEDGEMENTS

Lorna Annell toured me through her cousin Carl Feilberg's property containing the former Manitoba Prison Farm during my visit to the East Braintree area in the summer of 2016. Thanks to Stuart Hay at the Manitoba Legislative Library in helping to track down the photo of the strike leaders "on holiday" at the prison farm.

Killarney Flax Warehouses

I got a university education by attending classes in the winters and earning my tuition fees by working in rural Manitoba during the summers. For four years, between 1978 and 1981, my summer job allowed me to stay in 'hotels' owned by the Canadian Pacific Railway. They were not the sort of hotels that you might recall from bygone days, when the railway operated luxurious facilities in most of the major cities across Canada, such as Winnipeg's Royal Alexandra. No, these CP hotels were much less sumptuous. My room had no light except that from a hand-held flashlight and no running water unless you counted the occasional rainstorm, when water seeped through holes in the walls or roof. My bed was a folding cot and sleeping bag. I could not afford to stay in a real hotel—or even a campground—so every night I climbed into an empty boxcar that my employer used to ship its product to a factory in the United States, and hoped the train would not haul away my hotel room during the night. Three enormous metal-clad buildings in Killarney—standing mostly empty—take me back to those days in the CP hotel and tell a story about a little-known industry in Manitoba that used (and continues to use) agricultural waste to make high-quality paper.

When we think of paper manufacturing in Manitoba, we typically think of paper made from tree pulp at mills in Pine Falls (now gone) and The Pas (currently in ownership

The distinctive blue flowers of flax create a colourful mosaic on the prairies during Manitoba's summer. judy wilson photography

transition). What is less well known is that, for nearly 50 years, paper has also been made in the agricultural belt of southern Manitoba, using fibre extracted from the straw of flax plants. Straw is the part of a plant that remains after its seed is harvested; usually, it consists of stems and leaves. Flax straw is highly resistant to decomposition due to an abundance of hard fibres—strands made of cellulose and other tough chemicals. This attribute makes flax straw useful as an insulation material when people need to cover their septic tanks during our cold winters—it does not rot quickly as other grain straws do. Flax farmers can burn the straw or till it into the soil, both of which have associated costs and environmental problems. That is why, when a large American corporation called Kimberly-Clark began buying flax straw from Manitoba farmers in 1958, it seemed like an ideal solution, saving farmers from these problems and giving them an additional source of income. The company bought the straw shortly after the flax seed had been harvested, bundled it into box-shaped bales of about 40 pounds each, and transported the bales to

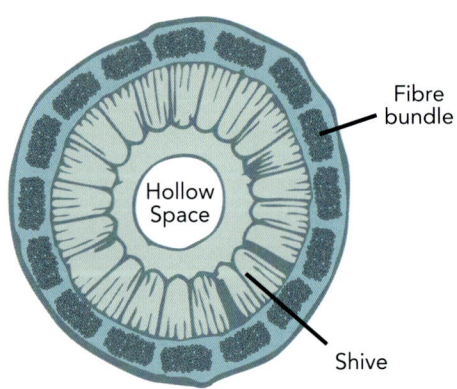

This cross-sectional diagram of a flax stem shows the cylinder of exterior "bast" fibres that enclose a central core of "shive." During processing by the mini, portable, or stationary mills, the bast and shive are separated. The finished fibre bales contain a small amount of shive that is removed fully during processing at a plant in the United States. GORDON GOLDSBOROUGH

one of several sites around the province where they would be piled into neat stacks.

Covered with a tarp to keep out moisture, bacteria acted on the straw in a process called retting, during which the outer layer of straw turned grey, over several months to a year or two. The well-retted straw was then passed through a "decortication mill" that shattered the stems, separating the outside fibres (called bast, that comprises about 20 percent of the stem volume) from the inner core (shive, the remaining 80 percent). Three tons of straw produced about one ton of fibre. Typically, the shive was discarded—burned or tilled into the ground—but sometimes used for livestock bedding or other purposes. The beige-coloured mixture of fibre and a small amount of remaining shive, called tow, was then packed tightly into 300-pound bales to be loaded into railway boxcars like my hotel room and shipped to the aforementioned plant. There, the straw was further cleaned and treated with chemicals to extract the pure fibre

and remove coloured ingredients, resulting in white pulp that could be spread out in sheets and dried to make paper renowned for its thinness and high strength. Flax fibre has been used since medieval times to make linen cloth. More recently, it has been made into fine paper for use in bibles, hymn books, and carbon paper. Until 1984, Canadian paper money contained a mixture of domestic and imported fibres, including flax. The most common use for flax fibre, however, was and is to provide the white paper tube for cigarettes.

The history of commercial paper-making using flax fibre goes back to 1921 when a plant at Jersey City, New Jersey owned by businessman Peter J. Schweitzer (and later by his son Louis) began making paper from imported European fibre. During the Second World War, the supply of fibre from overseas dried up so Schweitzer began developing domestic sources. Flax has been grown by North American farmers for over a century but was generally regarded as a specialty crop that was hard to grow and hard on the land. The city of Windom in southwestern Minnesota was considered the "Flax Capital of the World" because of the abundance of flax grown in its vicinity.

In 1945, Louis Schweitzer purchased a flax-processing plant at Windom that had manufactured rope during the war and, within four years, his firm was no longer dependent on imported flax. However, the transition was not smooth. Initially, the Windom mill failed to produce the quantity and quality of fibre needed for efficient paper production. In desperation, Schweitzer hired Carl Schneider, a Navy veteran and electrical engineer that he had met through a mutual interest in shortwave radio, and sent him to Windom to manage the unproductive mill. In the early 1950s, Schneider designed a radically different milling process that increased production dramatically and turned the Windom plant into a financial windfall. In time, Schweitzer's company was bought by the multinational Kimberly-Clark Corporation, becoming known as its Schweitzer Division. Demand for flax straw to feed the Windom mill grew, forcing straw buyers to venture farther in search of supply. In 1958, one of those buyers, LeRoy Slupe, was dispatched to southern Manitoba to investigate if it would be worthwhile to buy flax straw for shipment back to Minnesota. Regular straw buying in Manitoba began in 1964 and, within five years, the market was sufficiently lucrative that the company hired its first Canadian employee, Marcel Lahure of Carman, as a local straw buyer. He became a full-time,

This photo, believed to have been taken in the United States around 1973, shows an early prototype of a "mini mill" developed by Kimberly-Clark to process stacks of flax straw right in a farmer's field. The bales of flax fibre were loaded onto a truck, at right, while leaving a pile of waste shive, at left, for the farmer to burn or spread. The 300-pound fibre bales were moved manually at this time but, soon afterward, the company invented an electrically-powered "donkey" that ran along a track on the side of the trailer to carry and stack the bales with ease. Metals bands were used to bind bales into six-packs to be loaded by forklift into railway boxcars for shipment to the paper mill. LLOYD COLEMAN

A group of Kimberly-Clark staff standing in a flax crop includes my great-uncle Marcel Lahure (fourth from left) and LeRoy Slupe (right). SCHWEITZER-MAUDUIT CANADA

This aerial view of Killarney show the three 12,000-square-foot warehouses built by Kimberly-Clark in 1978 to store up to 6,000 tons of flax fibre awaiting shipment to the United States. Also visible in the photo is the portable office trailer beside one of the warehouses where I spent my summers from 1978 to 1981, the boxcars and loading platform to the left of the warehouses where flax fibre bales were loaded for shipment to the fibre processing plant, and grain elevators that were demolished sometime after 2007. SCHWEITZER-MAUDUIT CANADA

year-round supervisor in 1972. By this time, the company was buying 40,000 tons a year of baled flax straw from Manitoba, for which farmers were paid up to $14 per ton.

Because flax is grown in various areas of Manitoba, and trucking of flax straw back to Minnesota was costly, the company developed a portable fibre-processing mill that could operate in Canada to process and ship only the purified fibre to the paper mill in the United States. This portable mill, which began operating in Manitoba around 1970, would be set up at one of the company's straw storage yards—at Boissevain, Carman, Deloraine, Haskett, Manitou, Melita, and Souris—for periods of up to a few months each. Operated year-round by a crew of fifteen, often with two shifts each day, it would process flax that had been brought and stacked in the yard, then move to the next yard. Eventually, as flax processing in Manitoba began to eclipse that of Minnesota, a second portable mill began operating here. A further advance in portability occurred in 1974, when Kimberly-Clark introduced "mini mills" mounted on a semi-trailer. These mills could go right to the farm fields, process the straw that the farmer had stacked, and leave behind just a pile of shive when it moved to another field. No transportation of straw was required. Four of these mini mills, along with two portable mills, were operating in southern Manitoba by the late 1970s when I began working for Kimberly-Clark. We travelled throughout southwestern Manitoba, with occasional forays into eastern Saskatchewan, in search of flax straw. While each of seven-person crews of the mini mills processed straw in the countryside, I manned the company's office—a converted semi-trailer—that was parked beside the railway tracks in a nearby town. As truckloads of tow arrived to be loaded into boxcars, I would collect and analyze tow samples so that New Jersey would know what to expect when the boxcars arrived there. I maintained shipping, personnel, and payroll records, and did whatever other odd jobs needed to be done. I drove a forklift, tracked down crew members who had not shown up for work in the morning, communicated with the mills and the "home office" back in Windom, referred public inquiries to the appropriate manager, and a wide range of other tasks.

The period of highest flax production in Manitoba was the mid-1950s to the late 1980s, but the zenith of flax straw milling in Manitoba may have been in 1977. Typically, an acre of farmland produces between one-half and two-thirds ton of flax straw. That year, however, an unusually large

This view of a mini flax-processing mill shows it being fed with flax straw bales on a conveyor belt at right and finished fibre bales exiting the mill at left. A pile of waste shive dumped in a pile behind the mill was usually burned by the farmer after the milling was finished. RANDY QUANE

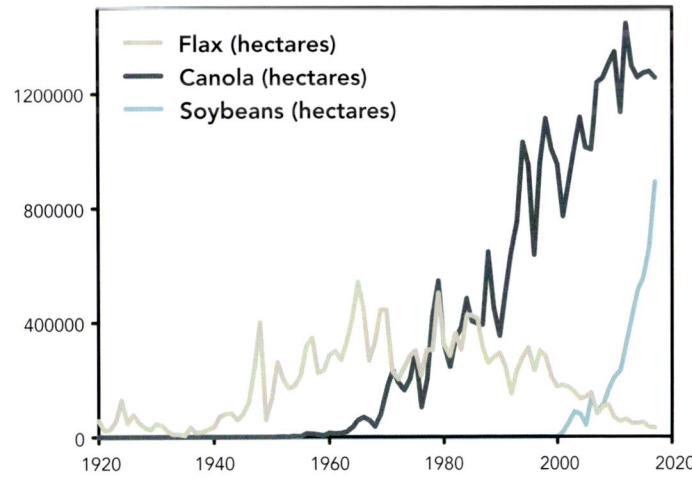

Statistics on the total hectarage of agricultural land in Manitoba sowed with flax, canola, and soybeans between 1920 and 2017 illustrate the long-term trends in these three oil-bearing crops. Flax reached its maximum popularity in the 1960s through 1980s but has waned considerably to the present, displaced on farm fields by canola (since the 1970s), soybeans (since 2000), and other plants. DRAWN FROM DATA COMPILED BY STATISTICS CANADA

At the flax fibre processing plant at Spotswood, New Jersey (near New York City), large rolls of finished flax paper are cut into a series of smaller disks to be used for making cigarette wrappers. SCHWEITZER-MAUDUIT CANADA

amount of straw was produced, from one to one-and-a-quarter tons per acre. Carl Schneider was quoted as saying that "I've been in this business 31 years and this is the heaviest crop I've ever seen." More flax straw was available than Kimberly-Clark—and its two Canadian competitors, Domtar Fine Papers Limited and Olin Holdings Limited (later owned by Ecusta Fibres Limited)—could handle. Yields vary widely from year to year so, rather than turn away

straw that it might need in the future, Kimberly-Clark decided to build four enormous warehouses to house the partially processed fibre. During the summer of 1978, I witnessed the construction of two of them along the railway tracks in Killarney and an additional one in Glenboro. The final warehouse in Killarney was built in 1979. Each metal-clad building measured 60 feet by 200 feet, each had a concrete floor. Rather than ship tow bales straight to New Jersey, they were stacked in piles in the warehouses. Gradually, over a period of years, the bales could be unloaded from the warehouses as warranted by demand at the New Jersey plant.

My grandfathers, both of whom were farmers, were remarkably consistent in the crops they grew. Each year, it was a choice of wheat, oats, or barley, and rarely anything else. (I do not recall that either of them grew flax.) In the past three or four decades, however, we have seen dramatic diversification in the crops that Manitoba farmers are growing. Crops that were once rare have

become common. Starting in the 1970s, and continuing unabated today, yellow-flowered canola has become a major crop species. Purple-flowered soybean acreage has exploded since 2000. On the other hand, wheat acreage has dropped dramatically, along with flax. From its height when the Killarney warehouses were built, the attractive fields of blue-flowered flax have decreased from a peak of 1,250,000 acres in 1979 to less than one-twentieth of that area today. The warehouses at Killarney were last used by the company in 2006 and stood mostly empty for over a decade, before being sold recently to local businesses. The Glenboro warehouse was also sold and is being used to store agricultural crops and equipment. The company is the only one still active at processing flax straw, the two Canadian firms having exited the market in 1984 (Domtar) and 2010 (Olin/Ecusta). Operating entirely in Canada as of

OPPOSITE Flax straw bales awaiting processing at a mill near Carman, June 2017. GORDON GOLDSBOROUGH

Interior view of a former flax fibre warehouse at Killarney, May 2017. GORDON GOLDSBOROUGH

1985, the company has a large stationary mill southeast of Carman, surrounded by dozens of large straw stacks, that produces higher-quality, lower-shive-content tow than the older mills. In 1995, Kimberly-Clark spun off its tobacco-related specialty paper business in Canada, USA, and France to create an independent, publicly-traded company called Schweitzer-Mauduit International based in Georgia. It continues to buy flax straw from all over southern Manitoba as well as Saskatchewan and North Dakota and processes about 50,000 tons annually. Mill portability is no longer a feature of the operation. The mini mills were taken out of service in 2002, scavenged for reusable parts, and eventually sold for scrap. One of the portable mills was kept as a backup for the stationary mill. All flax is now trucked into a vast straw storage yard around the stationary mill. Rather than loading the fibre bales directly into boxcars—which are fast disappearing as railways transition to standard-sized containers—they are packed into containers at the mill and trucked to Winnipeg to be loaded onto a train for transport to New Jersey.

Marcel Lahure, the first employee of Kimberly-Clark in Manitoba, was my great-uncle, a brother to my maternal grandmother. In the early 1970s, he evangelized the use of flax straw to farmers around the province, and oversaw the growth of an industry. In a blatant act of nepotism, he hired me—a university student needing summer employment—to run the mobile office that accompanied the mini mills. In addition to doing my job over the four months during my summer recess, I learned many lessons while working for Kimberly-Clark. I learned how to move (and occasionally derail) a boxcar all by myself and to stop a runaway boxcar before it broke onto the main line and smashed into a passing train. I learned how large dosages of caffeine pills could be helpful when you are sleep-deprived and want to visit your girl-friend (later, your wife) who was many hours drive away. I learned how to dispose of suspiciously leftover beer after a night of heavy drinking by your co-workers. (Believe me, you do not want to know any more about this one.) I learned the value of an ice-cold Slurpee on a hot day when you are working in an office trailer with no air conditioning—and taught that lesson to LeRoy Slupe and Carl Schneider. I learned how fast some sports cars can drive in reverse—over 60 miles per hour (it was very scary, now that I think of it). I met many fine people during those four summers, both among the crews as well as in the towns where we worked. The crew members were mostly young men, many of them (like me) away from home for the first time. Being young and flush with cash, they were prone (unlike me) to the sorts of excesses that people in similar situations throughout history have enjoyed during downtime. They smoked. They swore. They drank. They had sex. A lot. I remember the practical jokes. Being related to one of the bosses, I was mostly immune to them, but one time my little Austin Mini car was put up on blocks, just high enough so its wheels did not touch the ground, but not so much that I could see this, and wondered why my car did not move when I tried to drive away. In the course of those four summers, I travelled all over southern Manitoba and eastern Saskatchewan, spending weeks living in boxcars here and there, often in places that I had never known to exist. It was this experience, more than any other in my life, that made me passionate about the many wonderful places in rural Manitoba. It was, I think, the genesis of my project to map historic sites around Manitoba, to talk about them on the 'Abandoned Manitoba' radio series, and to eventually write books like this one. I just wish that I had taken more photos along the way.

ACKNOWLEDGEMENTS

I have fond memories of my summers spent on the road with the flax-processing crews of Kimberly-Clark Canada. Yet, my formal documentation of those experiences is woefully inadequate, as I learned when I sought to collect photos for this chapter. The few photos in my old albums were poorly composed and out-of-focus (due to lack of skill, not drinking). Luckily for me, others were more diligent. Judy Young, daughter of the late Lloyd Coleman, shared several photos from albums compiled when he was a foreman on the mini and portable mills, along with newspaper clippings from the 1970s that provided a wealth of information. Long-time mill employee Randy Quane provided great reminiscences and feedback on a draft of the chapter. Dean "Beaner" Graham, who began working for Kimberly-Clark in October 1974, at the age of 16, and still works for Schweitzer-Mauduit, filled numerous holes in my recollections, provided a copy of an old corporate video about flax processing, allowed me to copy photos from the walls of his office boardroom, and recreated a photo of me doing "shive testing." Grant Tweed gave me access to the cavernous flax fibre warehouses in Killarney.

Assiniboine
River Pillar

A mysterious pillar protrudes from the middle of the Assiniboine River about three miles downstream of Brandon. It is massive, standing over ten feet out of the water and twice as wide as it is tall. Made entirely of concrete and surrounded by water, the pillar is badly pitted and scarred from being battered by innumerable ice blocks and tree trunks floating down the river over a long span of time. What is it?

Sometimes, I like to imagine that I am living a century ago so I can consider how my present-day life is different from what I would have led in the past. One of my favourite scenarios is that I am a travelling salesman in rural Manitoba, going from place to place peddling my wares. I plan where to stay when I arrive at a town: a hotel if the town is a larger one and I am lucky enough to get a bed that I do not have to share with strangers, or the cold,

An antique postcard from Ninette, taken around 1912, illustrates how a railway station in rural Manitoba might have looked to a travelling salesman in the early 20th century. GORDON GOLDSBOROUGH PHOTO COLLECTION, 2018-0103

hard floor of the train station if my lucks runs out. If my journey is short, I can walk or bicycle to my destination. For longer trips, my faithful horse will pull my wagon or sleigh, or I may drive my finicky new automobile on the primitive highways that are just beginning to be built. For long trips, there is really only

one reliable means of transportation: the railway. Luckily, it has a daily or weekly schedule to most of the towns that I need to visit. As I disembark from a train on arrival at my destination, I see the railway employees unloading all manner of items: large sacks of mail; crates of food, clothing, and hardware; machinery; even

Concrete abutments and pier of the abandoned Grand Trunk Pacific Railway bridge, June 1940. LAWRENCE STUCKEY COLLECTION, S. J. MCKEE ARCHIVES, BRANDON UNIVERSITY

livestock sometimes. How easy the railway has made our lives! How did we live before it was built? This may be a question that many rural Manitobans ponder today, for an entirely different reason from mine. Many communities created by the arrival of a railway line now must face the demands of daily life without that once-essential connection to the outside world. Their railway line has been abandoned.

The concrete pillar standing in the middle of the Assiniboine River is a pier that was once part of a railway bridge over the river, built in the early twentieth century to service a branch line of the Grand Trunk Pacific (GTP) Railway between Brandon and the village of Brookdale to the northeast. The railway's right-of-way—a mostly straight-lined, raised soil and gravel berm where parallel metal rails would be laid—was constructed sometime before 1924 (and, in fact, is still visible in aerial photos today) but the rails were never installed. Massive concrete abutments on each riverbank and the pier in the

river were meant to support a steel truss bridge, similar in appearance to Winnipeg's Arlington, Louise, and Redwood bridges. After the decision was made not to complete the line, the trusses were removed in 1924 and probably reused somewhere else. But the abutments and pier could not be removed so easily and were simply abandoned. The southern abutment appears to be a popular party spot, judging from the graffiti splashed all over it and the numerous bottles strewn around that I saw during a visit in early 2017.

The former GTP bridge over the Assiniboine is an extreme case of railway abandonment, one that was abandoned before it was even used once, probably because it was never needed in the first place. More often, railways are abandoned after they have operated for many years. In the early days of railroading in Manitoba, when the future looked grand and federal politicians envisioned millions of immigrants spreading out across the prairies, a massive spider's web of railway lines was built. Many of the lines were of questionable necessity. In 1906, the American-owned Great Northern Railway opened its Dakota Subdivision running from Devils Lake, North Dakota northward to Brandon, intending to continue on to The Pas and eventually reach Hudson Bay. That northward extension was never built and the entire line was abandoned in 1936 for lack of business, leaving the farming communities of Bannerman, Desford, Hayfield, and others to blend back into the prairie from which they had come. Today, these places are all but forgotten. The reason for the Dakota Subdivision to be abandoned within thirty years of construction was that it was never really needed in the first place. Far too many branch lines had been built. The volume of traffic did not warrant their costs of construction, much less their ongoing maintenance. Prior to 1933, there were no regulations on railway abandonment and companies were free to respond at will to market forces. That year, the federal Railway Act was amended to require the companies to obtain permission from the Board of Transport Commissioners. During the Second World War, the need for efficient transportation of goods meant that lines were upgraded. But after the war ended, only the main lines were maintained while branch lines were neglected. They deteriorated or became obsolete—their wooden ties gradually rotted so they were unable to carry the loads they once did and the steel rails could not support the heavier railcars that began to run on them.

The first wave of formal branch line abandonments in Manitoba began in 1960 when segments of the Canadian National Railway (CNR)'s Wakopa and Oakland lines through southern Manitoba were closed. That same year, the Canadian Pacific Railway (CPR) abandoned its Reston Subdivision. These were followed by the CPR McAuley (1961), CPR Snowflake (1962), CPR Fallison (1962), CPR Kaleida (1962), CPR Lac du Bonnet (1962), CNR Victoria

A map of the CNR's Wawanesa Subdivision between Brandon and Belmont, submitted to the Hall Commission, marking the green (Group C) segment abandoned in November 1975 and the red (Group B) remainder abandoned in December 1983. REG FORBES COLLECTION, S. J. MCKEE ARCHIVES, BRANDON UNIVERSITY

Exhibit 8

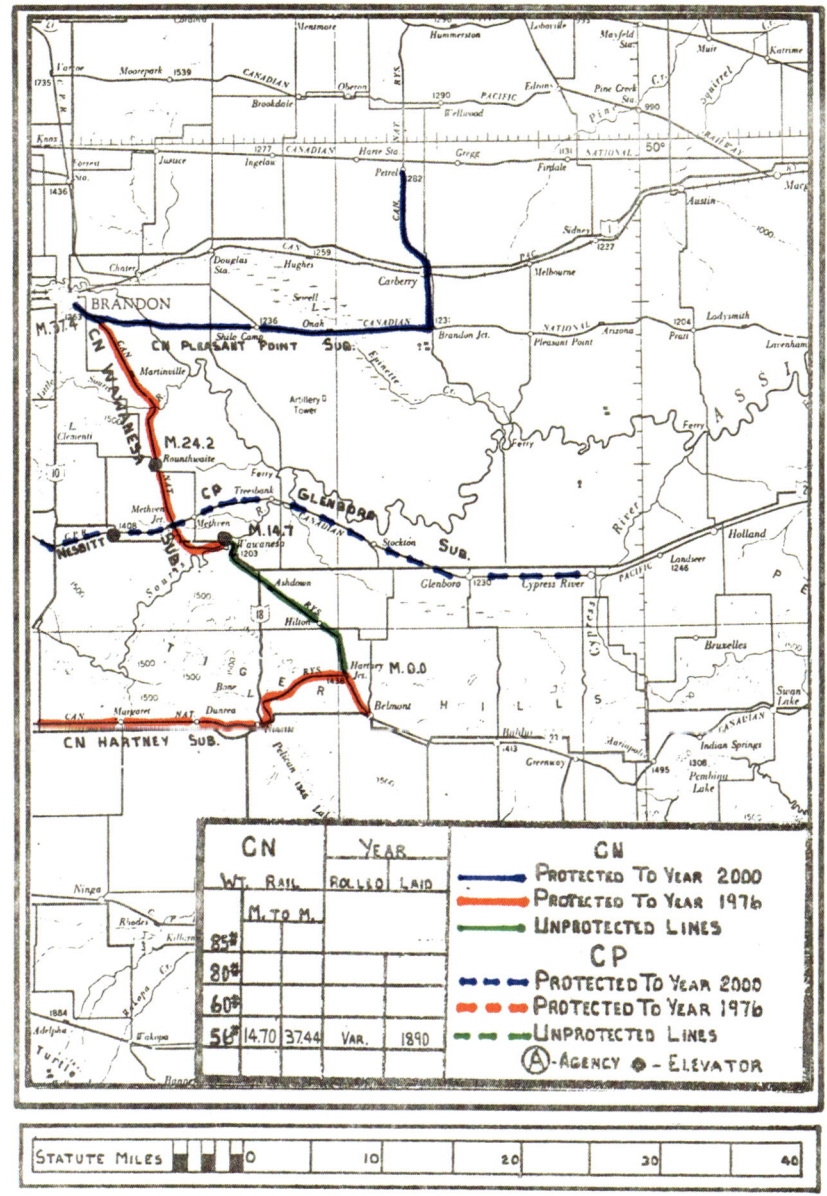

Wawanesa Subdivision

CHAMBER OF COMMERCE

PROGRESS OF MANITOBA

Birch River, Man.

January 21st, 1976.

The Birch River and District Chamber of Commerce
wishes to present the following reasons why they are
not in favour in rail abandment in the Sway Valley:

1. Loss of employment for railroad employees
2. Possibly eventual loss of elevators
3. Loss of our principle source of income,
   logging, agriculture, etc.
4. Loss of our pulpwood industry which
   employs many people.
5. Deterioration of our highways.
6. A slow death of our community.

BIRCH RIVER & DISTRICT
CHAMBER OF COMMERCE

A. Lowe
President
Mr. A. Lowe

A letter from the Birch River Chamber of Commerce, in the northern Swan Valley, to the Hall Commission gave six reasons for its opposition to abandonment of the CNR's Erwood Subdivision to the community. The line succumbed in April 2000. REG FORBES COLLECTION, S. J. MCKEE ARCHIVES, BRANDON UNIVERSITY

Beach (1963), and CPR Rapid City (1963) lines. A moratorium on further abandonments, enforced by the federal government, kept the rest of the branch lines in operation into the early 1970s. In December 1974, the government of Pierre Trudeau announced that it had subdivided the remaining rail lines across Canada into three categories. Tracks in Group A (of which there were 3,148 miles in Manitoba) were considered to be part of a "basic network" guaranteed to the year 2000. Group B consisted of rails to be maintained for one year until their final fate could be determined through further study, while the remainder in Group C were slated for immediate abandonment.

The government appointed a Commission of Inquiry to recommend on the fate of the Group B lines. Known formally as the Grain Handling and Transportation Commission, most people referred to it as the Hall Commission in recognition of its head, retired Supreme Court Justice Emmett Hall. It operated between 1975 and 1977, holding public hearings all over western Canada, including in numerous small communities around Manitoba. The sole member of the Hall Commission from Manitoba, Brandon's Reginald "Reg" Forbes, amassed a vast collection of files during that period and, luckily for historians, he saw fit to deposit the files in the archives at Brandon University. They provide an incredibly detailed insight into the deliberations of the Commission as it made recommendations affecting the fate of lines all over Canada. Contained in Forbes' papers are numerous heartbreaking appeals from earnest, hard-working people who begged the Commissioners to spare their railway line, citing statistics on the greater distance they would have to drive to transport their grain to market and the dire consequences for their communities if the line was lost. An example was a brief submitted in March 1976 by a group at Elgin, on the CNR's Hartney Subdivision (abandoned in June 1978):

> We are a very small community and we are struggling to maintain the town as best we can. We have a new community hall being constructed on voluntary labour, a good skating and curling rink, and a good school. We have a store, bank, garage, restaurant, blacksmith, pool room, post offices and barber shop in town. We are very concerned with what will happen to Elgin if our rail line and elevators are closed. What

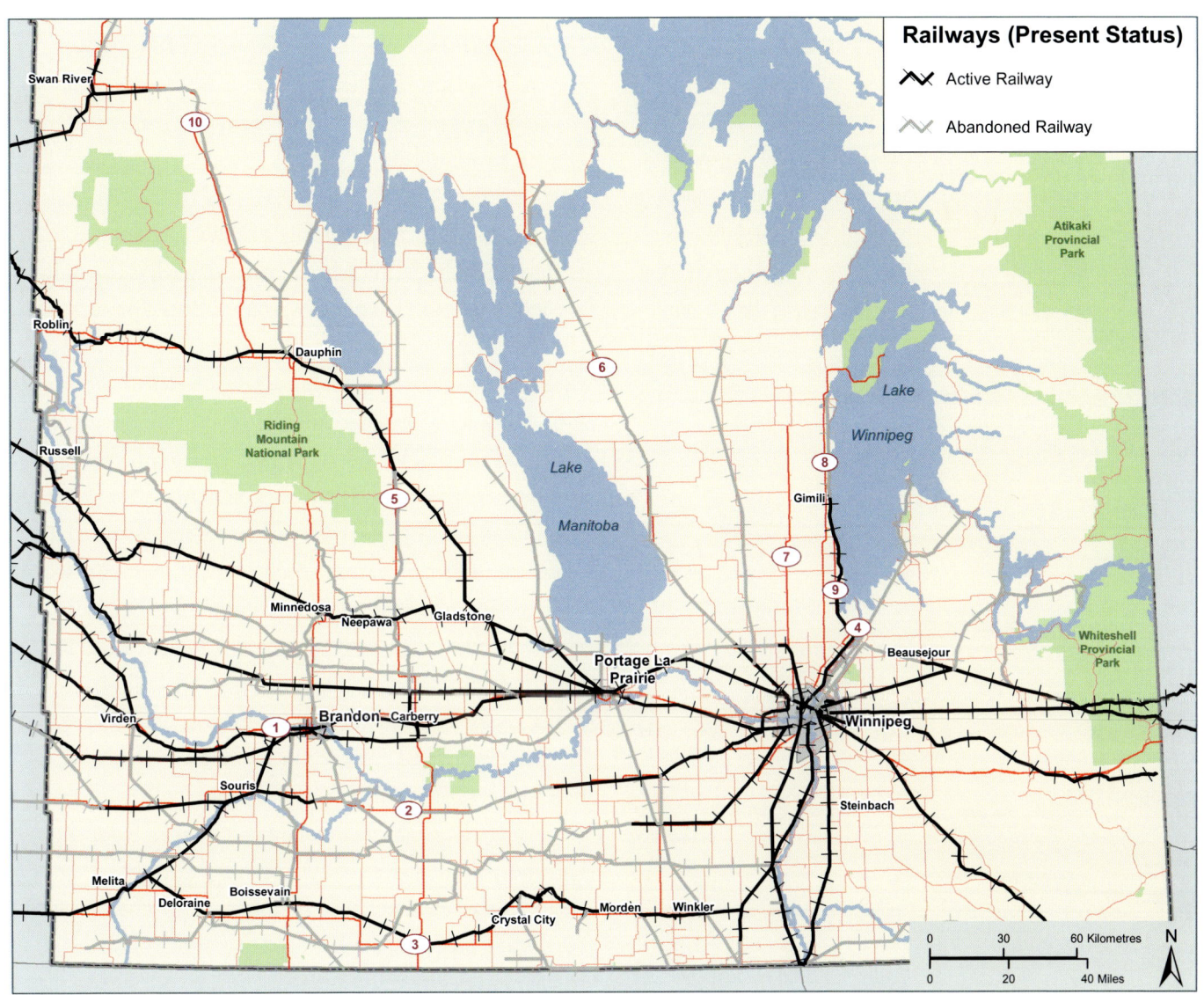

Railways (Present Status)

- Active Railway
- Abandoned Railway

A map of railway lines in southern Manitoba shows those presently in operation (black lines) as well as abandoned ones (grey lines).
MAP BY JENNIFER LIDGETT USING DATA FROM JIM PEARSON

will become of the businesses now located at Elgin, such businesses as garages, fuel oil dealers, lumber yards and fertilizer dealers? Last year there were 39 cars of fertilizer and 1 car of lumber came in by the railway. We wonder if our stores, banks, restaurant, and repair dealers could continue if farmers began to take their business to other towns. If farmers are delivering grain to another town they will soon begin shopping there and getting their repairs done there. In short the loss of business generated by

When the railway line through Rounthwaite was abandoned in December 1983, the Manitoba Pool grain elevator there was moved to Nesbitt, where a new crib annex was built beside it. Closed around 2001, it was sold into private ownership. The railway tracks at Nesbitt were removed in mid-2016. UNITED GRAIN GROWERS COLLECTION, UNIVERSITY OF MANITOBA ARCHIVES & SPECIAL COLLECTIONS

farmers bringing grain into town would slowly begin to kill what we have left in Elgin. If our town is going to disappear, we would prefer to let it die [naturally], not have it killed.

At a typical public hearing, a railway company representative would deliver a brief explaining what the railway wished to do with particular Group B lines. In most cases, the company's wish was abandonment on the grounds that the line was not economically viable. Most of the Group B lines served agricultural areas of the province, which meant that abandonment affected grain companies and farmers the most. The grain companies were generally pragmatic, arguing that even if they did not favour abandonment in principle, they could adapt so long as there was a period of adjustment and the abandonment was not immediate. This view was understandable because the companies operated facilities all over Manitoba, and in many cases other provinces, so the loss of business at one place would be balanced by an increase in business at other places. But farmers and businesspeople living in the vicinity of lines to be abandoned had no such balancing. Farmers would have to haul their crops farther to deliver them to market, thereby incurring greater transportation cost, while businesspeople would be put out of business. Farmers were especially angry at the railways which, they argued, had neglected branch maintenance and undercut themselves intentionally by introducing competing truck-based transportation, thereby making railway service to grain elevators less lucrative. Not surprisingly, local communities recommended that 100 percent of lines under consideration for abandonment should be retained, either fully or partially. At the opposite end of the spectrum, railway companies wanted to abandon 63 percent of the lines and retain 37 percent in some form. Occupying middle ground, but tending toward the local view, were the Manitoba government and grain companies which each recommended 96 percent for full or partial retention and only four percent for abandonment. In the end, the Hall Commission recommended the abandonment of 632.9 miles of Group B rails in Manitoba (including ones that were not in active use anyway), representing about 14 percent of the total. The abandonment affected the government-owned CNR disproportionately: 66 percent of recommended abandonments were on CNR lines versus only 34 percent on the CPR.

Consider just one example of branch line abandonment and its consequences. The Wawanesa Subdivision, built in 1890 by the Northern Pacific and Manitoba Railway Company (later a part of the Canadian Northern Railway and still later of the Canadian National Railway), ran southeast-northwest between Brandon and Hartney Junction (3.3 miles northwest of Belmont), about 37.4 miles in total length. Roughly 96% of the freight transported on the line was grain, picked up at warehouses or elevators at Hilton (mile 1.2), Ashdown (mile 5.8), Wawanesa (mile 11.4), Elliott Siding (mile 14.5), Rounthwaite (mile 20.9), and Martinville (mile 29.0). The close proximity of grain elevators arose in the days when grain was moved by farmers using horse-drawn wagons, so through the years, farm mechanization combined with economic forces led to elevator closures. By the 1970s, the only ones left were at Wawanesa and Rounthwaite. The railway argued that the entire line was in fair to poor condition and should be abandoned on grounds that, between 1972 and 1974, it had lost between $13,272 and $20,367 per year on the line. It would cost $5 million to replace lighter-density rails so the line could support the weight of modern, large-capacity hopper cars. The local community, provincial government, and grain companies all called for the Subdivision to be retained but the Hall Commission agreed with the railway and recommended its abandonment. The Group C segment between Hartney Junction and Wawanesa was abandoned in November 1975. An elevator on this segment, at Hilton, was closed and moved to Ninette where it continued in service until 1987. The remainder of the line, the Group B segment from Wawanesa to Brandon, was abandoned in December 1983, at which time the elevators at Rounthwaite and Wawanesa closed. The older elevator at Wawanesa was deemed not to be worth moving so it was demolished while a new elevator at Rounthwaite was moved to Nesbitt, on the designated "basic network."

The guarantee afforded by designating a line as Group A only

A pile of steel rails removed from the CPR Glenboro Subdivision in the Fall of 2016 are an abstract illustration of railway abandonment in Manitoba. GORDON GOLDSBOROUGH

extended to the year 2000. Now, in the twenty-first century, a new round of railway abandonment has begun. In September 2014, the segment of the CPR Glenboro Subdivision that included Nesbitt was abandoned and the former Rounthwaite elevator, having escaped closure in 1983, closed. It was sold to a local farmer who, as far as I can tell, is still using it to store his grain. In the fall of 2016, I was driving along Highway 2 and witnessed the removal of rails from the Glenboro line. In the town of

Glenboro, there was a massive pile of steel stacked along the right-of-way, awaiting shipment to a recycling facility. It was a visual and visceral sign of the abandonment that is going on all over the province right up to the present day.

There have been wide-ranging implications of railway abandonment for communities. Farmers needed more on-farm storage for their grain and larger trucks to move it to the few remaining elevators. Municipalities lost tax assessments from closed elevators, along with the financial support for local causes for which the grain companies (especially the cooperative ones) were renowned. The Rural Municipality of Oakland estimated that it lost $48,000 in annual tax revenue (about $120,000 in today's dollars) when the Rounthwaite elevator and rails were removed, while the Village of Wawanesa lost $21,000, or about 3% of its total revenue, when its elevator closed. As the folks at Elgin predicted, villages lost economic activity when farmers went

elsewhere to deliver their grain and did not patronize local businesses. (The single remaining grain elevator at Elgin is now privately owned.) Municipalities had to upgrade local roads to withstand heavier truck loads, especially during the critical spring period when "road restrictions" prevent heavily-loaded trucks from using certain provincial roads. And farmers faced greater fuel costs and vehicle purchases for longer hauls.

Ultimately, railway abandonment has contributed substantially to rural depopulation throughout southern Manitoba. Did the population of the area served by the Wawanesa Subdivision decline after its abandonment? Yes, primarily in the area farthest from Brandon. In the thirty-year period from 1981 to 2011, the combined populations of the Rural Municipalities of Oakland and Strathcona, and the Village of Wawanesa (all of which ceased to exist in the municipal amalgamations of 2015), decreased by ten percent, from 2,511 to 2,261, mostly due to a 36 percent decline in Strathcona.

(The highest population of the area was in 1931, at 4,256.) The communities of Hilton and Rounthwaite are essentially gone now except for a few persistent homes. Wawanesa is hanging on, despite the loss of its elevator and tracks, having benefitted from an influx of residents employed at the Shilo military base.

Life in Manitoba is generally a lot more comfortable than a century ago, and the means of getting from place to place is faster, easier, and more convenient than when I was a make-believe travelling salesman. But the abandonment of railway lines all over the province has undoubtedly changed community life in profound and devastating ways, some of which we have not yet fully faced. Visible signs of railway abandonment remain all over the landscape, in addition to the Assiniboine River pillar. Last summer, I was flying my drone in the "pothole country" south of Minnedosa. Interspersed amongst bright yellow fields of canola are hundreds of small, shallow lakes created when retreating glaciers thousands of years ago cleaved off chunks of ice that subsequently melted, leaving depressions that filled with water. My "drone's eye view" could see a heavily vegetated, straight line crossing one of the potholes. Clearly, it was not a natural phenomenon. A key clue was that the line continued on each side of the pothole, extending far into the distance. It was the right-of-way of the CPR's Varcoe Subdivision between Macgregor and Varcoe (near Miniota) that had been abandoned in two stages in the mid- to late-1970s. Its metal rails are long gone but the

The right-of-way of the CPR's Varcoe Subdivision, abandoned in the 1970s, ran straight through a small lake in the farmland south of Minnedosa. GORDON GOLDSBOROUGH

right-of-way will remain visible for generations to come, reminding future daydreamers of a time when railway lines were the lifeblood of Manitoba communities that are themselves becoming distant memories.

ACKNOWLEDGEMENTS

Ken Storie shared generously of his knowledge of the old concrete pillar sticking out of the Assiniboine River, and Christy "Mo" Henry at the S. J. McKee Archives (Brandon University) gave me unfettered access to the Reg Forbes and John Everitt collections that were essential to research for this chapter. Jim Pearson provided copies of his incredibly detailed and useful maps of railway lines, past and present, in Manitoba. Filmmakers Shaun Cameron and Graham Street indulged my obsession to find the site of the Martinville grain elevator during our travels in the Brandon Hills.

Negrych
Homestead

The people who settled in Manitoba in the late 19th and early 20th centuries were tough, both physically and mentally. They had to be. They were driven by a desire to create a new life of freedom in western Canada, and to make opportunities for their descendants. Their homes provided few of the creature comforts that we take for granted today: primitive heating in winter using wood or coal, no cooling in summer, a toilet in a stinky and mosquito-filled outhouse in the yard, no hot and cold running water at the turn of a tap, no electrically-powered lights and appliances, no communication with the outside world at the lift of a handset, and certainly no big-screen television and internet access. We assume that these wonderful conveniences came about gradually through the 20th century so, by the 1980s, most Manitobans lived a life of ease compared to their parents and grandparents. Therefore, it is curious to think that, as recently as 1990 in a relatively developed part of the province, some people eschewed a life of comfort to live essentially as their forebears had done.

This is the story of a remarkable site that is considered by heritage advocates to be the most complete and best-preserved pioneer homestead in Canada, and possibly all of North America. I am referring to the Negrych Homestead, located about 24 miles by road northwest of Dauphin or 12 miles northeast of Gilbert Plains. Operated today as a community museum, I tried several times over a period of years to visit it, always arriving when it was closed, until I finally managed to get there in the spring of 2017. I must say that it was one of the most moving experiences I have had during my decade on

Annie and Stephen Negrych stand at the entrance to their home, date unknown. ED LEDOHOWSKI

the road in search of historic places. Walking into the site seemed as though I had used a time-machine to jump back over a century, to see a log house almost exactly as it would have appeared when it was built in 1899.

In 1897, Wasyl (Basil or William in English) and Anna Negrych, accompanied by their seven children ranging in age from nine months to nineteen years, left their home in the highlands of western Ukraine and boarded a sailing ship in the German port of Hamburg, bound for Quebec City. The trip was gruelling and at least two of the 788 passengers

OPPOSITE The former Negrych Homestead overlooks the Drifting River at the left of this aerial view, with tree-lined farm fields at the right. In the centre of the grassed farmyard was an orchard, surrounded by a wooden rail fence. Several of the family's original plantings—rhubarb, apples, plums, sour cherries, hops, horseradish, and dill—still grow. The visible buildings include, from left to right, a Barn (1908), Bunkhouse (1908), House (1899), Chicken Coop (1902), Granary (1898), Barn (1902), Garage (1937), and Granary (1908). GORDON GOLDSBOROUGH

died in transit. On arriving in Canada, the Negrychs travelled by train to Winnipeg then, after a brief stay, continued on to Dauphin, where 53-year-old Wasyl bought a quarter-section of land for $10. Thirty-three-year-old Anna and the younger children stayed in an immigration shed at Dauphin while Wasyl and the older children investigated their new homestead. Wasyl and his brothers Anton and Jan, and his cousin Iwan, had purchased the four quarter-sections of one square mile.

The original Negrych farmhouse, built in 1899, measures 15 feet wide and 35 feet long, with a wood-shingled roof. Its walls are covered in homemade mud-plaster. The door, locked from the inside, can be unlocked using a homemade wooden key inserted through a hole in the wall. GORDON GOLDSBOROUGH

Unlike settlers who typically built homes near the outer edge of their land, near a "road allowance," the Negrychs built on the inner corners of their quarter-sections, along an old "colonization trail" that ran southeast-northwest through the property. The families created, in effect, a small Ukrainian village for themselves. Initially, the families built "buddas," temporary A-frame structures made of locally sourced poplar poles covered in cowhides bought in Dauphin. In 1899, after his initial home was destroyed in a massive prairie fire that swept through the region, Wasyl Negrych built another one, in a style typical of ones in the Carpathian mountains of eastern Europe. It still stands today. The 15-foot by 35-foot structure is made almost entirely of wood with minimal metal hardware. Its walls are squared tamarack logs covered inside and outside, along with the interior ceiling, with homemade mud-plaster—made by mixing clay, straw, cow manure, and water—made strikingly white by adding laundry bluing to the wet mixture prior to application. Unlike some such buildings, where the roof would be covered in thatching, the home's roof was covered with wood shingles. Following a floorplan popular in their Ukrainian homeland, the Negrych home had three rooms, all with wooden floors. The main entrance led into a central room that served as a kitchen, with an iron cook-stove, shelves, and a washstand. Beneath the kitchen was a root cellar excavated into the ground for storing vegetables through the winter. A small room off one side of the kitchen was used as a pantry. The largest room to the other side was a combined bedroom and sitting room containing "two iron beds, a rocking chair, extension dining room table, a treadle sewing machine, a small box heater and a coal oil lamp."

In their new home in Canada, the Negrychs had five more children, bringing their family to twelve children: six girls and six boys. They also built several other buildings on the site, including an earthen-floored bunkhouse (built in 1908 for the boys), cow barn, pigpen, chicken coop, three granaries (1898, 1908, 1940), and an icehouse, all made of logs. Inside the bunkhouse was a peech, a log-and-clay stove used for summer cooking. It also heated the bunkhouse in winter and provided smoke to cure meats in a lean-to beside the building. Surrounding the buildings was a vegetable, berry, and herb garden, an orchard (with plums, sour cherries, and six varieties of apples) enclosed with wooden rail fences, and small fields cut from the surrounding forest where the Negrychs grew grain and feed for their chickens, pigs, and cattle.

The barn on the Negrych Homestead dates from 1902. Its original thatched roof was replaced by a wood-shingled roof in 1942 when two layers of logs were added to provide room for a hay loft.
GORDON GOLDSBOROUGH

Wasyl Negrych died in February 1927, at the age of 83, and was buried in a little Ukrainian Orthodox cemetery a mile northwest of his home. Anna Negrych continued on until March 1944, when she joined her husband in the nearby cemetery. The youngest of their six daughters, Annie, born in 1907 and never married, continued to live in the original house into her 80s. Throughout her long life, Annie never had the house wired for electricity or a telephone. Lighting was provided by kerosene lamps, as it had been years earlier, and heat was provided by a stove fuelled by wood. There was no running water. Instead, Annie would dip a bucket in the Drifting River that flowed about 100 feet away from her house. However, she

In 1908, a bunkhouse was built of plastered logs to accommodate the family's six sons. Its floor was covered with a mixture of straw and horse manure. The sloped wood pieces on the right side of the bunkhouse trapped smoke from the peech to cure hanging meat and fish. Stephen Negrych lived in the bunkhouse as a child, and again after he retired from teaching, from 1968 to 1990 GORDON GOLDSBOROUGH

A clay oven, called a peech, inside the bunkhouse was used for cooking and it also provided heat during long, cold winters. GORDON GOLDSBOROUGH

did not lack for company. In 1968, her brother Stephen returned to the homestead to join her and their older brother Wasyl.

Born in 1903, Stephen Negrych had attended Wesley College in Winnipeg then, over the next 38 years until retirement, he was a teacher at a series of ten one-room schools. Like he had done as a child, the old bachelor slept in a bunkhouse a few feet away from the main residence. In 1983, Wasyl became ill and was moved to a personal care home in Dauphin, where he died on 17 December 1986. At that time, most of the farm machinery, animals, and building contents were sold at auction. With Bimbo, a small dog of indeterminate breeding, the two surviving Negrychs continued to live "off the grid" as their ancestors had done for generations, performing light chores during the day and reading in the evening by the light of a coal oil lamp. Occasionally, Stephen played his violin. Annie made meals on the old cookstove, fired by wood cut by Stephen in the surrounding forests. Finally, in the spring of 1988, Annie Negrych moved into a senior's home in Gilbert Plains and she died there on 16 December 1988. Stephen Negrych lived at the homestead until October 1990 when he moved into Dauphin. When he died at the Dauphin Hospital on 23 June 1992, he was the last of the pioneer Negrychs. He was buried in the same cemetery as his parents, along with Annie and many other members of his extended family.

The Negrych farm buildings, largely unaltered from their original appearance, survived far longer than most other pioneer farmsteads that were usually torn down when they were replaced by modern amenities. Late in his life, Stephen Negrych is said to have hoped the homestead that his parents built would be preserved for its historical significance in commemoration of his parents' pioneer spirit. In 1991, the local Lions

Club began developing plans before he died. Initially, that would have entailed relocating the buildings to the Selo Ukraina Museum south of Dauphin, home of the National Ukrainian Festival. However, that would have destroyed the context for the buildings—the fact that each building sits in the same spot as when it was first built—which is their most unique feature. The move never happened and, instead, the Gilbert Plains and District Historical Society stepped forward with a commitment to protect and preserve the buildings where they stood. Consequently, the 120-year-old Negrych Homestead is the oldest-known Ukrainian-Canadian dwelling in Manitoba on its original site.

The Negrych Homestead began opening for public visits in 1994 and work continued through the 1990s with the refurbishing of old buildings and the construction of a few modern replacements such as a piggery and an icehouse. Owned by the Municipality of Gilbert Plains, and leased to the Gilbert Plains and District Historical Society, it was designated as a provincial historic site in 1992, and as a national historic site in November 1996 (although the federal designation ceremony did not take place until August 2004). If you are interested in seeing this truly remarkable site, the Negrych Homestead is open daily in July and August, Tuesdays to Saturdays, from 10:00 AM to 4:30 PM, or at other times by appointment. When you arrive at the site, be reminded that it is almost a half-mile from the nearest public road along a twisting, tree-encroached driveway. There are no flush toilets and

Several members of the Negrych family, including Stephen, the last surviving child of the pioneering family who arrived in 1899, are buried in the cemetery of the former Saints Peter and Paul Ukrainian Orthodox Church about 1¼ miles northwest of the Negrych Homestead. On my first visit to the cemetery, I found it well tended. It was looking a little shaggy when I was there three years later, in July 2017. GORDON GOLDSBOROUGH

cellphone reception is spotty. But I can think of no better place to imagine you have been transported back a century and experience the fortitude with which hardy Ukrainian settlers set down roots in this region of Manitoba.

ACKNOWLEDGEMENTS

I thank Julie Russell, the Community Development Officer for the Municipality of Gilbert Plains, for allowing me to tour the Negrych Homestead out of season. My only regret is that we could not get the wooden key to unlock the door of the residence building. I had to content myself with peering in through its windows so I look forward to another visit someday to this wonderful "time machine" site. The indefatigable Ed Ledohowski shared his extensive knowledge of the Negrych site.

Camp Hughes

The region west of Carberry, in western Manitoba, is distinguished by vast expanses of sand deposited there about 12,000 years ago, at the mouth of a massive river—predecessor to today's Assiniboine River—that once drained into glacial Lake Agassiz. Today, the Carberry Sandhills are a popular tourist destination. Not as well-known is a site about one mile south of the Trans-Canada Highway, separated from the Sandhills by a shallow wetland known as the Douglas Marsh. For a few short years during the First World War, it was occupied by the second-largest city in Manitoba, roughly double the size of Brandon. It was a military training facility called Camp Hughes.

The main line of the Canadian Pacific Railway passed through this area in 1881 and a siding here was named Sewell by the visiting Governor General after a member of his staff. The open landscape and proximity to the railway made it attractive for army summer training camps in the early 20th century. Established as Camp Sewell in 1909, and used for the first time in June and July 1910, it hosted peacetime training of artillery, infantry, and cavalry units. Over 6,600 men and 3,500 horses spent time there during the summer of 1914. Following the British declaration of war against Germany in August 1914, the military began evaluating its needs for training and decided to expand Camp Sewell. It became Camp Hughes in September 1915, when it was renamed in

OPPOSITE The former Camp Hughes swimming pool filled with vegetation and assorted trash, July 2016. GORDON GOLDSBOROUGH,

An historical postcard of military recruits at Camp Sewell digging trenches for use in training, circa 1915. ROB MCINNES

honour of Major-General Sir Sam Hughes, Canada's Minister of Militia and Defence.

Nearly 15,000 soldiers from the burgeoning Canadian Expeditionary Force took up residence at the camp during the summer and autumn of 1915. The site was developed to its fullest extent in 1916 when it accommodated over 27,000 men, with all the amenities that one would expect of a city this size. The main camp along the railway tracks included a station and platform for arrivals and departures, administrative offices, vehicle maintenance buildings, 350-bed hospital, veterinary hospital, dental office, kitchens, armoury, two churches, prison, and post office. Between 60 and 70 tons of supplies arrived by rail each day. Perishables such as meat, dairy products, and

Military recruits at Camp Sewell practice using wooden batons meant to simulate a bayonet on their rifle, 1915.
SUYOKO TSUKAMOTO

ice were moved immediately into a huge, refrigerated storage building. A bakery made 25,000 loaves of bread each day. Also present was a parade ground, ordnance sheds, and a water tower fed from wells dug nearby. Garbage went into at least two dumps east of the camp. Troops were accommodated in over 3,000 cone-shaped canvas tents deployed in neat rows. An in-ground concrete swimming pool, operated by a civilian contractor along with hot baths and showers, was touted as the largest in western Canada. The east edge of the camp was allocated to civilian concessions, known as "The Midway." It had six movie theatres (named Allies, Empire, Dominion, Imperial, Strand, and Twin), a watch repair shop, tobacconist, tailor shop, bookstore, newsstand, soft drink shop, two banks, and photography studio, aligned along a "Main Street" with a low-lying spot where water would accumulate after rainfall. There were numerous mailboxes around the grounds to collect outgoing letters. Mail was delivered twice a day and, during 1916, the camp's post office handled six million regular letters along with 52,730 registered letters and 9,123 money orders. Downtime was occupied by games of baseball and football, and visits from family and friends were permitted during periodic Visitors' Days. The 196th battalion, whose recruits were drawn from universities across western Canada, published a newspaper. In addition to these sundry services,

An historical postcard of members of the 196th (University) Battalion dining at Camp Hughes in 1916. ROB MCINNES

BATHING PARADE, 10TH C.M.Rs. SEWELL CAMP 1915

An historical postcard of military recruits enjoying a refreshing dip in the swimming pool at Camp Hughes, 1915. MILITARY HISTORY SOCIETY OF MANITOBA LIBRARY/ARCHIVE

one private reported that "the girls from Brandon and elsewhere carried on a thriving business on the outskirt of the Camp boundaries hiding in the poplars during the day."

In the early days of the First World War, recruits were trained in the use of artillery, but by 1916 the focus had shifted to producing infantry troops destined for the trench warfare of European battlefields. They trained in military discipline, marksmanship, grenade-handling, and hand-to-hand combat techniques. At first, guns were in short supply so troops frequently used wooden batons to simulate bayonets and other "dummy weapons" rather than live ammunition. Fatalities among the trainees were few, attributed mostly to medical conditions, some pre-existing and others brought on by spartan living conditions. The camp hospital had 1,894 patients in 1915 and 3,815 in 1916. Some of them were admitted for basic medical treatment or surgery. In 1916, more than 300 men

Aerial view of the former Camp Hughes swimming pool, July 2016. GORDON GOLDSBOROUGH

square miles of land. A six-mile network of trenches dug by hand and with digging machines, along with grenade and rifle ranges, were constructed on the southwest portion of the camp starting in 1915 and completed the following year. Occupied by battalions of 1000 men for periods of at least 24 hours at a time, the eight-foot deep trenches, some of them built in a zigzag pattern, were meant to replicate those that troops would encounter on arrival in Europe. To make the experience as realistic as possible, railway ground flares fired in the air simulated mortar flares of the real battlefield. Some of the trainees pretended to be the enemy in opposing trenches on the other side of a "No Man's Land."

Training at Camp Hughes was suspended in 1917. After the First World War ended, the camp was used for summer training of militia through the 1920s and into the 1930s. Between 1933 and 1936, the moveable infrastructure was carried to the newly established Camp Shilo, south of the Douglas Marsh in the midst

were treated for venereal diseases while 55 suffering from tuberculosis were quarantined. That year, there were eleven deaths at the camp. Some would be buried elsewhere, but a cemetery on site, near the former hospital, contains the remains of six soldiers killed during exercises, along with a few civilians from the local area.

At its height during the war, Camp Hughes occupied about five of the Sandhills, and the rest was dismantled as part of an unemployment relief project during the Great Depression. During the Second World War, Camp Hughes was used occasionally for infantry training and an asphalt airstrip was constructed east of it. Military radio transmission towers were erected during the Cold War on the former rifle range but they were removed in the early 1990s.

Bruce Tascona and Grant Tyler of the Military History Society of Manitoba (MHSM) visited the former site of Camp Hughes in 1987 and found "a few rusted bits of relics including enamel cups and plates" scattered about, as well as a series of "ditches." Over the next several years, they mapped, photographed, and studied the site thoroughly and, in April 1994, succeeded in having Camp Hughes designated as a provincial historic site. Archeological excavations have been undertaken by the MSHM, provincial government, and staff and students from Brandon University. However, greater recognition of the historical importance of this site—said to have the best-preserved First World War trenches in North America—has come slowly. In 2004, a commemorative plaque was erected near the cemetery by the Manitoba Heritage Council. Declared a national historic site in 2011, it took five years for a plaque to be unveiled by the Historic Sites and Monuments Board of Canada. Ongoing advocacy is done by a "Friends of Camp Hughes" comprised of local residents along with the MSHM.

I visited Camp Hughes in July 2016 during the public ceremony recognizing it as a national historic site. In addition to the training trenches, I saw the concrete floor for a mechanical shop and concrete foundations for several other buildings, stubby concrete posts for supporting the train station and movie theatres, the swimming pool—now filled with vegetation and trash—and a single small concrete building whose function during the military occupation of the site is still subject to speculation. (Some think it was used by the bakery to allow bread dough to rise; its foot-thick, windowless concrete walls make me skeptical. It looks to me like a bank vault, similar to seven others that I have found around the province.)

The trench system at Camp Hughes is readily accessible. I encourage you to take an afternoon to walk the site

Aerial view of the practice trenches at the former Camp Hughes site, July 2015. Two people can be seen standing near the trenches, which gives an idea of their extensive size. GORDON GOLDSBOROUGH

The last remaining building at the Camp Hughes site, a thick-walled concrete structure of unknown purpose, July 2016. GORDON GOLDSBOROUGH

The concrete floor of a building at the former Camp Hughes site where it is believed that vehicle maintenance was done, July 2016. GORDON GOLDSBOROUGH

and contemplate the thousands of soldiers who once swarmed over the area. It is an important reminder of Canada's involvement in the First World War, which ended 100 years ago this year. The Friends of Camp Hughes produce a helpful interpretive pamphlet available at the trailhead. However, you should not visit the eastern parts, where buildings were located. There are several reasons for this, not least of which is that the land is leased by the government to a local rancher who has fenced it to keep in his livestock herd. Gates left open by oblivious visitors would allow the cattle to escape. More significantly, the area immediately south of the tent site has been used for military training using live ammunition. Unexploded ordnance—what military folk call UXOS—may remain at or just below the ground surface and could be triggered by an inadvertent kick or curious pickup. Bullets and grenades have been found during archaeological excavations. For those who willfully ignore advice to stay away in the name of safety, I will conclude with some sage words offered before I entered the range at Camp Shilo several years ago: "If you did not drop it, do not pick it up!"

ACKNOWLEDGEMENTS

Thanks to good work of the Military History Society of Manitoba over three decades, the Camp Hughes site was rescued from obscurity. Anyone wanting to know more about it should read military historian Bruce Tascona's excellent book *Camp Hughes, the War Years: A Story of the Canadian Military Training Ground During the Great War, 1914-1916*. I thank archaeologist Suyoko Tsukamoto for sharing generously of her knowledge of Camp Hughes and her personal collection of historical photos, Tighe McManus for providing a map of the buildings that once stood there, and Rob McInnes for allowing me to use postcards from his great collection.

Pine Falls
Paper Mill

I read the daily newspaper faithfully. I do read news online, but there is something about the experience of reading a *real* newspaper that I find more enjoyable. Each morning, I trudge groggily to the end of my driveway to pick up the paper and spend half an hour or so perusing its pages before heading off to work. Yet, I am the only person in my household to do so on a daily basis. When I asked my millennial kids when they had last read a newspaper, they each looked at me incredulously as though I had asked when they had last visited Mars. I suspect this is a common occurrence in a lot of Manitoba homes as we depend increasingly on the internet as a source for news. Pine Falls is probably aware of this trend more acutely than most places through the closure and demolition of their community's lifeblood: the

demise of the Pine Falls Paper Mill is not just about paper but about a world that is changing how it communicates.

Winnipeg businessman John McArthur was active in developing the forest resources of southeastern Manitoba during the first two decades of the 20th century. He formed the Manitoba Pulp and Paper Company (later shortened to Manitoba Paper Company) and served as its first president. He bought 2,000 acres of land and established a sawmill near Lac du Bonnet and a logging camp near Pinawa. In 1921, McArthur acquired a tree-cutting license for 729 square miles of federally-owned forests, called "Pulpwood Berth No. 1," intended to be used for the making of wood pulp. He selected a scenic spot alongside the Winnipeg River, within the Fort Alexander Indian Reserve (now the Sagkeeng First Nation), as the site for a newsprint mill. The process of making newsprint, the low-grade paper on which newspapers are printed, involved

On 3 September 1926, photographer Lewis Foote snapped this photo of Elisha Hutchings (left), John McArthur (centre), and Alexander "Sandy" Macdonald (right) visiting the new newsprint mill at Pine Falls. In 1910, all three men had been identified by a Winnipeg newspaper as being among the city's 19 millionaires at that time. McArthur would die four months later. ARCHIVES OF MANITOBA

removing the bark from cut trees then turning the bare logs into pulp using large stone grinders. The pulp was cooked in a mixture of water and the chemical zinc hydrosulphite (made by mixing zinc powder with sulphuric acid) to break apart the wood fibers and bleach out coloured impurities. The resulting white pulp

A view of logs waiting to be processed at the newly built newsprint mill at Pine Falls, June 1927. ARCHIVES OF MANITOBA

passable by car in good weather. On 5 February 1927, the first shipment of paper arrived at the printing plant for the *Manitoba Free Press*. The *Free Press*, predecessor of today's *Winnipeg Free Press*, was the only Winnipeg paper to use locally-made newsprint. The majority of the mill's output, sixty to eighty percent, was exported to the mid-western United States. Beyond the mill, another 300 to 400 seasonal workers toiled to supply it with spruce, fir, and Jack pine logs. Millions of cords of timber were cut along the east and west sides of Lake Winnipeg and brought to the mill on barges. Other were cut in the forests adjoining the Winnipeg River and, until 1965, were floated downstream to the mill—despite protests from Fort Alexander band members about negative impacts on their river fishery—and held in large booms until needed. Band members were paid to retrieve sunken logs out of the river. The practice of river booming ended in 1993.

As was common of industrial employers at the time, the Manitoba

was spread on screens to be dried into sheets of paper, smoothed, then rolled up for delivery to customers.

After obtaining a 99-year lease from Fort Alexander band members, and while negotiating an outright surrender of the land, McArthur began building his newsprint mill in October 1925. Completed in November 1926, the first paper was produced in January 1927. By June,

its two huge paper-making machines were fully operational. Four hundred people worked at the mill, producing up to 300 tons of paper per day that were shipped out on the Canadian National Railway's 19-mile-long Pine Falls line. The railway had been completed in January 1926 specifically to service the mill. Otherwise, access to the outside world was over a trail from Great Falls that was only

Paper Company took an active role in the lives of its workers, by building Pine Falls—the first planned town in Manitoba—in 1926. Designed by a landscape architect from Montreal under company supervision, its streets were laid down in concentric semi-circles and 110 company-owned homes were supplied with sewer, water, and telephone service. Residents were issued a company-owned lawn mower and were expected to use it regularly. A company-owned store (sold to the Hudson's Bay Company in 1946) sold groceries, dry goods, and hardware. There was a company-owned, five-classroom school, a modern 20-bed hospital, a hotel, and two staff houses for unmarried workers. Anglican, Roman Catholic, and United Church adherents all held Sunday services. A golf course was laid out, tennis courts were constructed, and a rowing club and rugby league were organized.

John McArthur died in January 1927 and, a little over a year later, the Manitoba Paper Company was purchased by the Abitibi Power and Paper Company of Montreal. From 1932 to 1935, the mill was closed as demand for newsprint dropped during the Great Depression, although the *Manitoba Free Press* continued to be supplied from the mill's existing paper stocks. Prosperity returned to the region after the Second World War and the mill was busy throughout the mid-20th century. By 1976, the mill—the only newsprint-making facility on the prairies—was producing 480 tons per day, enough for a million 48-page newspapers. It consumed 3.75 billion gallons of water a year and 265,000 megawatt-hours of

Spools of newsprint, ready to be shipped, at the newly built newsprint mill at Pine Falls, June 1927. ARCHIVES OF MANITOBA

Workers and paper-making machinery at the newly built newsprint mill at Pine Falls, June 1927. ARCHIVES OF MANITOBA

electricity, about 42 percent of the nearby hydro generating station's total output. Its timber supply came from a large area on the east side of Lake Winnipeg, over half-way up the lake, and also in the Interlake on the west side of the lake.

As environmental regulations became tougher through the 1970s and 1980s, it became increasingly difficult for the aging mill—one of the last in North America still using the sulphite process—to be lawfully compliant with its discharges into the air, soil, and adjacent river. Its effluent, discharged into the Winnipeg River with little or no treatment, contained wood residue and chemicals from the pulping process that were known to be toxic to fish. There was no legal requirement to monitor air-borne emissions, although most people assumed the mill was not compliant with air quality standards. The winter snow around the mill was usually a grey-black colour due to particles falling from the sky. Locals dismissed it as "the colour of money." In 1971, as a measure to reduce its impact on the environment, the mill switched to using sodium hydrosulphite as a replacement for the more toxic zinc hydrosulphite. I experienced firsthand the growing public awareness that the mill was a major polluter when, for four years in the late 1980s, I was based at Pine Falls doing environmental research. Being naturally curious about the inner workings of a paper mill, I asked for a tour. The company, suspecting that my motives were not so innocent, instructed my tour guide to steer me clear of the "dirtier parts of the mill."

In 1992, Canadian environmental regulations changed so that older mills like the one at Pine Falls had to comply with regulations on the dumping of effluent that had

The thermomechanical mill in operation, September 2005. JENNIFER LIDGETT

previously applied only to those built after 1971. The company was given three years to comply with the new rules. In 1994, after Abitibi threatened to close the mill, controlling interest was sold for $40 million to a group of employees led by mill manager Fern Pitre, with external backing, and renamed the Pine Falls Paper Company. To keep the mill viable, its workers agreed to a ten-per-cent wage cut for five years. The provincial government provided a $30 million line of credit to upgrade the mill's wastewater treatment plant to deal with effluent before it was dumped into the river. The ink on the agreement was barely dry when 1,800 pounds of a pesticide used in the paper-making process spilled accidentally from the mill into the Winnipeg River. To compound matters, the spill went unreported to authorities for four days and contaminated the downstream water treatment plant for the Sagkeeng First Nation.

An upgraded wastewater treatment plant came online in December 1995 and, the following year, a $36 million upgrade allowed the facility to produce de-inked pulp using 100 tons per day of recycled newspapers and magazines—shipped from as far away as Chicago—to produce newsprint containing from 20 to 40 percent recycled pulp. The Pine Falls Paper Company operated for four years then re-sold the mill to Quebec-based firm Tembec, which restored original salary levels. Between 1999 and 2001, at a cost of $124 million, Tembec built a state-of-the-art thermomechanical pulping (TMP) mill to reduce manufacturing costs by 20 percent, make better use of the available

In 1996, the Pine Falls mill spent $36 million developing the capability to de-ink old newspapers and magazines so they could be recycled into new newsprint. JENNIFER LIDGETT

fibre mixture of 75% spruce and 25% pine, and improve newsprint quality. TMP is a two-step process in which debarked logs (or sawmill wastes) are chipped, usually in the forest then trucked to the mill, then crushed at high temperature and pressure—without chemicals—to break the wood fibres apart.

Closure of the old sulphite mill had an immediate positive effect: the town no longer smelled of rotten eggs all the time. The new TMP mill, that became operating in March 2001, gave off a pleasant smell of wood shavings and produced so much waste heat that a heat recovery unit reduced the mill's usage of dirty coal that contributed to air pollution. Coal consumption also dropped because the TMP mill was mostly powered by hydroelectricity. Consequently, greenhouse gas emissions decreased by half. Its effluent was cleaner too. The mill had the capacity to produce up to 200,000 tons of newsprint per year using a mixture of new and recycled pulp. Things seemed to be looking up. Soon after it began operating, however, the mill lost one of its oldest customers, the *Winnipeg Free Press*, when the paper was purchased by Winnipeggers Ron Stern and Bob Silver. They preferred to buy newsprint from their own mill, located in Alberta. The economics of recycled pulp deteriorated until it was cheaper to cut down trees than to recycle old newspapers. The new TMP mill came at a cost to the Pine Falls community. Unlike the company that had for

Logs stacked awaiting transport to the Pine Falls mill, November 2005. JENNIFER LIDGETT

decades operated the town for the benefit of its employees, in mid-2005 Tembec announced that Pine Falls had to become self-sufficient and ended its support. Being too small to become an incorporated municipality, the 80-year-old town amalgamated with the adjoining village of Powerview, incorporated in 1951 while the Pine Falls Generating Station was being built, to become Powerview-Pine Falls.

The new TMP mill fell silent in September 2009, barely 8½ years after it had become operational, when 280 workers were locked out in a labour dispute over wage concessions demanded by the company. A new agreement could not be reached and, in January 2010, all employees were laid off. The mill was closed permanently in September 2010 with Tembec citing high costs and declining newsprint demand. A year later, the 250-acre site was sold to the Canadian subsidiary of an American firm that specialized in dismantling heavy industrial sites. By the spring of 2014, the paper mill that had dominated the economy and landscape in Pine Falls for more than 80 years was gone. In mid-2017, I visited the former mill site and flew over it with my drone. The only visible signs of this once huge facility were some piles of scrap steel, a hydro substation erected in early 2000 for the TMP mill, an old steam locomotive on display near the former mill entrance, a newer diesel locomotive that stood abandoned because its railway line has been removed, and the nearby Manitou Lodge hotel (built in 1948, now converted into a private, multi-user residence). There is no longer any

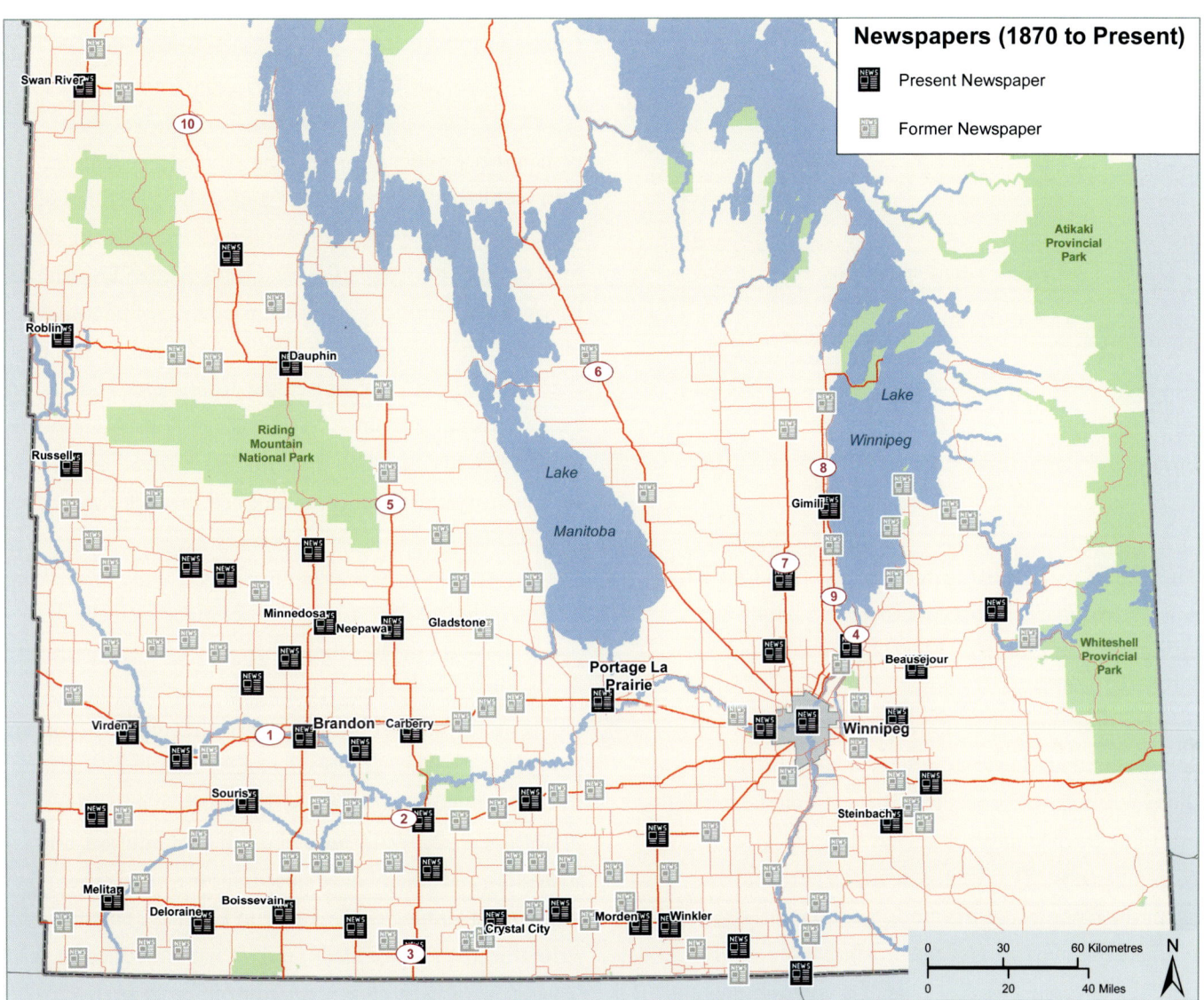

Newspapers (1870 to Present)

Present Newspaper

Former Newspaper

A map of Manitoba shows where, at one time or another, a daily, weekly, or intermittent newspaper was published. Ghosted symbols represent newspapers no longer in operation and black symbols are ones where a newspaper is still printed. MAP BY JENNIFER LIDGETT USING DATA COMPILED BY GORDON GOLDSBOROUGH FROM "A HISTORICAL DIRECTORY OF MANITOBA NEWSPAPERS, 1859–1978" BY D. M. LOVERIDGE, AND OTHER SOURCES

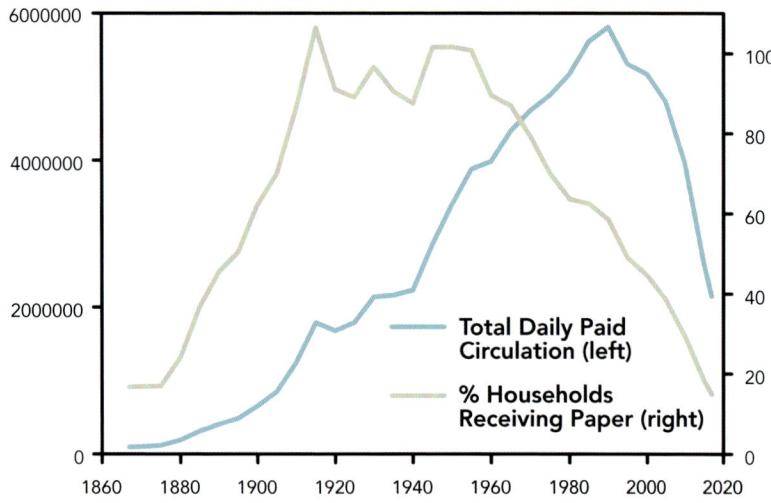

Total daily paid circulation of Canadian newspapers, and the proportion of households receiving a newspaper, from 1867 to 2017. REDRAWN FROM PAGES 3, 4, "REQUIEM FOR THE PRINT EDITION," COMMUNIC@TIONS MANAGEMENT INC., 30 NOVEMBER 2017

Chart legend:
- Total Daily Paid Circulation (left)
- % Households Receiving Paper (right)

commercial wood-cutting in the region. The Pine Falls newsprint mill closed because there was simply not enough demand for its products due to declining newspaper readership.

The first newspaper in western Canada was *The Nor'Wester*, founded at Winnipeg in 1859. By the 1870s, there were 34 newspapers published around Manitoba, including the *Manitoba Free Press* that appeared in November 1872. That total rose to 109 in the 1880s, 163 in the 1890s, 213 in the 1900s, and 242 in the 1910s. Numerous towns around the province had a newspaper, typically published weekly in smaller communities and daily in large ones, but the vast majority of them are now closed. Today, the Manitoba Legislative Library subscribes to 51 community newspapers. The Manitoba

Community Newspapers Association has 47 member papers with weekly circulations ranging from 515 to 43,719 copies, most of which have declined an average of 24 percent since 2000. Winnipeg-based media consultant Ken Goldstein has studied the diminishing fortunes of Canadian newspapers. He compiled charts showing the total number of newspapers read by Canadian households between 1867 and 2017, and the proportion of households receiving a newspaper during the same period. Ken shows that total daily circulation peaked around 1995 and has been in freefall ever since. Whereas nearly every Canadian home received a newspaper during the first half of the 20th century, the proportion dropped through the second half, standing today at just 15 percent.

Newspapers have resorted to all sorts of money-making tactics, including advertising that wraps around the front page and covers the headlines that were once sacrosanct to old-school journalists. They are putting their news online, frequently behind "pay walls" that oblige visitors to pay for access. They are seeking federal funding to ensure the survival of news-gathering by Canadian journalists. Newspapers, especially ones in small communities, are struggling and several have closed, most recently the 116-year-old *Grandview Exponent* in February 2017. As I write this, the *Portage Daily Graphic* has announced it is ceasing publication of its print edition; henceforth, it will be only an online newspaper. This past January, I carried out an admittedly unscientific poll among 30 students in my third-year undergraduate university class. I asked them where they got their news about the world, and asked them to raise their hands in response to a series of six options that I offered. Like my own kids, none of them read a daily newspaper. One student read a weekly newspaper and one student read magazines. Eighty percent of them used online media and about a quarter used other unspecified sources. Interestingly, none of the students admitted to having no source of news, which I suppose is encouraging. What it says is that the future generation of decision-makers will get their news in fundamentally different ways from their parents and grandparents. "Newspaper snobs" like me might decry this trend, pointing out that serendipity plays an important part of the news-paper-reading experience. I often notice headlines that might have otherwise escaped my attention, and lead me to learn about something wholly unexpected. Online media, on the other hand, are increasingly being designed to filter the news that they present to me, so I see only the items selected by "artificial intelligence" that meet my individualized criteria. The result could be a narrowed view of the world that confirms my opinions and biases, and does not challenge me with opposing ones. The growing numbers of websites presenting factually-questionable "fake news" threaten the foundation of the news-reporting business.

Meanwhile, life goes on in Pine Falls. For a while, there were plans to open a state-of-the-art sawmill on the former paper mill site. It would use local wood to make high-tech, cross-laminated timber for building construction, with wood wastes going to make bio-diesel. The deal fell through before it could be con-summated. Consequently, tourism is the mainstay of the town's econ-omy. Now that the era of large-scale industrial forestry in southeastern Manitoba is over, and is unlikely to come back, I wonder if there are plans afoot to change the name of the long-running 4P Festival. It touted the region's four economic pillars: Paper (making), Pea (growing), Power (generating), and Pickerel (catching).

ACKNOWLEDGEMENTS

My friend Brian Kotak, one of the last Environment Directors at Tembec Pine Falls, was a great source of information about the mill's final days. Jennifer Lidgett and Diane Dubé provided a large selection of photos. I am indebted to Ken Goldstein (Communic@tions Management Inc.) for providing me with his insightful paper on the diminishing fortunes of print news-papers in Canada. Darryl Holyk of the *Minnedosa Tribune* (the province's oldest, continuously published weekly newspaper) shared generously of his time to describe the trials and tribulations of operating a small, rural paper in Manitoba.

A view from beyond the perimeter fence of the TMP mill being demolished, June 2012. DIANE DUBÉ AND DAVE TORRES

Pine Falls Paper Mill   201

Scallion
Farm

Often, when I encounter a decaying old building for the first time, I know a lot about its history because I researched it before my visit: when and why it was built, by whom, and for whom. Sometimes, however, I discover an old building entirely by chance and know nothing of its past. Later, when I do some digging in the archives, it turns out to be nothing particularly special. In a few rare cases, I find that one of these discoveries is an important one.

Such a case was an old farmyard about 2½ miles northwest of Virden. I had seen it from afar a couple of times during travels in that region. Knowing that most abandoned farms do not have an interesting back story, I paid it little mind. Then, in May 2012, I decided to take a look up close. It was no easy feat. The yard site was a quarter mile from the nearest municipal road. Its driveway was encroached on both sides by large unkempt Manitoba maples.

The Scallion House as it appeared in May 2018. HOLLY THORNE

As I drew near, I noticed there were actually two buildings there. Both had been made of field stones gathered from the surrounding area that were split in half to make flat sides, then stacked back-to-back, flat sides out, to make a thick rock wall. One of them, a two-storey structure, looked like a giant dollhouse. Its north wall had fallen to show each of the rooms inside. The windows were all gone and the lathe-and-plaster interior walls were badly broken. Clearly, it did not seem safe. So, contrary to my usual practice, I did not venture inside. The other building was a granary, a squat, one-storey structure with a wooden roof, with a soil berm to the top of the rock wall on its east side, probably to help in loading grain into it. Unlike the house, the granary seemed in relatively good shape. To be honest, neither building impressed me much so I took a few photos, a GPS waypoint, and headed on my way. It was only months later, when I reviewed my notes from that trip and did background research, that

James William Scallion (1847–1926). *WINNIPEG TRIBUNE,* 26 APRIL 1926]

their significance became clear. The Scallion farmyard, established over a century ago, is connected intimately to the early engagement of farmers in Manitoba politics.

Sometime in the 1850s (family accounts vary), the Scallion family—William and Catherine along with their two daughters and two sons—came to Canada from County Wexford in Ireland and settled at Thorold, Upper Canada (today, Ontario), near Hamilton. The children were educated at local schools and the eldest son, James, planned

James Scallion's "The Grange" farm as it appeared around 1907. Note the house and left and stone granary at right that are still present at the site, unlike the barns in the middle. "VIEWS OF VIRDEN TOWN AND DISTRICT, MANITOBA," VIRDEN BOARD OF TRADE, EMPIRE-ADVANCE PRINT

to become a teacher. He attended the Toronto Normal School, taught school for a few years, then ran a store at Thorold in partnership with his younger brother, Thomas. The brothers must have been enticed by the possibilities of western Canada and, in 1882, they moved to Manitoba, initially settling at Stonewall before going on to the Virden area the following year. Together, they bought 640 acres of land near town and built the house and granary that I had found, along with a couple of barns and other outbuildings, most of them likewise made of stone. In the custom of the day, they named their farm "The Grange." The Scallion farm boasted the latest in technology. A power plant provided electricity for the house and barn at a time when few Manitoba farms were electrified. The granary was immense by standards of the time, being able to hold 12,000 bushels, with electric machinery to load and empty it. Within 500 yards of the granary, there was a siding on the Canadian Pacific Railway line that passed through the Scallion property. A loading platform on that siding permitted the Scallions to load their grain into boxcars for shipment without having to patronize a commercial elevator. That independence probably had an influence on James Scallion's views about farming and the rights of those who did it.

Eventually, the Scallion brothers increased their land holdings to 960 acres. They grew grain and raised livestock with the assistance of a pair of hired men. It is unknown when their sisters Hannah and Catherine joined them. It may have been after their parents died in Ontario, in 1887, or possibly earlier. In any case, none of the siblings ever married and they lived together for the rest of their days. Known for their hospitality, the Scallions were offered to visitors as a shining example of the success that could be achieved through hard work.

If James Scallion had done nothing more than develop his farm, he would scarcely be remembered nearly a century after his death. However, it was through his social

MANIFESTO

To the Farmers, Independent Electors, and all Friends of the People's Rights and Interests in Manitoba and the Northwest.

FRIENDS: You are aware that the election of Mr. R. L. Richardson, Member of the House of Commons for Lisgar, has been protested. It is well understood that the motives prompting this action do not spring from a desire to promote purity in elections and honesty in public life, but is a bold attempt—in fact, what may be termed a conspiracy —on the part of railway exploiters, predatory corporations and corporation politicians to crush out of public life a representative of the people who, by his fearless and untiring exertions in their behalf when their interests were being sacrificed to the greed of grasping combinations by representatives who betrayed the trust reposed in them by their constituents, has brought down upon himself the malignity of that combination, with all their powers fortified by the public purse and levies on subsidies granted from the public purse, for the purpose of accomplishing their purpose.

In January 1901, James Scallion published a "manifesto" in the *Winnipeg Tribune* in which he railed against "railway exploiters, predatory corporations and corporation politicians" for challenging the federal general election in November 1900 that saw the paper's founder and publisher, Robert L. Richardson, elected as an Independent for the Lisgar constituency. *WINNIPEG TRIBUNE, 17 JANUARY 1901*

activism on behalf of farmers that he came to prominence. He believed that farmers should have the right to sell their produce wherever they could get the best price, whether in Canada or the United States. He believed that farmers should be able to ship their grain directly to market and not be dependent on companies that paid low prices for grain and charged exorbitant "dockage fees," the fee to load a boxcar. In January 1903, he and some of his neighbours formed the Virden Grain Growers' Association and he was elected its president. Then, he travelled around the province to encourage other communities to follow Virden's lead. In March 1903, the Manitoba Grain Growers Association (MGGA) was established at Brandon, with Scallion as its president. He told the assembly that: "40,000 farmers had produced 100,000 bushels of wheat and they should all be wealthy but where was the wealth? Certainly not in the farmers' hands but in the homes of the manufacturers, railway promoters, and grain dealers." He served one

year as president then stepped down due to ill health, but he remained the honorary president for the rest of his life.

MGGA chapters formed in all of the major communities in the agricultural belt of Manitoba and the Association adopted socially progressive policies. In 1912, it admitted women as associate members and, the next year, it went on record as favouring "votes for women on equal terms with men." In 1914, its constitution was amended to recognize women as full voting members.

In 1906, Scallion was a founding member of the Grain Growers Grain Company, a cooperative that marketed the grain of its members in competition with private companies. Two years later, the company began publishing a farm magazine called the *Grain Growers Guide* that became, in 1928, *The Country Guide*. In 1917, the Grain Growers Grain Company changed its name to

A stone granary on the Scallion farm may be the oldest of its kind in Manitoba, May 2012. GORDON GOLDSBOROUGH

United Grain Growers. It would become one of the largest grain companies in the prairie provinces, operating grain elevators in hundreds of towns, with profits shared by its member farmers.

Scallion was politically active but claimed no party affiliation, voting for whichever candidate he believed was best qualified for the office. He is said to have resolutely refused attempts to nominate him for political office. In 1910, he joined a group of 800 farmers who went to Ottawa to lay their grievances before the federal government, especially relating to excessive freight rates being charged by the railways. His belief in free trade put him at odds with federal politicians who favoured protectionism. He put his views, forcefully and persuasively, before Prime Ministers Robert Borden and Wilfrid Laurier when they were in Brandon during visits to western Canada, in 1907 and 1910, respectively. To Laurier, he said:

> There are no trade arrangements the Canadian government could make with any country that would meet with greater favor or stronger support from the farmers of Western Canada than a wide measure of reciprocal trade with the United States, including manufactured articles and the natural products of both countries.

In early 1920, the MGGA changed its name to the United Farmers of Manitoba (UFM). Scallion was nominated as its president but withdrew his name due to continuing but unspecified health problems. The UFM was, in effect, a political party based on an ideology of non-partisanship and pragmatic, managerial government with special attention to rural concerns, later renaming itself the Progressive Party of Manitoba. In the provincial general election of 1920, it fielded 25 candidates, and had nine of them elected, while Liberal Premier Tobias Norris' majority government was relegated to minority status in the 55-seat Legislature, dropping from 41 to 20 seats.

Gaining confidence, the UFM was ready to take full advantage when, in March 1922, Norris' minority government resigned over allegations of corruption and fraud. In the general election held in July 1922, the UFM took 26 seats and gained a majority with several Independents who favoured UFM policies. However, they now had a problem. In the previous legislative session, their caucus had had no formal leader but, now that they were going to form Manitoba's first farmers' government, the UFM needed someone to become Premier. At least four candidates were considered, all but one with *bona fide* credentials as a farmer. Federal politician Thomas Crerar had farmed near Russell, while newly elected MP Robert Hoey farmed near Springfield and newly elected MLA William Robson farmed near Deleau. For his part, Ontario-born John Bracken had spent ten years as Professor of Field Husbandry at the University of Saskatchewan before being hired in 1920 as Principal of the Manitoba Agricultural College. In the course of interviews with the caucus, Crerar, Hoey, and Robson turned down the position, leaving Bracken as the sole candidate. He met with the caucus and impressed them sufficiently that they agreed unanimously to offer him the leadership. It took three more meetings before Bracken agreed reluctantly to accept the position. In July 1922, John Bracken was sworn in as Premier of Manitoba, with no political experience and never having cast a vote in any Manitoba election. Three months later, he gained the requisite seat in the Legislature when a postponed election was held in the constituency of The Pas. Bracken would go on to be Manitoba's longest-serving Premier—21 years—before jumping to federal politics in 1943 as leader of the Progressive Conservative party.

In 1918, Scallion, still in poor health, took a holiday in California then moved with his one surviving sister into a comfortable house on Lyons Street in Virden where he lived out his final years. He remained a prolific letter-writer and newspapers took to calling him the "Farmers' Premier" because of his continuing advocacy for the interests of western farmers. He sold "The Grange" to 38-year-old Scotsman Andrew Murray, who had arrived in Canada in 1911 with his wife and three children. They lived there for about five years before selling to their neighbour, Norman Gerrand, who operated the farm until his accidental death in the farmyard, at the age of 52 years, in 1948. The Scallion railway siding was removed sometime before 1954. I have not been able to determine how the Scallion farm—once a proud showpiece of innovation and efficiency—descended to its present state of disrepair, with all but two of the original buildings gone. Perhaps a reader can tell me?

James Scallion improved the lives of many farm families by working to ensure they received the highest possible return for their hard work. He played a key role in engaging farmers in the political process, helped to found the United Farmers of Manitoba, and he bore witness to its breakthrough in provincial politics. He was a founder of a cooperative grain company that was a major force in prairie agriculture until its disappearance in a corporate merger in 2001. But there was more. Before he died in April 1926, James Scallion made a final enduring contribution to his local community by donating $10,000 (about $140,000 in today's currency) toward the development of an endowment for the Virden Hospital and $5,000 for the Virden Cemetery where he would be buried. Yet, despite all his accomplishments and accolades during his lifetime, James Scallion is barely remembered in the Virden area. In 1975, the Canadian Permanent Committee on Geographical Names renamed a small river that flows through his former property, known previously as Little Bosshill Creek, as Little Scallion Creek. It seems to me that "The Grange"—crumbling though it may be—is as good a testament as any to this remarkable man.

ACKNOWLEDGEMENTS

I thank Andrew Cunningham for tracking down an early view of the Scallion farm.

St. Peter Dynevor Rectory

North of Selkirk, on a beautiful site overlooking the Red River, there is a boarded-up, 130-year-old building with a diverse past. It has connections to the early Selkirk Settlers, the treatment of tuberculosis in Indigenous people, and door-to-door sales by students from the "toughest school in North America." That building is the original rectory, or priest's residence, for St. Peter Dynevor (pronounced "dyna-vore") Anglican Church.

The church itself was a stone structure constructed between 1853 and 1854 beside the Red River, 2½ miles from present-day Selkirk, next to an older log church. Today, it is known as the "Old Stone Church" and is a provincially-designated historic site. One of its congregation's most famous members was Chief Peguis, who helped the Selkirk Settlers to become established when they arrived in 1812. The original St. Peter Dynevor Church was where Chief Peguis was baptized in 1840 and he built a small house near it, living there until his death in 1864. He is buried in its cemetery. Curiously, although the church is situated on the east bank of the Red River, its rectory was built on the opposite bank. Congregants living on the west side had to cross the river by ferry or, in later days, by a rowboat service that operated during the summer months.

Between 1862 and 1865, the 2½-storey rectory, like its namesake church, was built of locally quarried limestone

The Dynevor Hospital buildings with patients in front, 1920. ARCHIVES OF MANITOBA

blocks by Indigenous labour supervised by master masons Duncan McRae and John Clouston. Its stone walls are up to two feet thick, with wooden window frames and a roof of hewn oak rafters. Floors were covered in wooden planks. On the main floor was a kitchen, dining room, and pantry on one side with a parlour and study on the other. Upstairs were four bedrooms, in pairs on either side of a central hallway. The attic was used for storage. A stone chimney went up the centre of the building, probably to provide radiant heat to each floor. The front entrance into the home was enclosed by a small wooden porch.

The house's first owner was the Reverend Abraham Cowley, who moved in with his wife Arabella and five

The former St. Peter Dynevor Rectory as it appeared in July 2018. HOLLY THORNE of their six daughters in August 1865. Cowley, who had been sent from England to minister to largely Indigenous congregations, first at Fairford and later in the Parish of St. Peters, named his house Dynevor in commemoration of Lord Dynevor, "his childhood friend and spiritual mentor [who was] Canon Rice of Fairford, England." When Cowley died in 1887, he bequeathed Dynevor to the Anglican Church for use as a hospital. It stood empty for nine years before opening in 1896 as the Dynevor Indian Hospital— a Medical Mission of the Church Missionary Society—that was purchased, equipped, and operated by a local committee led by Anglican Archdeacon Robert Phair. Newspapers urged their readers to make donations in support of the new facility because "as the hospital has no endowment or other sources of support, the committee look to the Lord's people for the help necessary to carry it on." The first physician was Dr. Peter Rolston who, with his wife, tended to the patients without remuneration. A trained nurse was hired and, during its first year of operation, the hospital saw 1,341 Indigenous patients. A wood frame nurses' residence was constructed beside the stone building in 1901, and an addition made to the north side of the hospital in 1916 was intended for tuberculosis (TB) patients, bringing its total capacity to 65 beds.

In 1939, the hospital and surrounding land was sold to the federal government, who had primary responsibility for Indigenous peoples, to be used as a TB sanatorium for Manitoba's Indigenous populations. Its establishment acknowledged their staggeringly higher rate of TB infection, possibly due to lower levels of natural resistance. Between 1927 and 1947, the average death rate among Indigenous TB victims was thirty times higher than the general

Dynevor Indian Hospital, August 1937. ARCHIVES OF MANITOBA

population. The TB Hospital closed in 1957 and the building was repossessed by the Anglican Church.

Meanwhile, in 1951, the St. John's Cathedral Boys' Club was established for boys affiliated with St. John's Anglican Cathedral in Winnipeg's North End. In 1958, it opened a weekend school in Winnipeg then, in 1961, it obtained a lease on the former Dynevor Rectory. The following year, a full-time residential school for boys from grades 6 to 12 was established. Operated by a newly formed religious order called The Company of the Cross, the school was affiliated formally with the Anglican Church of Canada but with associate members from the Roman Catholic Church, United Church of Canada, and Dutch Reform Church. There was no requirement for the students to be Anglicans although everyone had to attend morning and evening prayers, attend Christian religious training during the day, and two services on Sundays. When it opened in the fall of 1962, the school hosted 60 boys. By 1965, there were 105 students, about two-thirds from Manitoba and the rest from Saskatchewan, Alberta, and British Columbia in the west, and Ontario and Quebec in the east.

One of its school's founders and teachers was former journalist Edward "Ted" Byfield, whose socially conservative views were expressed in the school's philosophy

The curriculum of the St. John's School stressed hard physical activity as the route to manhood. Snowshoeing was a common activity, as demonstrated by these students in February 1968. UNIVERSITY OF MANITOBA ARCHIVES & SPECIAL COLLECTIONS

Direct Sales

Direct sales, like that practised by the boys from St. John's School, take many forms. In the old days, peddlers travelled the province. There were home deliveries of milk, door-to-door salespeople selling pots and pans, encyclopedias, brushes, and cookies. There were home-based parties selling

The former J. R. Watkins Company warehouse and factory in downtown Winnipeg, July 2015 NATHAN KRAMER

plastic ware, cosmetics, and other goods. Today, the most common form is telemarketers and Internet sales. One of the largest direct sales companies in Manitoba, operating today to a lesser extent, is the J. R. Watkins Medical Company—shortened in the 1920s to J. R. Watkins Company.

The company was founded in 1868 by Joseph Watkins and it was based, for the majority of its history, at Winona, Minnesota. Its first product was a liniment whose ingredients included camphor, hot pepper extract, spruce oil, and other botanicals in an alcohol base. Later, Watkins introduced a cough remedy that consisted of 11 percent alcohol, chloroform, and heroin. A remedy aimed at "female complaints and diseases of women" was 20 percent alcohol. In time, the firm's line contained over 300 items, including veterinary goods, personal hygiene and household cleaning products, cosmetics, sauces and extracts, drink mixes, and spices of all kinds. The company did not have a network of stores or a paid sales force. Instead, it had commissioned "representatives" from communities across the United States and Canada. By 1993, at its 125th anniversary, the company had 9,600 representatives across Canada, of which 1,131 were in Manitoba.

In early 1913, the company came to Winnipeg, chosen due to its central

location in Canada, its excellent railway connections, and its proximity to the Minnesota mothership. Located initially at the corner of Home Street and Notre Dame Avenue, the building proved inadequate within three months. By late 1913, the company chose a vacant site at 90 Annabella, adjacent to the Canadian Pacific Railway main line and, in 1914, constructed an eight-storey structure designed by local architect John Woodman. The building, which served as warehouse and factory, featured numerous, large windows for improved interior lighting. Each floor had a large open area for processing, packaging, and storing products. Two large freight elevators ferried materials between floors. Between 1935 and 1939, the company purchased several rundown residential properties between its building and Higgins Avenue, demolishing them and creating a private fenced and landscaped green space. The open space remains today, though a fountain has long since been removed.

Many factors contributed to the decline of Watkins through the 1960s and 1970s. There were more companies, such as Avon, doing direct sales of similar products. Fewer households had stay-at-home women to whom door-to-door sales were pitched. The emergence of large grocery and retail chain stores meant there were more diverse options elsewhere. Television marketing raised the public profile of competing brands. More cosmopolitan, knowledgeable shoppers wanted greater selection than Watkins offered. Finally, the brand was viewed by some consumers as old-fashioned and stodgy, essentially "your grandmother's products." In short, the company did not keep pace with changing times. Watkins vacated the building in Point Douglas in early 1988 and henceforth supplied Canadians from its American headquarters. The building was sold to a clothing manufacturer that still uses the building for storage, and it has also had tenants through the years, although many of the upper floors are empty. In a tour in October 2016, I saw the remnants of a laboratory where Watkins product testing was done, a walk-in pill-drying oven, and discarded machinery used for milling, grinding, and packaging. Labels on switches indicated functions of long-gone machines: "Pine Oil Mixing Motor," "Tablet Room Line Shaft Motor," and "Cream Kettle Motor." In the basement was a large, multi-room vault for storing bonded products. A loading dock facing the CPR main tracks had, in its glory years, been used to ship products all over the country. Today, it is sealed off and is liberally festooned with graffiti.

Although it suffered hard times, declaring bankruptcy in the 1970s, and

A disused vault for the J. R. Watkins Medical Company, seen during my visit in October 2016, listed its Canadian office in Winnipeg as well as the headquarters and branches in the United States. GORDON GOLDSBOROUGH

is now a much smaller company than in its heyday, J. R. Watkins Company is still in business. Its signature "Watkins liniment," going back to 1868, is still a hot seller. When the company celebrated its 125th anniversary in 1993, a commemorative magazine noted that its best-selling product in the United States was double-strength vanilla extract. In contrast, the #1 product purchased by Canadians was toilet bowl cleaner.

of learning combined with hard physical labour and reinforced with corporal punishment. Described by Headmaster Frank Wiens as "the toughest school in North America," the students were pushed to extremes on the thinking that this would build character and courage. Many teachers and parents rejected the St. John's approach as "primitive, obsolete, naïve, unscientific and barbarous" but a few thought it was just the right thing for boys, especially ones with discipline problems. They were definitely not coddled and no one was on a first-name basis. Students were called by their surname, appended with a number such as "Smith 1" if there were several with the same one. Spankings were handed out liberally for such transgressions as uncompleted homework and poor marks on a test.

The school stressed vigorous outdoor exercises as part of its curriculum, including rowing on the Red River and Lake Winnipeg, an annual 80-km snowshoe march, marathon canoe trips, and

WINNIPEG **Free Press** weekend magazine VOL. 18, No. 5 · FEB. 3, 1968

WHY IS CHRIS JORGENSON MAKING SAUSAGES?

BECAUSE AT HIS TOUGH SCHOOL HARD WORK IS PART OF THE CURRICULUM

see page 2

The cover of the *Winnipeg Free Press'* weekend magazine on 3 February 1968 featured the son of MP Warner Jorgenson making sausage at the St. John's Cathedral Boys' School. PHOTO USED WITH PERMISSION OF THE *WINNIPEG FREE PRESS.*

snow-sledding using dogs bred specifically for the school. Instruction followed the provincial curriculum but was supplemented in numerous ways. Grade 6 boys, for example, were instructed in four languages—English, French, German, and Latin. All students were expected to work in addition to attending classes, with the school day beginning at 7:00 AM. They did all the janitorial work, cooked and served food, raised the sled dogs and cleaned their kennels, and worked with the school's herd of two dozen cattle and flock of 20,000 chickens. If any student complained, they were ignored because, as a 1966 school report explained, "Naturally youth will demand to be heard. This is only healthy and right. It is striving for adulthood. But only an adult generation that has taken all leave of its responsibilities would dream of actually listening." The teachers lived under equally spartan conditions, receiving communal room and board, and a salary of $1 per day. To raise funds for the facility, students went door-to-door selling sausages, ham,

side and back bacon, chickens, and honey that they had made as part of their duties. I suspect that many readers in Winnipeg will remember opening their front door to find a shivering boy on the step, offering meat products. It was direct sales at its most pitiful and needy. Who could refuse?

In 1966, the St. John's boys helped to put up a new building, in a H-shaped configuration, that provided additional space for dormitories, dining hall, classrooms, and a gymnasium. Each of them was expected to "volunteer" a half day of work on the job site. The old rectory was used for school offices and a classroom on the main floor, with additional classrooms on the upper two levels. New walls and "unsympathetic renovations" obscured most of its original interior layout, and a utilitarian staircase between floors replaced the original, more ornate wooden one. In 1988, the building was designated as a provincial historic site, which protected it from further radical renovation or demolition. There were ideas for it to be turned into "(1) a reception centre, an archive and accommodation for a chaplain; (2) a summer retreat for adults or; (3) a summer day camp for children." None of these uses came to fruition, probably because the school had more pressing matters to consider. As society moved away from a "spare the rod, spoil the child" mentality, enrollment waned through the 1980s, from a high of about 120 boys in the early years, to about 60 in 1989. In January 1990, sexual abuse charges were laid against one of its staff who had taught at the school off-and-on for 20 years. Five months later, in attempting to deal with the public relations nightmare, the school changed its name to Rupertsland College, a new headmaster was hired, and female students were accepted for the first time. However, the changes were too little, too late. In June 1990, after graduating eleven students, Rupertsland College closed, its entire board of directors resigned, and a receiver started to liquidate school assets. The Company of the Cross was unincorporated in November 1990. Years earlier, founder Byfield had moved to Alberta where he operated another St. John's School for a time and, later, published right-wing newsmagazines. He was also instrumental in the founding of Preston Manning's Reform Party of Canada.

In 1994, the former school buildings became home for a national non-profit addictions treatment centre for Indigenous people, with the first resident admitted in January 1995. It focused on Indigenous boys between the ages of 12 and 17 for stays averaging 90 to 120 days. The facility was later a satellite campus for a foundation based in the former Catholic orphanage at St. Norbert. In late 2016, the site was put up for sale with a cool $3.95-million asking price for the buildings and 324 acres of land. The old rectory's windows have had their shutters removed and are boarded up but painted to look like windows. There are several ominous cracks in the exterior and some of the stones in its thick walls are breaking into pieces. A small plaque in front of the building commemorates Boys' School Headmaster Frank Wiens, who died in 2010. I spoke to a realtor who told me that the building is considered unsafe and nobody is allowed to go inside. One of the last half-dozen surviving stone houses from the Red River Settlement era, it now stands empty after some 130 years of faithful—and certainly diverse—service.

ACKNOWLEDGEMENTS

I thank Murray Goodman for answering my questions about the former St. Peter Dynevor Rectory. As usual, the librarians at the Manitoba Legislative Library were wonderfully helpful. Ed Arndt and Neil Thiessen shared information on Watkins and its old warehouse in Winnipeg. My friend Don Forfar, who attended the St. John's Cathedral Boys' School for grades 9 to 12, credits his self-reliant, can-do attitude on life to his experiences there. I dedicate this chapter to the late historian Donna Sutherland, who helped me to pronounce Dynevor correctly and was always highly supportive of my work.

Manitoba Sugar Company Plant

Anyone who has driven along Interstate I-29 in North Dakota, between Grand Forks and Fargo, has experienced a curious aroma associated with a large industrial facility on the east side of the highway. Depending on the direction of the wind, you can smell it from miles away. Long-time residents of the Fort Garry suburb of Winnipeg probably recognize the smell as the same one that dominated their lives for decades. It is the odour of sugar beets, and a now-abandoned plant in Winnipeg tells the story of an agricultural industry that collapsed suddenly in the wake of industrial globalization. It is the sweet—or perhaps bittersweet—story of sugar manufacturing in Manitoba.

Sugar beets are the same species as common garden beets—known by the scientific name *Beta vulgaris*—that have been bred for high sugar content. About one-fifth of the total global sugar supply comes from sugar beets, most of which are grown in temperate areas of the world, in France, Germany, Russia, Turkey, and United States. (This compares to the other major sugar source, sugar cane, which is a product of tropical and subtropical areas.) The creamy white flesh of a sugar beet's cone-shaped tap-root contains between 12 and 21 percent sugar by weight. Eight pounds of beets make one pound of sugar. The soils of the Red River valley, from the American border to as far north as Teulon and extending westward to Winkler, Carman, and Portage la Prairie, are well suited to growing

OPPOSITE An aerial view of the former Manitoba Sugar plant at Winnipeg, November 2016. GORDON GOLDSBOROUGH

In January 1947, Wacław "Vance" Kuzia and my father-in-law Ludwik "Louis" Zbigniewicz were among 4,000 Polish war veterans who came to Canada seeking new lives. They were sent to Manitoba and put to work tending sugar beets. Kuzia worked near Emerson and lived in barracks at the edge of town. In a photo from his personal album, we see a group of veterans at work in sugar beet fields. HENRY KUZIA

sugar beets. Unfortunately, trials by the Manitoba Department of Agriculture and Immigration between 1900 and 1902, intended to demonstrate sugar beets as a crop for Manitoba farmers, gave disappointing results. Eight varieties of sugar beets were grown in plots around the province but their sugar content was deemed too low for commercial exploitation. Later study suggested the beets had been planted too late and were immature when tested for sugar so better results could have been achieved with good management. By the late 1930s, there was renewed interest in encouraging local sugar-making capability. Adolf Hitler was becoming belligerent and it was growing clear that global conflict loomed. Manitobans worried that, if war broke out, interruption of international shipping would jeopardize our sugar supply, which at that time came from overseas. In 1939, the Manitoba Sugar Company was incorporated, with financial backing from the provincial government, along with foreign shareholders Baron Charles de Neuman, who

owned textile and industrial plants in Europe and South America, and Jacob Goldschmidt, a Jewish industrialist who had fled Nazi-controlled Germany for the United States. Several Winnipeg men with links to the grain and building trades, led by lawyer Gordon Aikins, who would become its second president, also invested.

Manitoba's cold winters meant that beets produced during the summer would freeze rather than spoil, thereby extending the period of time during which the beets could be processed. In this way, it was believed that Manitoba would be able to produce refined, white sugar at competitive prices. Over 600 Manitoba farmers began to grow sugar beets experimentally during the 1939 growing season, with expectations they would be fully operational by 1940, to supply the new company with 1,500 tons of sugar beets daily. In January 1940, Premier John Bracken broke sod for a $2 million sugar processing plant ($35 million in today's dollars) in the Fort Garry area of Winnipeg, west of Pembina Highway just north of present-day Bishop Grandin Boulevard. The Winnipeg construction firm of Carter-Halls-Aldinger did the work and the plant opened for beet deliveries in the fall of 1940, with sugar produced at the plant appearing on Winnipeg store shelves in early October.

To learn about the process of beet growing, I spoke with Abe Martens of Kleefeld, who started growing them (along with other crops) in 1942, on a ten-acre plot that he moved around his farm on a four-year rotation. Depending on the weather, beet planting started in early

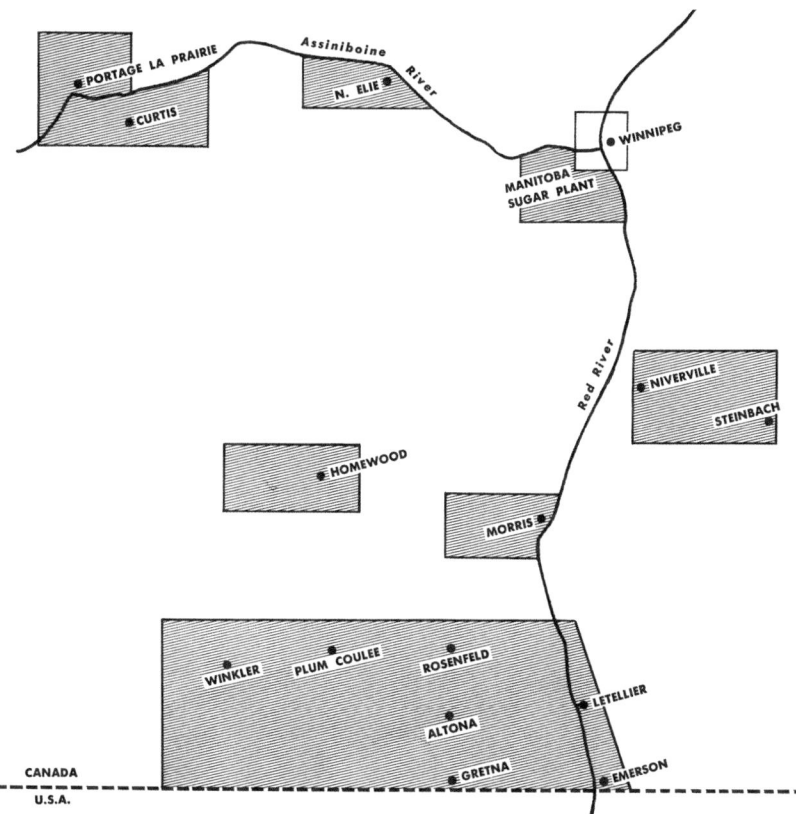

Of all the areas where sugar beets were grown in Manitoba, the area between Emerson and Winkler in southern Manitoba produced two-thirds of the shipments to the Manitoba Sugar Company. "THE MANITOBA SUGAR INDUSTRY" BY CLARK HOPPER, MANITOBA SUGAR COMPANY AND MANITOBA BEET GROWERS ASSOCIATION, NO DATE. MANITOBA LEGISLATIVE LIBRARY VERTICAL FILE

May and harvesting occurred over a month-long period in September and October. When Abe first started, a cluster of beet seeds was planted every 18 inches along a row. When the seeds had germinated, he had to thin out clusters where more than one seed had sprouted. Weeds that would compete with his beets for nutrients and sunlight had to be pulled. In the fall, he pulled mature beets from the ground, wiped off soil from the taproot, trimmed off the green top, then tossed the beet into his truck. Later, he fed the beet greens to his livestock or used them to cover the harvested beets if he could not ship them immediately. There was no waste. The whole process—planting, thinning, weeding, and harvesting—was a manual one. Abe observed that most families had lots of kids so labour was readily available. Otherwise, a beet farmer had to hire workers, paying them anywhere from 15 to 25 cents an hour, depending how hard they worked.

During the Second World War, sugar beets were tended by German prisoners of war and Japanese-Canadians displaced from their homes on the west coast. Later, new immigrants were put to work in the fields. My father-in-law Ludwik was among 4,000 Polish war veterans who arrived in Canada in 1946 and 1947 and were sent out to work on farms. His first job was to hoe beets in Manitoba. Eventually, mechanization came to Manitoba's sugar beet industry. At first, in the 1950s, Abe Martens bought second-hand thinners and harvesters from larger farms in the United States, eventually replacing them with newer, more efficient machines as he could. In time, with modern equipment, Abe could manage the entire sugar beet crop by himself. He needed only a few extra hands during the fall harvest of his 140-acre plot.

Between 1954 and 1983, the period for which statistics are available, a peak of 1,209 farmers tended around 28,000 acres of beets a year. The number of farmers declined over time, dropping to 434 by 1983, but the size of an average beet farm

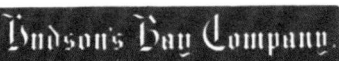
Manitoba's oldest firm, the Hudson's Bay Company, congratulated its newest, the Manitoba Sugar Company, in this October 1940 advertisement from the *Winnipeg Tribune.* Customers were advised that sugar from the new plant would be available on store shelves within days. *WINNIPEG TRIBUNE,* 5 OCTOBER 1940, PAGE 31

Campbell Soup Plant

Globalization has had other corporate victims in Manitoba besides the sugar beet plant. Another was the Campbell Soup Company's factory at Portage la Prairie. In January 1957, Manitoba premier Douglas Campbell (no relation to the soup makers) announced that the US-based firm would build a soup manufacturing plant here to supplement its existing plant at Toronto. Construction of the vast 125,000-square-foot plant, designed by the Winnipeg architectural firm of Green, Blankstein and Russell, began in June 1958. The plant consisted of

The former administrative office of the Campbell Soup plant at Portage la Prairie is abandoned, overgrown, and vandalized as can be seen in my photo from May 2018. GORDON GOLDSBOROUGH

five inter-connected one-storey brick buildings, four of which were used for manufacturing, and a separate one-storey brick building for administrative offices, employee cafeteria, corporate dining room, and changing rooms. A railway spur to the plant allowed up to five boxcars at a time to be loaded from its warehouse, and water came from a water tower beside the plant. Completed in mid-1960 at a cost of some $5 million, the plant became fully operational by the fall of 1960. It employed 170 people to take large quantities of peas, corn, potatoes, celery, onions, mushrooms, parsley, barley, poultry, and beef to produce 17 of the company's 21 varieties of soup, along with frozen food products, macaroni, and spaghetti. They did not make Campbell's signature tomato soup—immortalized by artist Andy Warhol's famous painting—because there were not enough tomatoes grown locally. This was the beginning of the era of "convenience foods" so it is safe to say that many of the products made at Portage fed a generation reared on foil-wrapped TV dinners.

In its first decade of operation, the Campbell's facility was expanded with a freezer-warehouse added in 1964, a mushroom-growing farm in 1966, and a product warehouse in 1968. By the latter year, the plant was making 30 varieties of soup, using 90,000 tons of raw materials annually. In August 1989, the company announced that the plant would close in December 1990, after 30 years of continuous operation, and transfer its production to the much larger Toronto plant. Two provincial political leaders stated publicly that they believed the closure was caused by the Canada-US Free Trade Agreement (CUSFTA) signed in January 1988. Company officials did not entirely deny the charge, blaming the closure on static sales during a period of increased competition from soup producers in Asia, Europe, and the USA. A growing diversity of convenience foods probably contributed to the declining market share for Campbells. Closing one of their two plants enabled the company to achieve greater efficiency of operation, using underused production capacity at Toronto. But if this was true, why did the company build the Portage plant in the first place? Clearly, they were losing market share. Today, 26 years after the closure, parts of the huge former factory are used for storage by local businesses and private persons, and part is a manufacturing plant for building materials. A large part of it remains unoccupied. The former cafeteria is vacant but has been used for filming a zombie movie. The administrative office is abandoned and overgrown, with moss growing on the floor of its lobby.

increased, from 14 acres per farmer in 1952 to 63 acres in 1983. Some farms were as little as a single acre, while others were larger, as much as 160 acres. An acre of land could produce from 6 to 20 tons of beets, which after processing turned into roughly 1 to 2½ tons of sugar. To gain the best possible price for their beets, in 1940 sugar beet farmers formed an association known initially as the Sugar Beet Growers Co-operative Association of Manitoba, and later the Manitoba Sugar Beet Producers' Association. Its founding President was a Roman Catholic priest, Louis Philippe Brunet of Starbuck. The Association negotiated on behalf of farmer interests; however, Manitoba Sugar was the sole buyer of beets so, ultimately, farmers had no recourse but to accept its terms. Their contract specified that they were obliged to purchase their seed from a company-approved source, plant beets in rows no closer together than 24 inches, use only fertilizers and pesticides approved by the company, and pay all costs to transport beets to the Winnipeg plant. In return, the company agreed to buy all the farmer's beets so long as they were within a quota set on the basis of their beet acreage. Payment was based on the crop's sugar content, which varied with the amount of rainfall and sunshine during the growing season. The farmer received an initial payment within a month of beet delivery and the remainder through the following year until the sugar had been sold.

In the fall of each year, farmers delivered truckloads of harvested beets to railway loading points at Elie, Ste. Anne, Niverville, Morris, Letellier, Portage la Prairie,

Open hopper cars from around southern Manitoba delivered mountains of sugar beets to the Manitoba Sugar Company plant, 1942. ARCHIVES OF MANITOBA

Newton Siding, Plum Coulee, Winkler, Horndean, Curtis Siding, Homewood, Rosenfeld, Emerson, Christie Siding, Teulon, Gretna, and Altona. The beets in hopper railcars (or in large open-topped trucks) were brought to the Fort Garry plant where they were stored in outdoor piles or, later, in a large, ventilated warehouse. (My wife recalls picking up beets that fell off the trucks and taking them home to be enjoyed by her pet rabbits.) Beets delivered in the fall were processed through the winter and into the following spring and summer. My uncle Bud, who farmed during the summer, found regular winter employment working in a warehouse at the sugar beet plant.

The first step in processing sugar beets was to wash and slice them into thin, noodle-like strips called cossettes. The cossettes were immersed in hot water to dissolve their sugar. Pressed to extract the sweet liquid, the leftover beet pulp was dried and used as cattle feed. Sugar was extracted from the amber-coloured liquid by successive evaporation, filtration, and centrifugation. The resulting white sugar crystals were dried, cooled, and screened to uniform size. The liquid was processed a couple more times to extract as much sugar as possible. The final residue was a thick, black syrup called molasses that could be used in animal feed or added back in small quantities to the finished, white sugar to make brown sugar. Complex aromas emanate from a sugar beet processing plant, arising from the decomposition of improperly stored wet beets, the sugar extraction process, and the leftover water sitting in large, outdoor holding ponds. I have heard descriptions of the smell from the Fort Garry plant that ranged from "sickeningly sweet" and "burnt rhubarb" to "molasses gone bad." If you want to judge the smell for yourself, drive by that beet plant in North Dakota.

In late 1956, controlling interest in the Manitoba Sugar Company was acquired by one of its competitors, the British Columbia Sugar Refining Company (known as BC Sugar, later operating in Manitoba under its subsidiary Rogers Sugar), which hoped to prevent competition from developing in Alberta and Saskatchewan. The company was subsequently taken to court by the Manitoba government over its monopoly in the western sugar market and the perceived impact on prices to consumers. The case was dismissed by the Manitoba Court of Queen's Bench. BC Sugar

A view of the newly opened Manitoba Sugar plant in Fort Garry, 1942. ARCHIVES OF MANITOBA

invested in the Winnipeg plant, which it believed to be inefficient in its operation, by building, in 1962, an enormous concrete silo beside the plant for storing 10 million pounds of the finished sugar prior to shipment. (Two more silos were constructed later.) Despite these improvements, the sugar plant closed in January 1997, putting 82 full-time employees out of work and leaving 230 sugar beet farmers—but not Abe Martens, who had "seen the writing on the wall" and quit beet growing the previous year—with no option to sell their produce or sell their specialized beet harvesters. A major factor contributing to the closure was a General Agreement on Tariffs and Trade (GATT) negotiated in 1995 that allowed the United States government to restrict Canadian exports of sugar-containing products and to levy barriers on refined sugar from Canada. The United States was Manitoba's principal market for refined sugar so, when that market was lost, there was no choice but to close the plant. In its final year of operation, the plant processed 360,011 tons of beets to produce roughly 78 pounds of sugar for every man, woman, and child in Manitoba.

Despite the plant's closure 21 years ago, its external structure remains intact, with "Manitoba Sugar Company" in large, white letters still emblazoned on its side. The five huge sugar silos still stand, but appear to be unused. Also visible are the now-empty holding ponds once used to treat wastewater. The original factory, along with several others built south of it, are now occupied by logistics and metal-processing businesses. Today, according to the Canadian Sugar Institute, the only growers of sugar beets in Canada are in Alberta and Ontario. Most sugar in Manitoba stores comes from a plant at Taber, Alberta or from sugar cane imported from the tropics and processed at Vancouver. The abandoned Manitoba Sugar Company building reminds us that we live in an increasingly globalized world, where our foods and other products come to us from far away. Now that the NAFTA between Canada, United States, and Mexico is being renegotiated, I wonder what other corporate closures may occur in the aftermath? The Manitoba Beet Growers' Association remained in existence long after the plant closed and has endowed an excellent exhibit about the former sugar industry at a museum in the village of St. Joseph.

Bags of white sugar sold in Manitoba stores once touted proudly that they were a "product of Manitoba." ANNUAL REPORT 1983, MANITOBA SUGAR COMPANY, MANITOBA LEGISLATIVE LIBRARY

ACKNOWLEDGEMENTS

Retired farmer Abe Martens gave generously of his time to talk with me about the "glory years" of the sugar beet industry in Manitoba. Henry Kuzia shared wonderful photos of his late father and other Polish veterans working in sugar beet fields near Emerson. Camille Fisette-Mulaire of the St. Joseph Museum showed me the excellent collection of beet-growing equipment and documents there.

Fort Ellice Trail

People who experience the Canadian prairies for the first time see them as a vast, featureless plain and wonder how the earliest Indigenous travellers were able to navigate. For generations, they followed trails defined by topographic features such as rivers, lakes, and hills, leaving no marks on the landscape as they went. This changed in 1800 when fur trader and explorer Alexander Henry the Younger arrived at the confluence of the Red and Pembina rivers—site of today's Pembina, North Dakota. He began to build wheeled vehicles to transport his gear across the vast prairies that lay westward. An early prototype of what later came to be known as the Red River cart used slices of three-foot diameter trees as wheels, replaced in later versions by wooden, spoked wheels. With two wheels fastened to an axle under a rough, wooden cart pulled by an

oxen, horse, or mule, the contraption could carry loads of 500 to 1,000 pounds. Typically made of locally-obtained hardwood—oak, elm, and ash—held together by wooden pegs, they had no metal parts. The axle had no lubrication so the carts were atrociously noisy. Around 1942, an old-timer would reminisce that "You could hear them coming for miles before you could even see them." Brigades of ten carts, or longer trains of a mile or more, followed each other single file, their narrow wheels carving deep ruts into the virgin soil. These ruts marked the routes of the first prairie highways between the far-flung outposts of civilization established by companies trading for fur. Among these primitive highways in Manitoba, arguably the most important was the Fort Ellice Trail, named for its destination near present-day St. Lazare.

Established around 1840, the Fort Ellice Trail went by several other names, depending on one's final destination, and it was not a single route. In a westward direction,

A Metis brigade of Red River Carts on the Fort Ellice Trail might have looked something like this photo of "The Half-Breeds' Ox and Cart Train" taken in mid-1881 by American photographer F. Jay Haynes during his visit to Manitoba ARCHIVES OF MANITOBA

it was known as the Saskatchewan Trail, Fort Carlton Trail, or Fort Edmonton Trail, becoming the Fort Garry Trail in an eastward direction. It was some 600 miles in length, beginning at Upper Fort Garry. The first part of the trail should be familiar to Winnipeggers, as it mostly

Trails to Fort Ellice are shown as dashed lines on this excerpt from an 1878 map of prairie Canada. "MAP OF PART OF THE NORTH WEST TERRITORY SHEWING THE OPERATIONS OF THE SPECIAL SURVEY OF STANDARD MERIDIANS AND PARALLELS FOR DOMINION LANDS" COMPILED AND DRAWN BY ALEX LINDSAY RUSSELL, OTTAWA. HTTPS://WWW.FLICKR.COM/PHOTOS/MANITOBAMAPS/2830613749/IN/PHOTOLIST-5J8CRK, FORTELLICETRAIL1878.TIF

followed today's Portage Avenue. Heading westward out of the city, it hugged the north side of the Assiniboine River, essentially along what would later be Highway #26, to arrive at the "Prairie Portage" (now Portage la Prairie).

Those travellers continuing west had three options. A northern route roughly followed the modern Highway #16. It crossed the Whitemud River three times, the first at Westbourne (known then as First Crossing). The community on the east side of the river at the third crossing

was known as Palestine but, in 1882, was incorporated as Gladstone. At Tanner's Crossing over the Little Saskatchewan River, the town of Minnedosa was established. The last stopping place was Shoal Lake before the trail descended 240 feet into the Assiniboine River valley then climbed back up to reach Fort Ellice on the west side. By this route, the distance between Upper Fort Garry and Fort Ellice was 217 miles. Assuming that a fast brigade could travel twenty miles a day in dry weather, the trip to Fort Ellice could be completed in eleven days. A train that was heavily laden or travelling on wet terrain might average only ten miles a day so the travel time would double, to around three weeks. A central route of the Fort Ellice Trail headed southwest from Portage la Prairie until past today's Sidney, then turned northwest to join the northern route at a point east of Shoal Lake. Its only major river crossing was the Little Saskatchewan southwest of Minnedosa. The distance and travel time were about the same. A southern route continued past where the central route branched north and crossed the Assiniboine River at a series of rapids about five miles as the crow flies southeast of present-day Brandon, continued west to the vicinity of Virden then headed northwest to Fort Ellice, arriving from the west. The distance between Upper Fort Garry and Fort Ellice was 235 miles by this route. It was 15 miles longer than for the more widely used northern route but was probably faster and easier because

it entailed only a single Assiniboine River crossing—where there was a well-gravelled and shallow approach on each riverbank—compared to several river crossings on the northern route, including an eight-foot-deep ford of the Assiniboine at Fort Ellice.

Metis freighters in the employ of the Hudson's Bay Company or privateers working on their own account formed the bulk of traffic on the Fort Ellice Trail. However, one might encounter people travelling for a variety of other reasons too, including surveyors, missionaries, settlers, and sundry members of the British gentry. Explorer John Palliser, for whom the Palliser Triangle is named,

A view of Fort Ellice from the north, 1890. The large building on the right side, with a covered balcony on the second floor over the entrance, was the Chief Factor's residence. ARCHIVES OF MANITOBA

An aerial photo, taken in October 2017, of the treeless area on the right side of the Assiniboine River, east of Brandon, that was occupied by Brandon House No. 1 from 1793 to 1811.
GORDON GOLDSBOROUGH

Brandon House

A long-forgotten spot along the Assiniboine River, near the crossing of the Fort Ellice Trail, are the remains of Brandon House. Situated about eighteen miles as the crow flies east of present-day Brandon, and established in 1793, it was the first post of the Hudson's Bay Company (HBC) on the southern Canadian prairies. Its purpose was two-fold. Company officials—who had previously traded for furs only at faraway York Factory—hoped that, by bringing trade goods closer to where Indigenous peoples lived and trapped, they would pre-empt the Canadian and American traders who were encroaching into their traditional trading territory. In addition to receiving and shipping furs, Brandon House was a provisioning post that acquired food for HBC workers. Its location on the expansive prairies meant it was a logical place to make pemmican using locally-obtained bison meat and berries. Pemmican was an essential food for the voyageurs who transported furs and trade goods back and forth between York Factory and the growing network of HBC posts across the plains.

In mid-October 1793, Brandon House was built about two miles west of the junction of the Souris and Assiniboine rivers, on the north side of the Assiniboine. Soon afterward, the North West Company, an HBC competitor, built a post nearby. Around 1800, the X Y Company built a post in the area too. With three fur trading companies operating in close proximity, this once-isolated spot became the epicentre of prairie commerce and exploration, at least for a few years. In 1805, the North West post was moved several miles downstream. Brandon House (referred to now as No. 1 to distinguish it from other posts with the same name) was abandoned in 1811 in favour of Brandon House No. 2, which operated several miles northwest, from 1811 to 1821 on the south side of the river, then back on the north side from 1821 to 1824. In October 1828, Brandon House No. 3 (or No. 4, depending how you count them) was established nine miles northwest of Brandon House No. 1. By 1832, it was abandoned too and this reach of the Assiniboine River slid back into obscurity.

For a period of nearly forty years, Brandon House played a key role in the prairie fur trade. My friend Tom Mitchell, an historian at Brandon University, argues that without Brandon House, establishment of Lord Selkirk's Red River Settlement (which became Winnipeg) would have been impossible. Several noted historical personalities passed through the place during its period of activity. Explorer David Thompson spent the winter at the North West post in 1797. Fur trader and surveyor Peter Fidler was at Brandon House No. 2 in 1816 when its supply warehouse was plundered by Metis leader Cuthbert Grant and a group of his men on their way to the Red River Settlement. There, they confronted Governor Robert Semple, killing Semple and twenty Selkirk Settlers, resulting in what came to be known as the Battle of Seven Oaks.

Interest in the Brandon House area was renewed in 1928, when amateur historian (and professional physician) David Stewart perused old HBC files to estimate the former location of Brandon House No. 3. Accompanied by fellow physicians Sidney Peirce and Charles Baragar, he confirmed its location. Baragar, at the time President of the Brandon Rotary Club, convinced other club members that it would be a good idea to erect a permanent marker at the site in time for its 100th anniversary. A fieldstone cairn was duly dedicated at a hugely-attended ceremony on 7 October 1928.

That cairn, erected 90 years ago, is still standing, and there are other reminders of the fur trading history of this region. In the early 1980s, the Manitoba government carried out an archaeological survey of the Brandon House No. 1 site, and Tom Mitchell and I re-visited the spot in October 2017. We found several shallow pits in the ground that were either the remains of fur trade buildings, or excavations made by the archaeologists. On a bank of the Assiniboine River nearby, low water levels revealed thousands of clam shells whose contents might have been eaten by the post's occupants then dumped back into the river.

However, what I found most interesting about the site was what was *not* there. Despite the passage of some 200 years since Brandon House was abandoned, there were no trees growing on its site. An aerial view of the site showed clearly a rectangular tree-less area where the fur trade post was once situated. There were knee-high grasses but nothing else. As a professional botanist, this puzzled me. I asked some of my university colleagues and they were equally perplexed. We think there may be some factor preventing trees from growing and can think of at least two possible explanations. The soil may be so heavily compacted from traffic around the HBC post that tree seedlings cannot grow through it. This, to me, seems unlikely. Alternatively, there may be some toxic material in the soil that prevents tree growth. They had tanned leather at Brandon House, and one of the many methods for doing this involved toxic metals. For a better understanding of this important historic site in western Manitoba, more research is clearly needed.

used a portion of the Fort Ellice Trail during his reconnoitering of the southern prairies in 1857. He was followed in 1858 by university professor Henry Yule Hinde, who made pioneering studies of the geological and biological resources of the territory.

In August 1871, a crossing on the trail's southern route was immortalized when Treaty No. 1 was signed at Lower Fort Garry. It defined the western-most boundary of the treaty area as the "Grand Rapids." That spot—where the Fort Ellice Trail crossed the Assiniboine River—was chosen because it was well-known to most anyone familiar with the prairies. Through the 1870s, members of the North West Mounted Police patrolled the plains using the Fort Ellice Trail and, in 1885, units of the Royal Winnipeg Rifles and Winnipeg Light Infantry followed it to the North West Territories on their way to confront Louis Riel.

In September 1881, Presbyterian minister Andrew Baird used the Fort Ellice Trail on his way to establish a church at Fort Edmonton. After

In this view of the Fort Ellice site from 1919, the chimney from its blacksmith's forge and a pair of buildings were the only remaining structures. All are gone now. ARCHIVES OF MANITOBA

a paper presented to the Manitoba Historical Society.

The site occupied by Fort Ellice at that time overlooked the Assiniboine River valley, about 2½ miles southeast of present-day St. Lazare and about eight miles east of the Saskatchewan border. However, this was not the original site where the fort had been established in 1831 by the Hudson's Bay Company, that site being some distance to the west, nearer Beaver Creek. Its purpose as stated by instructions from the HBC Council was "to protect the trade of the Assiniboines and Crees of the Upper Red River District from the American opposition on the Missouri."

The fort's name recognized Edward Ellice, a London-based agent and supplier for the North West Company who, after its 1821 merger with the HBC, remained active in the new company. (Ellice would also be commemorated by a street in Winnipeg.) Fort Ellice was rebuilt at its later site, in 1862, on a plateau overlooking the meandering

Assiniboine River. It had a commanding view, which enabled the HBC to keep tabs on traffic (friendly and otherwise) passing on the river below, and on the surrounding plains. The facility was not heavily fortified. A wooden palisade scarcely taller than a man enclosed a square compound with several wooden buildings. An opening in the north side of the fence was the entrance for those wishing to trade. To their left as they entered was the building where trading was done. To their right was a warehouse. Straight ahead was a wooden boardwalk leading to the grandest building, a two-storey residence and office of the Chief Factor. On the east side were storehouses and a dairy. A low building on the west side contained quarters for the men and a carpenter's shop. There was a single cottage for families, a blacksmith shop, and an outdoor bake oven.

Baird arrived at Fort Ellice in its final days, as a trickle of settlers arriving in the region was turning into a spate. The need for the Fort

a brief stop at Winnipeg, where he purchased "a horse and buckboard, a tent, a blanket and buffalo robe, some bacon, hardtack and other supplies," Baird headed on his way, arriving at Fort Ellice more than week later. He was greeted warmly by HBC Factor Archie McDonald and invited to lead a church service the following day. During his stay at the fort, Baird became sufficiently familiar with its layout and operation that, fifty years later in February 1931, he was able to describe it in detail in

Ellice Trail waned as new, faster means of transportation were becoming available. During the short-lived age of steamboats in Manitoba, Fort Ellice was about as far upstream in the shallow Assiniboine that a steamboat could reach. When currents and water levels were favourable, the trip aboard a boat such as the ss *Alpha* (described in my previous book) could be completed in a fraction of the time compared to a Red River cart. In May 1880, for instance, an upriver trip from Winnipeg to Fort Ellice took the *Alpha* 19 days, towing a barge heavily laden with "400 sacks of flour, 74 sacks of bacon, 50 barrels of pork, and 320 chests of tea." However, the return trip to Winnipeg, travelling with the current, took just five days. The travel time dropped even more with the arrival of the Canadian Pacific Railway in western Manitoba in late 1881. Homesteaders began arriving in abundance. The days of the fur trade and bison hunting on the plains were over.

A panoramic aerial view of the Assiniboine River valley and the former Fort Ellice site as it appears today, looking toward the east. GORDON GOLDSBOROUGH

Fort Ellice cairn unveiled on 10 June 1935, as seen in June 2018. GORDON GOLDSBOROUGH

Fort Ellice was abandoned in 1889. However, it lived on via the names of two rural municipalities established in its former territory: Ellice, named for the fort itself, and Archie after Archie McDonald, both incorporated in December 1883. (These municipalities are now merged as the RM of Ellice-Archie.) Most of Fort Ellice was made of wood so very little of it would survive for long. By 1930, only a pair of buildings and a stone and concrete chimney from the blacksmith shop remained. However, there are at least three cemeteries at the site. One of them, marked with durable stone crosses, contains the more affluent people who died at the fort. The graves of less important people in the other cemeteries, if marked at all, have since disappeared as their wooden markers rotted away.

On 15 July 1930, realizing that an important historical landmark was at risk of being forgotten, municipal and provincial politicians gathered at the site, along with 4,000 onlookers, to lay the cornerstone of a monument near the former fort's palisade, overlooking the Assiniboine River. Despite the best of intentions, it would take another five years, and the active involvement of local First World War veterans, to complete construction of an impressive eight-foot-high stone cairn. The cairn, with a metal plaque affixed to its side, was unveiled at a ceremony on 10 June 1935. It featured two prominent maples leafs at its top along with a brief summary of the site's history. The project was not government-sanctioned and, although many people believe the site to be a designated national historic site, it is not. (Maybe it should be?) Through the 20th century, the site was used by the surrounding community for baseball games and other recreational pursuits. When I first tried to visit the site of Fort Ellice in October 2011, I was turned away by a large sign advising that permission was required to enter the privately owned property. The situation changed in June 2012 when the Nature Conservancy of Canada, recognizing the historical and ecological significance of the site, purchased it with plans to provide free public access. I was one of the first to visit the cairn and overgrown cemetery with permission of the new owners.

Today, Manitoba's southern prairies are criss-crossed by an extensive network of highways and travel times between points are measured in hours, not days. The long-abandoned Fort Ellice Trail is largely forgotten except at spots here and there where someone has erected a commemorative marker. I have found nine such markers, most of them on the northern route, including near Arden, Birtle, Gladstone, Minnedosa, and Strathclair, but also two on the southern route, near Austin and Miniota. Two of the markers, at the White Horse near St. François Xavier and at Neepawa, were installed by the provincial government in the early 1960s. The trail itself is mostly on private property and its cart ruts have been obliterated over the years by plows and other farm machinery. However, I heard that remnants can still be seen in a few places if you look carefully. Last May, I visited a site south of Austin, where landowner Janice Wiebe believes the trail had crossed West Squirrel Creek. After leaving

a log "stopping house" operated by Scottish immigrant John McKinnon, travellers used his toll bridge over the creek. Several gullied approaches down to the creek were still clearly visible. Although weathered by the passage of 140 years, so individual cart ruts were not visible, it seemed improbable that they could have arisen in any other way than through erosion by repeated traffic. Sticklers who want to know the exact route of the Fort Ellice Trail need only consult maps from the 1870s that were drawn by surveyors preparing the prairies for agriculture. Now stored at the Archives of Manitoba, these wonderful maps clearly show the prairie trails, allowing anyone with an interest to revisit a time when screechy wooden carts were the vehicle of choice on the highways of the past.

A grave marker in the overgrown Fort Ellice Cemetery, June 2015. GORDON GOLDSBOROUGH

ACKNOWLEDGEMENTS

I owe profuse thanks to Tom Mitchell for making me aware of the old prairie trails, and drawing my attention to the historic Assiniboine River crossing and fur trade post sites east of Brandon. Those wanting to know more about the Assiniboine River Rapids should consult Tom's excellent 2018 paper in *Manitoba History*. I am grateful to the good folks at the Nature Conservancy of Canada, especially Kevin Teneycke and Christine Chilton, for permitting me to visit Fort Ellice in June 2015, for which Marcel Fouillard was my guide. Janice Wiebe toured me on the remains of the trail on her property.

Pointe du Bois

Company-owned houses at Pointe du Bois, seen in a promotional booklet published in the mid-1920s by the City of Winnipeg Hydro-Electric System. ARCHIVES OF MANITOBA

"You can't go home." I suspect the former residents of the town near Manitoba's oldest, continuously-operating hydro generating station would agree with this sentiment. They could drive on its streets, marked by signs with familiar names, and pass by the sites of homes, churches, and stores in their memories. However, they would find no actual buildings. With just a few exceptions, the "company town" of Pointe du Bois has been wiped from the map, leaving generations of Manitobans disconnected from their roots.

In December 1902, sixty men employed by the Winnipeg General Power Company began blasting and moving rock at the Winnipeg River, 6½ miles southeast of Lac du Bonnet at a site referred to as Pinawa, to begin construction of a hydroelectric generating station—the first in the province designed to operate

OPPOSITE These company-owned houses at Pointe du Bois, seen here in June 2013, were demolished a few months later. CATHY WHITE JUSKOW

year-round. When the facility began operating within a year and a half, its electricity—made by passing river water through a turbine linked to a generator—was transmitted along a 55-mile power line to Winnipeg, where the domestic demand for electricity and the cost of the city's expanding streetlight system was growing. In late July 1904, the company merged with another local firm, the Winnipeg Electric Street Railway Company that operated the city's streetcar system, to become the Winnipeg Electric Railway Company (WERC).

Within months, Winnipeg's city council, concerned that a WERC monopoly on power production would lead to higher prices, decided

to build its own power station on the Winnipeg River, 30 miles by river from the one at Pinawa. In June 1906, just as the WERC station began operating, Winnipeggers approved overwhelmingly, by a margin of 2,382 to 382 votes, an expenditure of $3,250,000 (or $91 million in today's currency) for the city project, described as "the greatest victory for municipal ownership in the history of the Canadian West." The spot the city chose, after an adventurous canoe trip to the site by the project engineers and nine members of the city council in October 1906, was called Pointe du Bois, meaning "wooded point" in French. In due course, the land was leased from the federal government, renewable in twenty-year periods in perpetuity. Construction of a dam to hold water at the waterfall site would provide a "hydraulic head" of 47 feet with a power output of 45 megawatts, eventually rising to 78 megawatts. The new generating station would be operated by the City Light and Power Department, renamed the Winnipeg Hydro Electric System in 1921, and usually shortened to Winnipeg Hydro.

A four-storey brick and concrete building near the Pointe du Bois Generating Station, used to house non-residential staff, as it appeared in August 1926 soon after construction. Designed by Winnipeg Hydro's engineering staff and built by the McDiarmid Construction Company of Winnipeg, the building had verandahs on the side facing the Winnipeg River. In its basement was a cook's residence, boiler room, and storeroom. On the ground floor was a sitting room with an open fireplace, reading and writing room, dining room, kitchen, pantry and pastry room, and wash room. The second and third floors had identical layouts, each with seven single bedrooms, one double bedroom, and communal lavatories. Space in the attic could be used for four or five additional bedrooms when needed. The building is now vacant and likely to be demolished. MANITOBA HYDRO

The new hydro generating station was designed by the Toronto engineering firm of Smith, Kerry and Chace, and built by John Gunn and Sons Limited of Winnipeg, one of the largest construction firms in western Canada. It would take two years after the municipal vote for construction to get underway, and work would continue over the next three years. The first step was to build a 28-mile tramway from Lac du Bonnet, bridging the Winnipeg River and Pinawa Channel, through difficult terrain to Pointe du Bois. Completed in September 1908, a steam train running on the tramway provided fast and inexpensive delivery of materials and workers to the construction site, relative to what WERC had incurred to build its plant at Pinawa. The full potential of the Pointe du Bois site was not yet fully realized when, on the evening of 16 October 1911, the city street lights turned on for the first time using electricity from the new facility. Only five of the planned sixteen turbines had been installed in its powerhouse. Turbines were added as funds and demand dictated—in 1914 (2), 1919 (1), 1921 (1), 1922 (2), 1925 (2), and 1926 (3)—completed the plant. Meanwhile, in 1924, a coal-powered standby plant was built on Amy Street in Winnipeg to assure a supply of electricity to essential services when the power went out or Pointe du Bois' output did not meet demand.

Power from Pointe du Bois was carried to Winnipeg over 60,000-volt transmission lines that ran 77 miles in a mostly straight line to the city. On arrival at a terminal station built on Rover Avenue in Point Douglas, the voltage was reduced to 12,000 volts then re-transmitted by six underground lines to Sub-Station No. 1 on King Street in the Exchange District. There, the voltage was reduced again, this time to a range as low as 120, as desired by consumers. Four underground lines from the Rover station went to Sub-Station No. 2 at the corner of McPhillips and Logan. In 1919, a second transmission line from Pointe du Bois to Rover was built, along with Sub-Station No. 5 on Scotland Avenue at Stafford. It received 60,000-volt power from the Rover station and re-transmitted it sixty miles to Portage la Prairie, the first delivery of power from Pointe du Bois to a site out-side of Winnipeg.

Initially, the primary domestic use for electricity was home lighting and, in 1917, the average Winnipeg customer used just 573 kilowatts-hours (KWH) per year. Unlike today, where Manitoba Hydro encourages its cus-tomers to be "Power Smart" by conserving electricity, the city government did its best to get Winnipeggers to use as much electricity as possible, so revenue would pay off the construction costs. On the main floor of a new two-storey office building on Princess Street, it displayed a dazzling array of household conveniences to encourage residents to switch from wood- or gas-powered appliances to electric ones. In 1924, a second showroom opened on north Main Street. In 1926 alone, they sold 32,121 electric lamps, 1,620 electric ranges, 629 electric water heaters, 396 electric vacuum cleaners, 320 electric washing machines, and 315 electric toasters. A glamourous new showroom, opened in

Company-owned houses at Pointe du Bois, July 1966. CATHY WHITE JUSKOW

Aerial view of Pointe du Bois powerhouse, control structure, and town, circa 1974. GEORGE PENNER

Built on Winnipeg's Princess Street between 1919 and 1920, this two-storey building housed offices of the City Light and Power Department on its second floor and a showroom for new electric appliances on its main floor. Occupied by Winnipeg Hydro into the late 1950s, and later by another branch of the city government, it was renovated but vacant at the time of this October 2016 photo. ERIC DE SCHEPPER

1935 in the Boyd Building on Portage Avenue, urged Winnipeggers to use even more electricity, and the company hired its first home economist to provide buyers with tips for using their purchases. As consumption increased, so did production on the Winnipeg River. Individual usage reached 4,008 KWH in 1930 and 6,672 KWH in 1950. (For comparison, it was 20,700 KWH in 2015.) Eventually, increasing demand resulted in the construction of the Slave Falls Generating Station, four

miles downstream from Pointe du Bois, between 1930 and 1931. Its eight turbines—installed between 1931 and 1948—could generate an additional 68 megawatts of power, transmitted over a line directly to Sub-Station No. 5.

In the early days, it took more than 50 men to operate the Pointe du Bois Generating Station. Most aspects of plant operations were manual. To lower its 97 spillway gates, for instance, two men equipped with mallets swung them in tandem to knock out three-foot-long wooden logs holding each of them open. Work was done at all hours of the day or night so men were on duty 24 hours a day/365 days a year. They were obliged to live at the site because the only way in and out was an hour-long trip aboard a bus—equipped with steel wheels so it could run on the tramway—that made two trips a week to Lac du Bonnet. Single workmen lived in a residence built for the construction workers until 1926 when a four-storey brick staff house was built, while

rental houses were constructed for married men and their families, in two groups called the "North Camp" and "South Camp." All the buildings were heated by wood from a company-owned sawmill and none had running water. It cost a lot to bring food from the outside world, so whenever possible, workers and their families tended gardens, hunted, trapped, and fished to feed themselves. The community was ethnically diverse—Icelanders, Britons, Italians, Ukrainians, as well as Canadians, and families were large. The Pointe du Bois School opened in 1913 and, because there were no land-owning taxpayers on whom to assess school taxes, students were taught by teachers paid by the City Light and Power Department. The town's other amenities included a privately-owned grocery store, a multi-denominational church (later, there would be separate Anglican and Roman Catholic churches), and a community hall for dances, concerts, and movies. There was a medical clinic staffed by a company-employed nurse, a swimming beach on the river, and skating and curling rinks. Recreational pursuits included tennis, baseball, curling, skating, hockey, trapping, and fishing. There was a social club for married men (single men were admitted eventually) called the Noble Order of Benedicts, complete with elected officers, passwords, and biweekly meetings. It had 46 members in 1927 and its assets included a "pool table, moving picture machine, piano, curling rocks, bowls, panatrope, and all necessary furniture, etc." There was an equivalent group for women called the Ladies Social Club where they chatted, drank tea, and planned the community's festivities at Christmas, Valentine's Day, and Halloween. In later years, there were active 4H, Girl Guide, and Boy Scout groups for the kids.

In 1931, houses became served with municipal water supply lines and sewage collection systems, with a water treatment plant located in the powerhouse. In 1943, a new school offering instruction in grades 1 to 11—named for pioneering power engineer John Glassco—became the pride of the community:

> Modern as television, this house of learning is well-nigh perfect. It is expected that some day the school will be expanded to include an auditorium. Contrary to the usual routine interior decoration for schools, the Pointe du Bois school is bright, smart and colourful throughout and one hopes that other schools will follow the example …

Pointe du Bois's resident population grew from 169 people in 1935 to 350 by 1947. However, the beginning of the end for the local way of life dates to 1941, when an all-season road was built to Lac du Bonnet. It now became possible for people to come and go more readily, and commute to work from other communities. The resident population began to decrease slowly, to 300 people by 1980. Glassco School closed in 1981, by which time it was hosting only elementary classes, and its building was used as a recreation centre (with an outdoor swimming pool) and for Hydro administrative offices. In 1990, Winnipeg Hydro commissioned an engineering study to examine the state of the town's sewer and water infrastructure. The original cast-iron water mains had been replaced by PVC pipes between 1968 and 1970, and a new wastewater treatment plant was built in 1972, but the study concluded that

In August 1913, a school was established in the village of Pointe du Bois. Replaced by the present brick structure in 1943, a school described as the "finest rural school in Manitoba" was named in honour of early power engineer John Glassco. The school closed in 1981 and the building was in use by Manitoba Hydro for administrative offices when this photo was taken in August 2016. MARIA ZBIGNIEWICZ

Built in 1915 near the Pointe du Bois Generating Station, a house made of hand-cut granite blocks is believed to have been constructed by Italian stonemasons who had previously worked on the dam construction project. It was used as a private residence for power utility workers and their families until 1959, after which it was a staff house. The building was demolished by Manitoba Hydro in late 2013, a couple of months after I took this photo. GORDON GOLDSBOROUGH

considerable work had to be done to bring the services up to modern standards. There simply were not enough people using them to warrant the expense. By 1996, as a result of automation at the power station, there were only 79 residents and a quarter of the houses were vacant. No work had been undertaken by the time Winnipeg Hydro was acquired by Manitoba Hydro in 2002, completing the consolidation of power suppliers in Manitoba that had begun with the purchase of the Winnipeg Electric Company (the former WERC) in 1953.

The new owners realized that the century-old station —the oldest facility in its province-wide system, operating beyond its life expectancy—needed an upgrade. Work began in 2012 to replace the original spillway and, in 2014, the new structure began operating. The old spillway was sealed off, leaving just a skeleton like at the Pinawa Generating Station that had closed in 1951. The original powerhouse and generators continued to be used. As for the town, Manitoba Hydro is in the business of producing electricity, not preserving heritage. It tore down some of the oldest houses when it took possession and decided against doing any maintenance on the rest, with further plans to remove all the Hydro-owned buildings in town— which was all of them.

Four reasons were given for the decision: 1) with an all-weather road to the site, there was no longer a need for a residential community because plant workers could live elsewhere and commute to Pointe du Bois; 2) the replacement of the original spillway with a new, mostly automated one reduced the need to have employees on-site because the plant could be operated remotely from Winnipeg, 3) the buildings were 80 to 90 years old and had structural problems, mold, lead paint, and asbestos floor tiles and ceiling insulation, with essential repairs estimated to cost $6.8 million; and 4) upgrading of the town's basic water and sewer systems would cost an estimated $900,000. Consequently, the policy was that when someone moved out of a house, nobody was permitted to move in. Demolition of the 44 Hydro-owned buildings began in 2013. The last residents of Pointe du Bois were told to be gone by 1 January 2015 and each was offered a cash incentive to buy a home elsewhere or a vehicle to commute to work.

Today, the meandering paved streets to nowhere in Pointe du Bois are reminders of hydro history, with names commemorating long-time employees and managers of Winnipeg Hydro: Briggs Road for Lee Briggs (1928–1955), Glassco Avenue for John Glassco (1909–1944), McLeod Avenue for Kenneth McLeod (1922–1935), Sanger Avenue for John Sanger (1912–1951), Storey Boulevard for Thomas Storey (1929–1960), and Square Place for Samuel Square (1912–1953). Here and there are abandoned reminders of the former residences—for example, a children's swing set—but most tangible signs of the once-thriving community are hidden by tall grass and weeds. The workers needed to operate the plant commute from Lac du Bonnet or elsewhere. The old staff house is now closed. Steam

Locomotive No. 3 that once ran on the tramway now pulls the Prairie Dog Central train in Winnipeg. The output of the Pointe du Bois Generating Station pales in comparison with stations on the Nelson River in northern Manitoba that produce thousands of megawatts, especially considering that it is generating less power now than when it was in full operation. Four of its sixteen generators have been removed permanently and five more are idle pending essential repairs that may never happen. When I toured the 107-year-old powerhouse recently, it was producing only 30 of its theoretical maximum of 78 megawatts. There is no more visual a sign that the equipment is old than the built-in swastika adorning several of the generators. They were not built by Nazis but date from earlier times when their Swedish manufacturer used the symbol as a corporate logo.

It is probably a matter of time before Pointe du Bois joins the old Pinawa station and is decommissioned entirely. Then, the community

will live only in the memories of the people who consider it to be their hometown. Recently, I spoke with Cathy White Juskow, who was born at Pointe du Bois and lived there for the first 17 years of her life. Her father worked at the station and her mother was a homemaker. Cathy attended Glassco School until grade 7 when she began taking a bus to Lac du Bonnet. She has fond memories of her childhood in this close-knit community and she helped to organize a reunion in 2013, just before the building demolition began. She administers a "Memories of Pointe du Bois" group on Facebook where she and other former residents can grieve their lost community. She is reluctant to go back because she will never be able to go home. That place is gone.

ACKNOWLEDGEMENTS

Cathy White Juskow shared generously of memories and photos from her childhood in Pointe du Bois. I thank Manitoba Hydro for giving me an excellent tour of the Pointe du Bois and Slave Falls Generating Stations.

Winnipeg
Masonic
Temple

I confess that I am not a big fan of salad. If someone puts one in front of me, I will eat it. I may even enjoy it but I will definitely never crave it in the way that others do. One of the reasons for my attitude is that I do not typically get a choice in its ingredients. However, if I can control what the salad contains, I enjoy it more. One of the things I liked about restaurants of my youth was that many of them offered a "salad bar" with a wonderful assortment of choices. I didn't realize at the time that many of these restaurants shared a common ingredient: Oscar Grubert. This innovative entrepreneur had his hands in so many Winnipeg restaurants that it is hardly possible that anyone living in Winnipeg from the 1960s to 1980s escaped his influence. One of his most famous restaurants occupied a building in downtown Winnipeg that today stands empty and quiet, a brick and stone structure renowned for nearly 75 years for its interesting masonry.

Freemasonry is the oldest and maybe the largest male fraternal organization in the world, with origins among the stonemasons who constructed many of the fine stone buildings across Europe. Later, members who were not actual masons were accepted into the fraternity, becoming "Accepted" Masons, which is the basis for the term "AF & AM" (Ancient Free & Accepted Masons) by which Masons are sometimes known. At one time in Manitoba, it had members throughout all

A view of the former Winnipeg Masonic Temple as it appeared during road construction in June 2018. HOLLY THORNE

View of the Winnipeg Masonic Temple, 1900. ARCHIVES OF MANITOBA

strata of society, especially among the privileged classes. For instance, of the seventeen Premiers of Manitoba in our first century of provincehood, from 1870 to 1970, twelve were Masons. Organized Freemasonry came to the Red River Valley in November 1864, over five years before Manitoba became a province and two years before Canada became a nation. The first Masons in Manitoba established the Northern Light Lodge as a branch of the Grand Lodge of Minnesota, with John C. Schultz (an adversary of Louis Riel and later Lieutenant Governor of Manitoba) as Worshipful Master and merchant A. G. B. Bannatyne as Warden. In 1866, the lodge received its own charter from the Grand Lodge of Canada and, in May 1875, the Grand Lodge of Manitoba received its charter as the governing body for all other Masonic lodges around the province.

At first, the Masons met in a room above the store of their brother, A. G. B. Bannatyne. By 1894, the Grand Lodge occupied space on the top floor of the Western Canada Loan and Savings Company Building at the north-west corner of Portage Avenue and Main Street. A fire destroyed the building on 16 November 1894 and the Masons lost everything. Rather than occupy space in part of another building, the Masons decided to build their own home for the Grand Lodge of Manitoba. Excavation at the corner of Donald and Ellice began in July 1895 on what was described at the time as the only Masonic

Temple in Canada, and only the second in North America. Designed by local architect George Browne, a cornerstone was laid on 15 August 1895. By the time it was completed, it was a grand three-storey brick and stone structure. In its first floor were offices, library, banquet hall and kitchen, two large vaults, janitor's residence, lavatory, and furnace room. On the second floor were meeting halls, a general waiting room, and small rooms for educational purposes. The top floor, with a 14-foot-high ceiling, was intended for storage with two rooms for meetings of the Scottish Rite and Knights Templar, two branches of freemasonry.

The Masonic Temple was the centre of Masonic activities in Manitoba for 74 years, until 1969, when the Grand Lodge moved to a new building on the south side of Confusion Corner. The old temple was sold to a group of local investors for around $100,000 and they took possession in December 1969. Plans to open two or three "atmosphere restaurants" in it were announced, and a designer was dispatched to Europe to research what sort of restaurants they might be. In September 1971, a restaurant and dance club called The Rec Room opened, featuring lunch and dinner service in a licensed dining room and dancing until 1:00 AM on a "pulsating plexiglass dance floor." Humorous advertisements masquerading as personal classified ads were placed in local newspapers. It all sounded groovy … or should I say Grubee? The man behind it all was Oscar Grubert.

Born in 1929, at Winnipeg's St. Joseph Hospital of Polish immigrant parents, Oscar Grubert spent his

Oscar Grubert was apparently delivering buckets of his Champs fried chicken when this photo was taken in February 1964. UNIVERSITY OF MANITOBA ARCHIVES & SPECIAL COLLECTIONS

childhood at River Hills, a small village near Whitemouth in eastern Manitoba, where his father farmed and operated a general store. He attended school in Winnipeg's North End and, in 1954, received a law degree from the Manitoba Law School. He practised law until 1960, by which time he realized that his interests were elsewhere. Three years earlier, hoping to copy the success of Winnipeg's newly-opened A&W Drive-In Restaurant, Grubert had partnered with two other ambitious young lawyers, Bill Goldberg and Meyer Gilfix, to open the Champs Auto Dine on north Main Street. Its menu was diverse and the new businessmen quickly found themselves "losing their socks." While attending a restaurant industry seminar in 1958, Grubert heard about the great opportunities of a simplified menu specializing in chicken. He was advised to contact a fellow from the United States who was keen to sell franchises in such a business. He duly wrote to "Colonel" Harland Sanders of Shelbyville, Kentucky

In early 1964, Oscar Grubert opened an outlet for his Champs fried chicken in the Pembina Hotel in southern Winnipeg. The hotel still stands but the chicken is long gone GORDON GOLDSBOROUGH PHOTO COLLECTION, 2018-0015

to seek more information. Sanders came to Winnipeg—allegedly carrying a battered suitcase and checking into a fleabag hotel because he could afford nothing better—and urged Grubert and Goldberg to visit his first Canadian franchise in Saskatoon. Grubert would later say that "Bill and I borrowed the money to fly there and as we approached the location of the restaurant we saw cars

lined up three miles down the bloody street. Just to get that chicken." They returned home and signed a deal for the Manitoba franchise of Kentucky Fried Chicken. In 1959, he began selling the Colonel's "finger-lickin' good" chicken, under the name of Champ's Chicken, from an inaugural outlet at the corner of Sherbrook Street and Notre Dame Avenue. Within five years, he had six locations around the

In June 1965, Oscar Grubert opened his Champs Motor Inn in Winnipeg's Osborne Village. He envisioned it would be the flagship in a chain of entertainment hotels. Within five years, he had sold it to the Kives family (of K-Tel fame), who renamed it the Plaza Inn. The hotel, later renamed the Osborne Village Inn, has been closed since 2015. HOLLY THORNE

city, employed 135 people, and bought some 300,000 Manitoba chickens a year. By 1969, he had 500 employees and owned a chicken farm and processing plant at Neepawa. A decade later, he had 25 chicken restaurants in Manitoba, North Dakota, and Minnesota with an annual sales volume of $25 million.

There is a photo of Grubert delivering buckets of chicken, but it is unclear if he actually enjoyed his own product. He was a devout Jew and the chicken was not Kosher. Unkempt and often profane, by all accounts he was a hard worker who

would think nothing of donning an apron and pitching in when visiting one of his busy restaurants. A business profile in 1976 described him as being "still partial to crap-table fashions and expanded to Buddha-like girth, his round face has the melancholy, rather doubtful expression of someone who's just heard a prurient joke he doesn't understand." He was scrupulously honest, so much so that one of his acquaintances observed that, of all the businessmen he knew, "and I include myself, Oscar's the only one who hasn't, somewhere along the way, screwed somebody to gain

an advantage." When shown that it would be financially advantageous to sever his relationship with Kentucky Fried Chicken, he responded that "I couldn't do that to The Colonel."

Grubert grew his Winnipeg-based business into an international food and beverage empire. By the late 1970s, his Champs Food Systems Limited had 1,500 employees and 39 full-service and fast-food restaurants. He travelled widely to research new restaurant concepts that he could try in Winnipeg, arguing that if they could make it here, they would be successful anywhere. He wanted his restaurants to provide a memorable experience for customers, arguing that "next to sex, the second most enjoyable personal activity is dining out in a restaurant." He opened a succession of Winnipeg restaurants and bars through the 1960s, 1970s and 1980s with such names as Butcher Block, Koko's, Mama Trossi's, The Garden Creperie, Chances R, Thomas Button's, G. Williker's, T Bones, Sam Brero's, Carlton Street Fish Market,

Strawberries, The Palomino Club, and Blue Jeans Cabaret. Their menus were diverse, although hamburgers seemed to have been a Grubert favourite. In 1969, he bought an established drive-in restaurant called Kavanaughs and renamed it Kamps, with plans to turn it into an extensive chain throughout North America. His hopes were just as high for his Grubee's hamburger and roast beef sandwich restaurant, opened in 1975, as an attempt to develop a higher-end, fast-food format with the advertising tagline, "thank goodness for Grubees, thank Grubees for goodness." Four Grubee's were open in Winnipeg by end of 1975 with plans for three more in 1976. However, many of his restaurant ideas were abject and immediate failures. Bobby Orr's, a pizza restaurant named for the famous hockey player, and H. Salt Esq., an English-style fish and chip shop, were two such examples. Kamps also did not succeed as he had hoped. Known for "shoot-from-the-hip brand of entrepreneurship, rather than cautious market analysis," Grubert would sometimes tweak the format of a failing restaurant until its fortunes reversed. Such was the case for the old Masonic Temple.

The Rec Room, Grubert's first attempt in the old building, was not a success. Within five months of opening, Grubert reconfigured it as GG's Cabaret and Supper Club, and a few months later as GG's Cabaret and Discotheque. This version fared only slightly better, closing after about two years. In April 1975, after renovations that included construction of a two-storey kitchen addition at the back of the building, it reopened as Mother

In the era of disco and leisure suits, Grubee's restaurant on Portage Avenue, seen here in May 1979, was Oscar Grubert's innovative entry into the competitive burger market. It combined an upscale hamburger with his signature salad bar. Grubert was convinced, as he was for his other entrepreneurial ventures, that Grubee's was a recipe for success and copies would soon be opened far and wide. UNIVERSITY OF MANITOBA ARCHIVES & SPECIAL COLLECTIONS

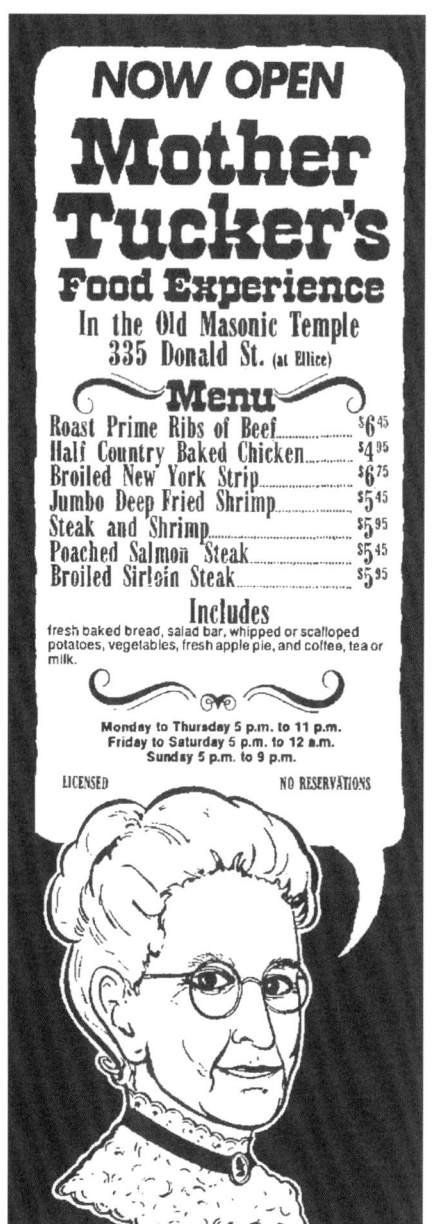

NOW OPEN

Mother Tucker's

Food Experience

In the Old Masonic Temple
335 Donald St. (at Ellice)

Menu

Roast Prime Ribs of Beef	$6⁴⁵
Half Country Baked Chicken	$4⁹⁵
Broiled New York Strip	$6⁷⁵
Jumbo Deep Fried Shrimp	$5⁴⁵
Steak and Shrimp	$5⁹⁵
Poached Salmon Steak	$5⁴⁵
Broiled Sirloin Steak	$5⁹⁵

Includes

fresh baked bread, salad bar, whipped or scalloped
potatoes, vegetables, fresh apple pie, and coffee, tea or
milk.

Monday to Thursday 5 p.m. to 11 p.m.
Friday to Saturday 5 p.m. to 12 a.m.
Sunday 5 p.m. to 9 p.m.

LICENSED   NO RESERVATIONS

Tucker's Food Experience. The idea was to provide a fine dining experience at reasonable prices. On the menu were such staples as prime rib, chicken, steak, shrimp, and fish, with a focus on all-inclusive meals, not single entrees. All diners received, in addition to their main course, fresh baked bread, whipped or scalloped potatoes, vegetables, fresh apple pie, and coffee, tea or milk. Most significantly from my perspective, Mother Tucker's offered a state-of-the-art salad bar. It featured no fewer than 60 ingredients, laid out in large bowls from which diners could take as much or as little as they liked. I recall being overwhelmed by more choices than I had ever thought possible, and seeing people walk away with plates piled high with all sorts of salad variations. On the second floor was Tucker's General Store, a fully-licensed lounge furnished in early 20th century Western general store décor. The high-ceilinged third floor was unused, at least until the 1990s, when it was equipped with 110 theatre seats, a stage, and lighting for use in "bare-bones theatrical productions." Speaking of bones, there were periodic stories through the years that the old building was haunted. A woman who worked in the foyer at Mother Tucker's, for example, claimed she heard, on numerous occasions, a person walking down the stairs from the second-floor lounge. Nobody would appear and she would check to find the staircase empty. Was it a real paranormal phenomenon, or the result of an over-active imagination or too little sleep? Personally, I am inclined to the latter point of view.

Mother Tucker's was, by far, the most successful restaurant in the Masonic Temple building, operating for 24 years, and introducing such other innovations as a roast beef

In April 1975, an early advertisement for Mother Tucker's Food Experience (before adoption of the more familiar "granny" logo) touted entrees ranging in price for $4.95 to $6.45. In addition to the chosen meat, the deal included "fresh baked bread, salad bar, whipped or scalloped potatoes, vegetables, fresh apple pie, and coffee, tea or milk." *WINNIPEG FREE PRESS,* 12 APRIL 1975, PAGE 36

carvery. When Oscar Grubert found a successful restaurant format, he worked to replicate it, by announcing grandiose plans—mostly unfulfilled—to open branches all over the continent. In the case of Mother Tucker's, he did open ones at Calgary, Edmonton, Ottawa, Toronto, and Vancouver, as well as Chez la Mère Tucker in Montreal. The name also spread into several major cities in the United States.

Although Grubert was primarily a restauranteur, he made brief forays into the sports and entertainment businesses. In July 1966, his Champion Productions brought the Rolling Stones to Winnipeg, transporting them to the Winnipeg Stadium concealed in a Champs chicken truck. He brought professional fastball to the city, naming his team the Winnipeg Colonels, and served on the Board for the World Hockey Association's Winnipeg Jets. In June 1965, Grubert opened his British-themed Champs Motor Inn in Winnipeg's Osborne Village. The first entertainer in its Rolls-Royce Lounge, an import from London, England, was picked up at the Winnipeg airport in a Rolls-Royce courtesy car. The Cock 'N Bull restaurant, with seating for 125 people, featured a barbecue for grilling steaks with a "true cooked outdoors" taste. A special ventilation system kept the room free of cooking odours. Grubert envisioned the Motor Inn would be the flagship in a chain of entertainment hotels. Within five years, however, he had sold it to the Kives family (of K-Tel fame), who renamed it the Plaza Inn. Today, it stands vacant awaiting redevelopment.

Generations of Manitobans have fond memories of Oscar Grubert's restaurants and the salad bar was one of their most memorable features. Grubert did not invent the concept of the salad bar but he certainly popularized it. In this photo from November 1978, the executive chef of Thomas Button's (centre) inspects its salad bar, along with a customer (left) and a Champs publicity director (right). UNIVERSITY OF MANITOBA ARCHIVES & SPECIAL COLLECTIONS

In the fall of 1979, Champs Food Systems celebrated its 20th anniversary by inviting the spritely 89-year-old Harland Sanders for a return visit to Winnipeg. Over the course of three days, the Colonel was photographed with scores of children who were said to have been "hardly more thrilled than if it had been Santa Claus." He took a boat cruise on the Red River with company

View of the Winnipeg Masonic Temple during its time as the home of Mother Tucker's Food Experience, February 1979. CITY OF WINNIPEG, HISTORICAL BUILDINGS AND RESOURCES COMMITTEE

management and their families, had his photo taken with the Winnipeg Colonels team, and gave hundreds of autographs. One lucky kid had her name drawn from among 100,000 entries for a free bucket of Champs chicken every Sunday for a year. (I wonder how sick of fried chicken she got after eating that much?) A little over a year later, Sanders passed away but his Kentucky Fried Chicken (rebranded as KFC a year after his death) is, today, the world's second-largest restaurant chain.

Mother Tucker's closed in 1999 and was replaced by Chris Walby's Hog City, a pork barbecue and sports bar named for the noted Blue Bombers football player. Oscar Grubert had a stake in this venture too. It operated for less than a year. In 2002, a Mexican-themed restaurant called Blue Agave Tequilaria opened and was closed by the end of the following year. Around 2004, the building was purchased by Peter Ginakes, owner of the Pony Corral restaurant chain, who promised to restore the building to its former glory. On the outside, windows were replaced, bricks were sandblasted and repointed, and a new roof was installed. When Ginakes began to restore the interior, he encountered two big problems. It lacked an elevator deemed essential for any successful redevelopment of the upper floors, and its plumbing, heating, ventilation, and air-conditioning systems were hopelessly obsolete. In early 2006, Ginakes removed the entire interior, right to the bare brick walls, leaving nothing intact. Heritage advocates were outraged but the damage was done. He intended to spend $2.5 million on renovations but nothing further happened after the building was gutted. In 2008, Ginakes leased the building to a local engineering firm that planned to turn the ground floor into retail space, possibly as a restaurant or bar, with its offices on the second floor, and six loft-style apartments on the top level. When the firm's employees balked at moving from their suburban office, plans were dropped in favour of subdividing the 16,500 square feet of space into 24 to 30 apartments. After the firm failed to exercise its option to purchase the building, it was put up for sale in 2010. Meanwhile, it has sat vacant for the past decade.

Salad bars are not nearly as common as they once were. Restauranteurs found they led to excessive food wastage that did not warrant the hard work needed to keep them clean and safe for diners. However, some places still proudly offer a salad bar. One such place is Mother Tucker's, still going strong but not in western Canada. Oscar Grubert and his son moved to Toronto where they continued the concept, having sold 19 of their KFC outlets in Manitoba back to the corporation in 1981. Grubert died in 2014 but his son Nolan carries on the family business with restaurants in Ottawa and the Toronto region. They still specialize in buffet-style meals that include the venerable salad bar along with a soup bar, bread bar, and ice cream bar. In the final analysis, Oscar Grubert's success in Winnipeg may be attributed to the fact that he catered to our legendary reputation for bargain-consciousness. We want an upscale dining experience at a cut-rate cost, and Oscar provided it. The undoing of Mother Tucker's Food Experience, at least in Winnipeg, was probably the expanding options and tougher competition that accompanied the arrival of deep-pocketed American burger and steak chains that served the same market demographic as Oscar Grubert.

Today, Winnipeggers have dining options that are far more numerous and diverse than anything in the 1970s. Nevertheless, I suspect that many readers will have fond memories of good times at one of Grubert's many restaurants. Every time that I pass the old Masonic Temple, I think of Mother Tucker's and its role in broadening my own culinary horizons. However, whenever I really want to remember Grubert and his many contributions to Manitoba's restaurant landscape, much as I might enjoy a salad, it will be with fried chicken.

ACKNOWLEDGEMENTS

Thanks to Lewis St. George Stubbs and his dogged digging in the University of Manitoba Archives, and especially its *Winnipeg Tribune* collection, I had much more information on Oscar Grubert and his numerous business ventures than I had expected when I began working on this chapter. Avrum Rosner shared his memory of seeing Mick Jagger step out of a Champs chicken truck. Shelley Ostrove spoke with me about his experiences working as Grubert's publicity man.

In 2006, the interior of the former Masonic Temple was gutted so the building could be brought up to modern building codes. The fir studs and floor joints are visible in this photo of the second storey taken nearly a decade later, in April 2015. CITY OF WINNIPEG, HISTORICAL BUILDINGS AND RESOURCES COMMITTEE

York Factory

Aerial view of York Factory in 1923, looking northeast toward Hudson Bay. Since this photo was taken, a large portion of the riverbank has disappeared. HUDSON'S BAY COMPANY ARCHIVES

My most memorable experience last summer was sitting in the stern of a speedboat on the mighty Nelson River, downstream of Manitoba Hydro's Limestone Generating Station. I stared at the twin wakes of its gas-guzzling engines as they propelled us with the collective thrust of 830 horsepower toward Hudson Bay, at heady speeds of up to 50 miles per hour. As we passed mile after mile of pristine boreal forest along the river banks, I could not help but think how fast, comfortable, and incredibly fun my experience was compared to those of travellers from centuries past. They had to endure weeks of manual paddling to get to York Factory, a former fur trade post at the mouth of the historic Hayes River, about 550 miles northeast as the crow flies from Winnipeg.

York Factory, also known by the Cree name Kihci-wâskâhikan ("the Great House") and known originally as York Fort, was arguably the most important site in western Canada relating to the fur trade by the Hudson's Bay Company (HBC). Starting in the late 1600s, it was the primary place where trade goods from England were delivered then shipped inland to posts all over the HBC domain. In turn, furs taken in trade from Indigenous peoples were collected here for shipment back to England to be made into coats, hats, and other apparel. The name Factory does not mean it was an industrial site. Instead, it was the residence of a Factor, an archaic British term for

the overseas manager of a commercial enterprise, in the same way that the residence of an Anglican Rector is a Rectory. The original York Factory, referred to by historians as "York Factory I," was first established in 1684 on the north bank of the Hayes River, next to a small creek, about five miles inland from the river mouth. Damaged by shifting spring ice, in 1715 it was moved farther inland to "York Factory II," remaining there until a severe flood in May 1788 convinced the Factor to move to higher ground half a mile upstream, the present-day site of "York Factory III." There, the post remained in operation until 1957 when it was closed permanently.

There were once as many as 50 buildings at York Factory, but today, the largest survivor, the Depot, was constructed between 1831 and 1838 to replace an earlier structure, making it roughly 180 years old. It is the oldest wooden building in western Canada. (A close contender, the second-oldest wooden building, is the Grey Nuns Convent in Winnipeg, built between 1845 and 1851.) Despite its age, the Depot is solid. When I visited it in 2017, one of my travel companions remarked that none of its floors squeaked when he walked over them. The building is huge—measuring 100 feet by 105 feet, and enclosing about

Some of the graves in the York Factory cemetery have stone markers but the vast majority, mostly those of Indigenous people who lived and worked there, are unmarked. A few died from infectious diseases such as tuberculosis but concerns over the release of disease pathogens as the cemetery eroded are probably unfounded. GORDON GOLDSBOROUGH

18,000 square feet of space—and mostly two storey except for one part that has three, with a lookout on top where workers could see approaching vessels from Hudson Bay and Indigenous people coming to trade. Because of its massive size, the Depot was designed with windows facing into a central courtyard. This provided interior lighting as a better alternative to candles, which could be dangerous in a wooden structure. Furs taken in trade were stored in a series of buildings to the south of the Depot while other goods were kept in warehouses on the north side. Between the warehouses, in front of the Depot, was an extensive food garden surrounded by a picket fence and an enormous flagstaff. The entire site was surrounded by a wooden palisade barely taller than a man. It had mostly fallen by 1916, when the remainder was removed.

Beyond the palisade were homes of the resident Muskego Cree and Metis workers and their families, called the Home Guard Cree by the HBC. There was a church mission

school for Indigenous children and an Anglican church, a "blubber house" for rendering fat from beluga whales caught in Hudson Bay into oil for on-site lighting and sale, tradesman's shops, a boat house, a carpenter's shop, and a stable. Near the church was a cemetery containing the graves of at least 160 fur traders and Indigenous people, and a stone building for storing gunpowder far enough away from the main facility to minimize the risk from explosions. Its stout walls were constructed between 1838 and 1840 of locally quarried limestone, bricks imported from England, and stone nicked from Prince of Wales Fort at Churchill.

Water was (and is) a persistent problem at York Factory. The entire region is covered with at least three feet of peat with a thin layer of vegetation on top so that, when you walk anywhere, your feet sink into the wet, spongey ground. Historically, drains were dug to help in conducting water away from buildings, including an elaborate wooden collector drain in the courtyard of the Depot. Drain maintenance was a perennial job of post workers, and HBC carpenters built boardwalks between most of the buildings to make it easier to walk on the springy ground. Beneath the surface, two or three feet down, the soil of silt and fine sand is frozen year-round—called permafrost—which would have been a major impediment to burying people in York Factory's cemetery. I will come back to this topic later.

The size of the resident European population at York Factory varied over time, peaking at around 60 by 1860. Most were single men under contract to the HBC although a few married officers brought their wives. There were children, some the product of relationships between HBC men and local Indigenous women. Scots— from the mainland or offshore archipelagos of Orkney, Shetland, and Hebrides—generally comprised over half the total population. They worked long, hard days in the period from April to mid-October, when the shipments of supplies arrived from Britain. Ships anchored in Hudson Bay, two miles offshore in a spot called "Five-fathom Hole," because the Hayes River was too shallow. Packages were offloaded into small, flat-bottomed skiffs that could operate in water as shallow as four feet, and transported to York Factory to be carried into warehouses for temporary storage. Eventually, they were redistributed and shipped out in York boats heading upstream on the Hayes to HBC posts as far east as Fort William (today, Thunder Bay) and as far west as the Rockies. Furs returned to York Factory from inland

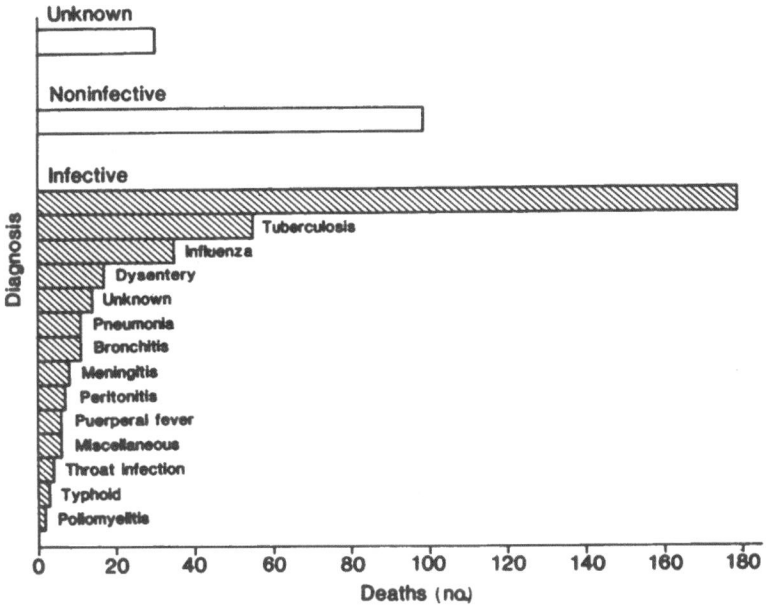

Causes of death of people (European and Indigenous) at York Factory between 1801 and 1900, determined from post logs and other sources, by Dr. William B. Ewart. *CAN. MED. ASSOC. J.*, 1983.

posts were packed, stamped or burned with a distinctive YF brand, and loaded for the voyage back to Britain. Winters were comparatively less busy and time was spent producing trade goods and provisioning the factory with firewood, fish, game, and other necessities. The work week was usually six days, with Sunday as the day for rest and religious ceremonies. Ten to 14 days of holiday were interspersed through the year, on Coronation Day, St. George's Day, Easter, and Christmas, and sometimes also Guy Fawkes Day, the reigning monarch's birthday, and St. Andrew's Day.

The 16,000-square-foot Depot Building, built between 1831 and 1838, and shown here in July 2017, was the main structure at York Factory, housing the trading store and warehouse space. Most of it was two storeys except for a three-storey portion with a lookout at the top that provides a panoramic view of the surrounding area. It is among the oldest, if not the oldest, surviving wooden building in Manitoba. Boardwalks surrounding the building, and around the site, facilitate walking on the wet, spongey peat that covers the entire area. GORDON GOLDSBOROUGH

To keep people working at peak efficiency, workers generally ate well, and some of the officers were said to have attained generous proportions. Sugar, tea, and oatmeal were imported from Britain but the bulk of food consumed at York Factory was obtained locally or shipped from inland posts. Despite the shortness of the growing season at this northern latitude, and the prevailing wetness of the soil, crops of turnips and, less commonly, potatoes, carrots, onions, parsnips, radishes, horseradish, buckwheat, peas, beans, cucumbers, cabbages, lettuce, endive, mustard, cress, flax, and barley were grown with limited success in the factory's gardens. (It is even rumoured that dandelions were imported from Scotland as a source of hardy greens and a treatment for scurvy, and they thrived to become a tenacious weed.) Domestic animals kept as a meat source included geese, turkeys, and chickens, with a few pigs and cattle, while the Home Guard Cree working for the HBC hunted for wild geese, caribou, ducks, and other waterfowl, and caught whitefish, jack, and other fish. They also carried mail between posts, tended the gardens and gathered wild hay for the livestock, rafted wood cut upstream on the Hayes down to the post, and helped to load and unload freight. Medical afflictions—accidents on the job and various communicable and non-communicable diseases—were generally no more common than in other communities at that time.

Leisure time was spent variously. Some men competed in foot races, played matches of an early version of football, swam, boated, skated, or snowshoed. Those inclined to quieter pursuits played cards, chess, checkers, cribbage, or dominoes. A post library opened in 1856, providing newspapers, magazines, and books for those who were literate, and letter writing was popular. More cultured gentlemen, usually among the officers, conducted scientific experiments and made astronomical and meteorological observations. Some collected specimens of local plants and animals for scientific study. Gambling, drinking, fighting, and general carousing were the preferred pastimes of a few, with the social ills that typically accompanied them.

To the Europeans who stayed at York Factory for periods ranging from weeks to years, it was an outpost of civilization surrounded by vast expanses of wilderness. Some viewed it favourably; others were not so impressed. Letitia Hargrave, wife of Chief Factor James Hargrave, wrote in 1849 that York Factory was "by far the most respectable place in the Territory." Another resident noted that he "took leave of Fort York, its fogs, and bogs, and mosquitoes, with little regret." I cannot speak to the prevalence of fog, but I certainly witnessed the bogs, and the mosquitoes were absolutely fearsome during the night we spent in a building near the Depot (within a fenced compound to protect against wandering polar bears).

By the late 19th century, as boats and railways began operating in southern Manitoba, it was becoming more efficient to supply northern HBC posts from the south. York Factory's status as the HBC's administrative and provisioning centre began to erode. The staff complement declined from the 1870s. Relegated to a district headquarters, it was demoted further in 1901 when the

former York Factory and Norway House districts were combined into a single Keewatin district with headquarters at Norway House. (York Factory regained headquarters status in 1911, as part of the HBC's Nelson River district, losing it again when the railway arrived at Churchill in 1929.) Maintenance of the buildings

and drains was neglected. The powder magazine's floor collapsed in 1905 and, henceforth, the limited quantities of gunpowder passing through the facility were stored in the Depot. By the end, the once-grand factory was a mere trading post in the HBC's extensive network, staffed by a handful of people. In 1933, it lost

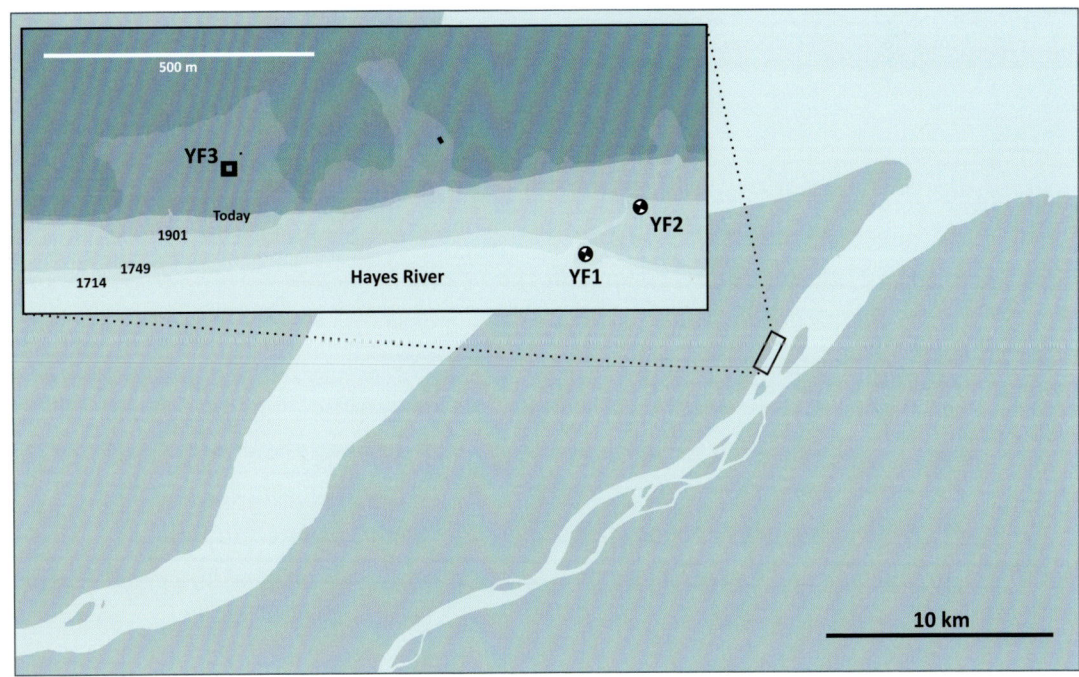

The York Factory site, on the north shore at the mouth of the Hayes River, has been prone to marked riverbank erosion since its establishment in 1684. The locations of the shoreline as it may have appeared in 1714, 1749, 1901, and today are shown. As a result of erosion, the sites of York Factory #1 (1684–1715) and York Factory #2 (1715–1788) are now in in the river. REDRAWN FROM MAPS IN THOMSON AND STEPHEN (2010) AND THE ARCHIVES OF MANITOBA

Rapid erosion of the riverbank at York Factory, seen here in June 2005, is putting the historic Depot Building at risk. KEN SKAFTFELD

the customs port of entry that it had had since the 1880s. Designated as a National Historic Site in 1936, the Depot closed as a fur trade facility in June 1957, ending 169 continuous years of trading, by which time all the outbuildings were gone except for the power magazine (now roofless), a small wooden library and a few other buildings dating from the early to mid-20th century.

The Home Guard Cree relocated inland, to Shamattawa, Split Lake, York Landing, and other places, and today their descendants are members of Fox Lake Cree Nation, Shamattawa First Nation, Tataskwayak Cree Nation, War Lake First Nation, and York Factory First Nation. Without resident guardians, vandalism ensued. From 1959 to 1962, the HBC leased the land, excluding the Depot, to a company pensioner who agreed to protect it from damage, while the company initiated discussions with the federal government about taking over the site. Designated as a provincial historic site in 1960, there was no tangible progress for several years. It took an outsider to get things moving. In 1966, a member of the Minnesota Historical Society visited York Factory and was sufficiently alarmed by its dilapidated state that he wrote to Premier Duff Roblin. That letter is credited with provoking provincial, federal, and company officials to reach an agreement. In July 1968, in a ceremony at Lower Fort Garry, the HBC sold the deed to the Depot and its land for $1 to Jean Chretien, the newly appointed Northern Affairs minister. Chrétien accepted the transfer but did not commit to any development, arguing that the site would first have to became more accessible.

York Factory remains as inaccessible today as when Chrétien took possession 50 years ago. Staffed by two seasonal Parks Canada employees from June and mid-September, the government does routine maintenance, makes repairs when resources permit and where disaster looms (such as when the rotting drain in the Depot's courtyard began to collapse in 2002), and provides tours to visitors who, given the remote location, are not especially numerous. In 2016, for example, just 232 people—three-quarters of them from Manitoba—signed a guest book in the Depot. The biggest threat to the site is the nearby riverbank, which is eroding at an alarming rate of up to three feet per year, caused by a combination of ice scouring during the spring melt, wave action during the open-water period, and unstable permafrost underlying the entire area. This is not a new problem, having been the reason for the abandonment of the previous sites of York Factory, between 1684 and 1788. Those two spots are now on the bottom of the Hayes River, several hundred feet from shore. Comparison of the site today with photos taken in the 1920s indicate that over 160 feet of the land between the Depot and the Hayes River has been lost in the past 90 years and, if erosion continues at its present rate, Parks Canada estimates the Depot will topple into the river within 100 years. It is unknown to what extent the melting of permafrost due to global climate warming will cause erosion rates to accelerate so the demise of the Depot may happen even sooner.

An engineering study in the early 1980s concluded that the only viable means to stabilize the riverbank would be to armour several hundred feet of shoreline, upstream and downstream of the Depot, using large boulders. The approach, calling riprapping, would cost in the range of $1.9 to $2.7 million depending on the source and method of delivery of the stones. A group of geotechnical engineers who volunteered their time to re-examine the problem in 2005 endorsed the earlier conclusion, and

raised the cost to $4 to $6 million based on inflation. As an alternative, they proposed a less costly means of shoreline armouring using a timber wall combined with grading the upper bank slope and covering it with erosion control blankets. This would protect against "sunny day" erosion but would be largely ineffective against "extreme spring thaw and ice jam events." Essentially, the protection of York Factory will be enormously costly, if done properly. One is left to wonder if the expense is warranted given the limited budget under which Parks Canada is presently operating—dollars spent protecting York Factory will be taken from worthwhile projects elsewhere—and the relatively few visitors who will benefit. Meanwhile, Parks Canada has adopted a "managed salvage approach" in which archaeologists have identified, through systematic

At low tide, numerous metal artifacts arising from centuries of human occupation at York Factory can be seen littering the exposed mudflat at the base of the eroding riverbank, June 2005. KEN SKAFTFELD

Tables inside the Depot Building at York Factory display some of the wide array of artifacts revealed by shoreline erosion, July 2017. GORDON GOLDSBOROUGH

excavations in the 1970s and early 1980s, and detection of shallowly buried objects using ground-penetrating radar, important historical resources to be removed as they are threatened by erosion. Drains and pumps installed beneath the Depot and in the cemetery in the 1990s help to keep them as dry as possible.

One of the intriguing aspects of the bank erosion at York Factory is the potential impact on its old cemetery. Graves from the original two sites have already been washed away and it is likely the present one will be eroded too. In 1983, Winnipeg physician William Ewart published a paper on the causes of death among residents of York Factory, based on his examination of records kept by its Factors and Manager between 1714 and 1946. His concern was that some of those people died from infectious diseases such as typhoid, tuberculosis, influenza, pneumonia, and dysentery. For example, six Indigenous people

died of smallpox in July 1782. If their bodies were buried in ground that subsequently froze, they would not decompose as would happen otherwise. If microorganisms responsible for the fatal diseases could survive in a frozen state, this would mean, when erosion caused some of the bodies to be revealed, the disease agents would be released, putting at risk the health of people at York Factory today. Naturally, Parks Canada staff were alarmed by this possibility so they commissioned a consultant to investigate it more fully. In his report, never made widely public, he conceded that he could comment only on the "burial locations, burial practises, and the likelihood of bodies being preserved in a frozen state," and not on the possible survival of disease-causing microorganisms. The cemetery site was probably chosen specifically because, unlike the surrounding area that was entirely underlain by permafrost, it was not fully frozen so would have made for easier grave digging. Deceased people would have likely been buried in shallow graves, only to a depth of a foot or two, where full decomposition would occur. He concluded the probability of re-infection from exposed corpses was low.

In the meantime, erosion is revealing numerous long-buried metal artifacts from the slumping face of the riverbank in front of the Depot. During our visit to York Factory, we saw a display of such things as cannon balls, musket balls, and a large whipsaw. We arrived late in the day and were toured around the site by Parks staff. We saw the cemetery, remains of the powder magazine, and the Depot, one of only two intact buildings still standing.

(The other is the library.) We were told it was used mainly as a warehouse, with trading taking place in a separate building, but that a room on its main floor was eventually turned into a store during the declining period in its history. After a barbecue hosted by our boat driver, we bedded down for a few hours of restless sleep, in my case being awoken very early by the aforementioned mosquitoes. I got up to wander around and send up my drone for some aerial photos. As the tide came in by 8:30 AM, we were on our way home, having been there for barely 15 hours.

As we rocketed back to the boat launch by the Limestone Generating Station, I thought about the site and what it represents for the history of Manitoba. Without York Factory and its logistical support for inland fur traders, the development of southern Manitoba would have played out quite differently. Without Europeans arriving from the north, the prevailing influence would have come eventually from the east, from eastern Canada and the United States. Whether or not western Canada would have come under British rule is debatable, and without the arrival of Scottish farmers in 1812—who passed through York Factory on their way south to settle near the confluence of the Red and Assiniboine rivers—the ethnic composition of our province would have been altered markedly. The Red River Settlement established a bulwark of the British Empire in western Canada that helped to thwart the expansionist tendencies of our neighbours to the south. The trading relationships formed across the northern plains by HBC traders—most of whom retained British loyalties, and who retired to the Red River Settlement—meant the sentiment of this region through the 1800s remained more closely allied to that of Britain than to the United States that was newly enlarged by vast territory acquired in the Louisiana Purchase. Had circumstances of the past two centuries been even a wee bit different, Manitobans today might be declaring their allegiance to the flag of the United States of America. In short, York Factory had a profound effect on almost everything about conditions here today. Consequently, I think we should play greater attention to this overlooked spot that, in the not-too-distant future, will be lost forever to the erosive power of the Hayes River.

ACKNOWLEDGEMENTS

My understanding of York Factory benefitted enormously from information provided by Bob Coutts, Sharon Thomson, and Chris Kotecki. Mike Payne's excellent book *The Most Respectable Place in the Territory* describes daily life at York Factory during its most active years. Geotechnical engineer Ken Skaftfeld generously shared his files from a fact-finding visit to York Factory and its eroding riverbank in June 2005. I thank Ryan Bernier, Glen Cook, Dave Ennis, Chris Thompson, and Reed Winstone for their camaraderie during our July 2017 expedition to York Factory, and Clint Sawchuk and his sidekick Wayne "Grizz" Bjorndalen for getting us there and back, safely and very, very quickly.

A road sign that I found south of Deloraine in October 2011 urged caution when approaching a monument for the former Croydon one-room schoolhouse. GORDON GOLDSBOROUGH

Conclusion

You and I have travelled a lot of territory together in the course of this book. At this point, I could conclude—as I did with my previous book *Abandoned Manitoba*—with some general remarks about how abandoned places illustrate the ways in which Manitoba has changed through the years, ranging from our evolving transportation network to rural depopulation and the agricultural production of food. However, I am worried about the present state of affairs in the study of Manitoba's history so I would like to leave you with two weighty questions to ponder. How should we respond to a looming crisis in Manitoba's museums and archives as repositories of our collective memory? What should be the roles of government and the general public in the commemoration of historic places? I will tackle each of these questions in turn.

How We Dis(re)member the Past— The Decline of Memory

Museum and archives are essential to the practice of history. Both are important repositories of historical artifacts, documents, books, and other items. If there is a distinction to be made, it is the standard of care. The primary focus of a museum is to present its collections for public viewing and pay less attention to how those items are preserved. I do not mean to imply that museums do not care for their collections or do not have materials in storage. In fact, museums often have sizable collections that the general public rarely sees. Regretfully, the conditions under which museum collections are stored, especially ones in small communities, are frequently less than ideal. The focus of archives, on the other hand, is to protect items under conditions that preserve them for the future, without necessarily making them readily available to the public. An archive is less about presentation, and more about protection. Some archives do have public

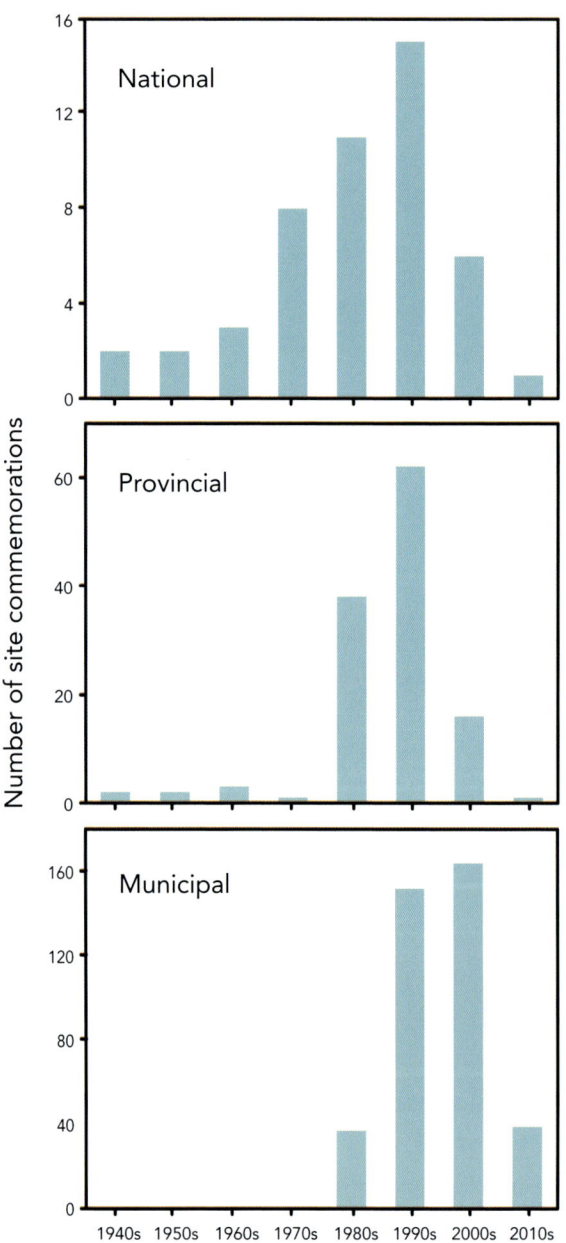

The trends in commemoration of historically significant sites, at the federal, provincial, and municipal levels in Manitoba, show a marked decline in the past decade GORDON GOLDSBOROUGH

outreach programs and, unfortunately, some do not provide storage conditions any better than those of museums. Generally, there are many more museums than archives in Manitoba and most communities, especially smaller ones, have them as a combined facility. For the sake of my argument, therefore, I will treat museums and archives as the same. Many of the smaller ones are, in my view, at risk of closing which puts their collections in jeopardy. The important and unique information they preserve will be lost if provision is not made for its transfer elsewhere. Some have already closed and more will follow in the near term. Why? The reasons are many and I will list them a little later.

But wait, you ask, why is he talking about museums when this book is about abandonment? The reason is that the story behind each of the places we visited in this book did not spring fully-formed from my mind. Each was the result of many hours of research in libraries, museums, and archives. If we lose any of these facilities and the collections they hold, it seems to me, we lose essential knowledge about ourselves. If you are, like me, a person who finds history fascinating, you should be concerned by anything that threatens our store of historical information on which future stories will be based. Manitoba has more than 200 museums and at least 25 archives and these statistics are undoubtedly underestimates because they do not include small, informal ones. (For example, I like to think that I have a rather nice little archive developing in my basement. It is not counted here.) Many of them date back decades and started as a result of modest, grassroots efforts. When they are gone, nothing will replace them.

I will illustrate my point with two museums, both now closed. The first is the Chapman Museum located about twelve miles northwest of Brandon. Like several other museums in Manitoba, the Chapman Museum was founded by a farmer with a penchant for collecting. Albert "Ab" Chapman and his wife Harriet had been collecting for years when they decided, in 1967, to open their collection to public viewing as a Canadian centennial project. Ab Chapman was a busy guy. In addition to running his farm, he was a councillor and reeve for the Rural Municipality of Daly for 42 years, from 1950 to 1992. He was president of the Union of Manitoba Municipalities (1974 to 1979). He served on the board for the Ninette Sanatorium and was a member of the Manitoba Municipal Board. Along the way, he also found time to raise three children. By all accounts, he was passionate about local history. When his wife died in 1979, he redoubled his efforts to preserve and present history through his private museum. In time, it consisted of sixteen historic buildings, all over a century old, including no fewer than *five* one-room schoolhouses, a general store, an Anglican church, a blacksmith shop, railway buildings (from the former siding of Pendennis), pioneer homes, and a wide array of farm and domestic equipment documenting prairie life at the turn of the 20th century. The Chapman Museum was open seven days a week, year round (by appointment in the winter) and no admission was charged although donations were welcome. In 1986, he had more than 900 visitors. This was clearly a labour of love. In 2014, a year after Ab Chapman died, his daughter and her husband, who lived on his original farmstead and operated the museum for several years while he was in declining health, closed it after 47 years in operation.

Another rural museum, also started by a farmer passionate about preserving our local history and heritage, closed in 2014. In this case, he had begun collecting in 1945 and he opened it during Manitoba's centennial year, 1970. His museum featured houses from several time periods, a former railway station, and a church, along with over 80,000 artifacts including farm equipment, vehicles, and tools. I had a personal connection to this museum. My grandparents helped to renovate some of its buildings and machinery, and my sister worked there during the summer, giving tours, cutting grass, and doing other light maintenance. After he died, his family continued to operate the museum for another 22 years. They are now in the process of winding up the museum and have asked me not to identify it until they complete arrangements for the dispersal of its collections. This is an important part of the story.

What happens to the contents of a museum when it closes? To some extent, the operators are at liberty to do as they see fit. One option is to return donated items to the original donors or their descendants. This is often not possible, or desirable, so the conscientious ones try to find another museum to take them. The sticking point is that the receiving museum should accept donations in good faith, as a contribution to their ongoing collections. Antiques and

other collectibles can have considerable monetary value so the donor museums try to ensure their donations stay in the public domain and do not end up in someone's private collection. Only as a last resort are items sold, given away, or discarded. For example, I helped the folks at the Chapman Museum transfer a collection of precious school district records from the early 20th century to the provincial archives and a pair of beautiful school banners to the Manitoba Museum. A unique collection of Manitoba-made bricks has been given to a museum at Argyle where, one day, we hope there will be an exhibit on local brickmaking. Meanwhile, the family that is shutting down the undisclosed museum (which had basic deaccession policies in place) is doing an admirable job—more onerous than I think they realized at the start—at finding good and appropriate museum homes for as much of its collection as possible. Numerous museums and archives across Canada, large and small, have been grateful recipients of thousands of its artifacts.

My two example museums illustrate the challenges faced by small facilities all over Manitoba. It is a virtual certainty there will be more casualties in the years ahead, attributable to one or more of at least six reasons. First, museums are frequently established as a result of single-generation enthusiasm with little to no long-range succession planning. If the facility is started by a group, there is at least some possibility it will continue when one of the founders moves, dies, or loses interest. I wonder if either of the founders for my two examples gave any thought to the burden he was imposing on the other members of

There are lots more abandoned places to see in Manitoba. This aerial view shows the long-abandoned Salt Plains race track along Yellowhead Highway #16, where from 1966 to about 1983, the Gladstone Stock Car Club raced stock cars. In July 1968, a 23-year-old school teacher from Gladstone was killed when his car went out of control and slammed into a safety barricade made of heavy wooden poles. When I took this picture in July 2017, the former track was a livestock pasture. In places, its edges were still marked by automobile and tractor tires, some embedded in rows in the ground. GORDON GOLDSBOROUGH

The sun sets, literally and figuratively, on the Chapman Museum in this photo from September 2017. HOLLY THORNE

his family? It was entirely understandable that they might grow tired and resentful of the commitment that their forebear made for them, perhaps years before they were born.

Second, museums should be mindful of an old maxim from the real estate business that everything depends on location, location, location. A museum in a farmyard, far from a busy paved highway, far from a major urban centre, is unlikely to attract many visitors. Increasingly, gravelled roads (or, heaven forbid, dirt roads) are seen as a major impediment by city-dwellers who

are unfamiliar with them. Neither of my examples was in a particular good spot to attract anything but local visitors who were already aware of them. Even well-designed road signs in strategic spots can do only so much to convince a traveller to drive miles out of their way.

Third, most museums are partially or wholly dependent on volunteers to staff the facility, answer questions, lead tours, do maintenance, and perform a myriad of other tasks. Most organizations that depend on volunteers report increasing difficulty in finding and keeping

them. In an increasingly self-centred world, volunteerism is not so popular anymore. Volunteers are growing older and less able to help. All but the most dedicated volunteers are subject to eventual "burn-out."

Fourth, unless a museum has explicit, multi-year financial support from municipal or provincial governments, it is dependent on a diminishing number of one-time grants, bequests, and other unpredictable funding. This is never a good formula for longevity. Museum operators who brag about never having accepted public dollars to support their operation are either independently wealthy or delusional.

Fifth, museums must stake out a niche that makes them unique among the many other facilities vying for public attention. Far too often, museums try to have a little of everything so there is nothing to distinguish them from a host of others offering exactly the same things. If there are two places with the same stuff, and one is conveniently located, the other one does not stand a chance. At the same time, museum displays cannot be static. Unless new things are offered from time to time, what is the incentive for anyone to visit more than once?

Sixth and finally, many museums are unwilling to confront the reality of declining public interest, attendance, and revenue. People visit museums because they are interested in what they will see there and museums must change to ensure what they offer is compelling to each new generation. If museum attendance is motivated by nostalgia for items on display, what will happen when people no longer have emotional connections to them? Take, for example, the butter churn that is a staple of many rural museums. Once widely used to turn cream into butter, they are popular to museum visitors who have first-hand experience using them in their youth. Today, very few people have ever used one. Rural depopulation means there are many fewer people with agrarian roots who will find old agricultural implements from Manitoba's "Settlement Period" fascinating. Museums that focus solely on this period are, in my view, ultimately doomed.

I do not claim to have a solution to the problems facing small museums around Manitoba, and every situation is different, but there are a few things to keep in mind. In my view, it is better to have a few well-funded, stable facilities than many under-funded, unsustainable ones. It is preferable to keep artifacts and archival documents in regional facilities in each major part of the province rather than in just a few, huge repositories.

A justifiable complaint that I hear regularly in rural Manitoba is that, all too often, precious items end up in Winnipeg where they are far away and subject to limited hours of availability. However, keeping them locally incurs an obligation to provide suitable conditions for storage. Proper storage of historical materials means providing not just *any* space, but a space with proper standards for long-term preservation. This means an environment with constant temperature and humidity; security against microbial, insect, and rodent pests; and measures to avoid or minimize such disasters as broken water pipes, leaking roofs, and theft. Basements, for example, are the worst possible place to put important historical documents. (Yes, I know, I am guilty of this with my personal archive.) When a facility is operating, there should be opportunities for professional development and networking of its personnel so they can keep abreast of new approaches and challenges. Most importantly, I think, addressing the dilemma facing museums and archives will require creativity and collaboration at all levels, and although I believe that government leadership is essential, there should be genuine public involvement in the planning process.

The crux of the problem—the disservice we do to future generations when we allow precious historical treasures to end up in a dumpster—is that small museums and archives are closing at the same time as larger facilities are getting full or have a narrowing collection mandate, and are consequently turning away important materials.

The Abandonment of Historical Commemoration

There are several named highways in Manitoba, including the Pine to Palm Highway (#75, known in the United States as the Jefferson Highway, from Winnipeg to New Orleans), Trans-Canada Highway (#1), Yellowhead Highway (#16), and Red Coat Trail (#2). However, I suspect that few people know about the Northern Woods and Water Route (NWWR). Designated in 1974, the NWWR is 1,500 miles in length and runs from Winnipeg to Dawson Creek, BC. From the Perimeter Highway, the NWWR travels on #6 into the Interlake through Lundar and Eriksdale, onto #68 across The Narrows through Ste. Rose du Lac, on #5 through Dauphin, then north on #10 through Ethelbert, Swan River and The Pas, finally heading into Saskatchewan.

In August 1980, the Manitoba government acknowledged the eastern end of the route by developing a small wayside park alongside Highway #6 just outside Winnipeg's Perimeter Highway, in the Rural Municipality of Rosser. An opening ceremony was attended by Don Orchard, the Minister of Highways and Transportation in the government of Sterling Lyon. The park had a small parking lot, a handful of trees, probably an Orbit trash receptacle, and a concrete monument with the NWWR logo embedded in it, with a metal plaque that described the route and its significance to tourism. Unfortunately, interest in the NWWR seems to have petered out by the late 1990s as I could find no press coverage of it after 1999. Interest in the little wayside park waned correspondingly.

A monument for the Northern Woods and Water Route, unveiled along Highway #6 in August 1980, is an example of commemoration gone awry. In the nine years since I first visited it, the site has looked like this photo from June 2018. GORDON GOLDSBOROUGH

Today, the road into it is overgrown and you have to walk through knee-high grass to reach the monument. For all intents and purposes, it has been abandoned. This troubles me because I feel that whomever installs a monument incurs an obligation to maintain or remove it. An abandoned monument is a public statement that its subject is no longer worthy of commemoration.

A monument, plaque, or sign can be a useful way to preserve the memory of an important historical site, even if no vestige of it remains. Around Manitoba, there are many sites that have been commemorated as important by one or more level of government. At last count, 55 sites had been designated by the federal government (as well as 21 historic events and 40 historic persons), 126 by

Northern Manitoba is disproportionately littered with abandoned facilities, such as this gymnasium floor at the 1980s construction camp for Manitoba Hydro's Limestone Generating Station on the Nelson River downstream of Gillam, August 2017. MARIA ZBIGNIEWICZ

the provincial government, and 649 by one of the many municipal governments (excluding the City of Winnipeg). There is a distinct trend in these commemorations over time and, unfortunately, it is a worrisome one. All levels of government, with one exception, have slowed or stopped their involvement with historical commemoration. (The exception is the City of Winnipeg which is busily designating historic buildings, especially in its downtown core.) The federal government still designates the odd place, person, or event in Manitoba but there are curious delays in its activity. It took 26 years, for instance, for the Metropolitan Theatre in Winnipeg to receive its plaque in early 2018, though the official designation was made in 1991. The provincial government made only eight designations from the 1940s to 1970s, then became actively engaged in the 1980s (38) and 1990s (62). The total dropped to 16 in the 2000s. So far, eight years into the 2010s, it has made only one designation, in 2011 and seems disinclined to make any more. In fact, damaged plaques from several previous designations have been removed and are in storage.

I have been told they will stay there until the unlikely day there are funds to restore them. Today, suggestions to the provincial government to designate places of historical importance are politely referred to the pertinent municipal government for consideration. Unfortunately, at the municipal level, the record of activity is about the same as for the province as a whole. Outside of Winnipeg, there were no municipally-designated historic sites until the 1980s, when 37 were selected. The "golden age" of municipal designation was in the 1990s (152) and 2000s (164), but has dropped to a mere 39 in the 2010s.

What is happening? Does the marked drop in historical designations in the past decade mean there are no more deserving places to be designated in Manitoba? I doubt it. I can think of numerous things that warrant recognition. One example: the role of bridges in the development of Manitoba's highway network; see the chapter on the Gervais Bridge in my previous book. Instead, I think it is evidence that the provincial government sees its priorities to be in other areas than the commemoration of heritage. Municipalities could fill the gap at the local level but, for the most part, they lack expertise and advice on what to do. They usually only act reactively, not proactively.

In the meantime, grass roots efforts such as the project that I have led for the Manitoba Historical Society over the past nine years are ongoing. The MHS project to map historic sites does not entail the erection of monuments, plaques, or signs but it serves the same underlying purpose: it draws public attention to important historical places. In fact, I believe we are democratizing the process of designating historic sites by putting responsibility in public hands. Our inventory of historic sites numbers 6,931 as I write this and the total grows daily. Why wait for a government to put its official stamp of approval on an historic site when it is possible for us to do it now? I encourage everyone, including you readers, to visit our interactive map of historic sites (http://www.mhs.mb.ca/sites), see what it is missing based on your experience, and contact me at www.abandonedmanitoba.ca to add them. We all benefit from capturing information about obscure places that have historical interest, and future generations will benefit from preserving information that may only exist in the heads of a few people who will soon be gone.

It is June 2018 as I finish this last paragraph and I am itching to hit the road in search of places to add to our historic inventory. I have 253 sites on my personal "to find" list and I would rather be out climbing around old abandoned buildings than writing about them. If you are similarly inspired, I encourage you to head out. Manitoba is a beautiful province and there is so much to see if you are adventurous and not dissuaded by dirt roads. Make sure, when you do, to take along your camera—and ideally a GPS receiver to get geographic coordinates for the sites you find—so you can share them. Maybe you and I will meet somewhere out there and explore together the many stories of abandoned Manitoba.

Appendix: Site Coordinates

Additional information and photos for each of the sites are available on the website of the Manitoba Historical Society at the web links shown.

CHAPTER	SITE	LATITUDE	LONGITUDE	URL
Assiniboine River Pillar	Assiniboine River Pillar	49.84287	-99.85119	http://www.mhs.mb.ca/docs/sites/gtpbridgepier.shtml
Bowsman Biffy Burn	Bowsman Biffy Burn Monument	52.23504	-101.21320	http://www.mhs.mb.ca/docs/sites/biffieburn.shtml
Brookeville Quarry	Brookeville Quarry	49.62626	-95.60007	http://www.mhs.mb.ca/docs/sites/brookevillequarry.shtml
Caddy Lake Airfield	Caddy Lake Airfield	49.84102	-95.18781	http://www.mhs.mb.ca/docs/sites/caddylakeairfield.shtml
Camp Hughes	Camp Hughes	49.87846	-99.56034	http://www.mhs.mb.ca/docs/sites/camphughes.shtml
Churchill Naval Building	Churchill Naval Building	58.74762	-94.12045	http://www.mhs.mb.ca/docs/sites/churchillnavalbase.shtml
Conclusion	Limestone Gym Floor	56.52115	-94.12930	http://www.mhs.mb.ca/docs/sites/limestonegeneratingstation.shtml
Conclusion	NWWR Monument	49.99023	-97.34082	http://www.mhs.mb.ca/docs/sites/woodswaterroute.shtml
Conclusion	Salt Plains Raceway	50.16462	-98.70358	http://www.mhs.mb.ca/docs/sites/saltplainsraceway.shtml
Conestoga Campground	Conestoga Campground	49.81018	-97.06788	http://www.mhs.mb.ca/docs/sites/conestogacampground.shtml
Crabby Steves	Crabby Steves	50.54433	-97.23038	http://www.mhs.mb.ca/docs/sites/crabbystevesdancehall.shtml
Davidson Dairy Farm	Carter Farm	49.42674	-96.39650	http://www.mhs.mb.ca/docs/sites/carterfarm.shtml
Davidson Dairy Farm	Davidson Dairy Farm	49.44224	-96.38934	http://www.mhs.mb.ca/docs/sites/manitobadairyfarms.shtml
Davidson Dairy Farm	Schau Farm	49.39597	-96.39873	http://www.mhs.mb.ca/docs/sites/schaufarm.shtml
East Braintree Prison Farm	East Braintree Prison Farm	49.61074	-95.64906	http://www.mhs.mb.ca/docs/sites/prisonfarm.shtml
Elva Grain Elevator	Brookdale Flat Warehouse	50.04827	-99.56277	http://www.mhs.mb.ca/docs/sites/brookdalewarehouse.shtml
Elva Grain Elevator	Elva Grain Elevator	49.21581	-101.11699	http://www.mhs.mb.ca/docs/sites/elvaelevator.shtml
Emerson Fox Barn	Emerson Fox Barn	49.01469	-97.21040	http://www.mhs.mb.ca/docs/sites/foxbarn.shtml

CHAPTER	SITE	LATITUDE	LONGITUDE	URL
Emerson Fox Barn	Hill Barn	50.03092	-98.40070	http://www.mhs.mb.ca/docs/sites/hillbarn.shtml
Emerson Fox Barn	Izon Barn	51.15627	-100.11101	http://www.mhs.mb.ca/docs/sites/izonbarn.shtml
Emerson Fox Barn	Kane Barn	49.28008	-97.34109	http://www.mhs.mb.ca/docs/sites/kanebarn.shtml
Emerson Fox Barn	Reeves Barn	49.90169	-100.35938	http://www.mhs.mb.ca/docs/sites/reevesbarn.shtml
Fort Ellice Trail	Brandon House No. 1	49.67531	-99.62733	http://www.mhs.mb.ca/docs/sites/brandonhouse.shtml
Fort Ellice Trail	Fort Ellice	50.41140	-101.28783	http://www.mhs.mb.ca/docs/sites/fortellice.shtml
Fort Ellice Trail	Fort Ellice Trail	49.92428	-98.94632	http://www.mhs.mb.ca/docs/sites/manitobaagriculturalmuseum.shtml
Fort Whyte Quarries	British-American Cement Plant	49.95093	-97.27652	http://www.mhs.mb.ca/docs/sites/britishamericancementplant.shtml
Fort Whyte Quarries	Fort Whyte Quarries	49.82162	-97.21525	http://www.mhs.mb.ca/docs/sites/canadacementplant.shtml
Fort Whyte Quarries	Steeprock Quarry	51.44238	-98.79740	http://www.mhs.mb.ca/docs/sites/portlandcement.shtml
Gilbert Plains Beef Ring	Gilbert Plains Beef Ring	51.09570	-100.47085	http://www.mhs.mb.ca/docs/sites/gilbertplainsbeefring.shtml
Grainfields School	Grainfields School	51.16946	-101.28059	http://www.mhs.mb.ca/docs/sites/grainfieldsschool.shtml
Grand Rapids Tramway	First Railway Monument (Dominion City)	49.14235	-97.15601	http://www.mhs.mb.ca/docs/sites/firstrailway.shtml
Grand Rapids Tramway	Grand Rapids Tramway	53.16470	-99.27143	http://www.mhs.mb.ca/docs/sites/grandrapidstramway.shtml
Introduction	Kennedy House	50.06570	-96.96970	http://www.mhs.mb.ca/docs/sites/kennedyhouse.shtml
Introduction	Port Nelson	57.04880	-92.60033	http://www.mhs.mb.ca/docs/sites/portnelsonbridge.shtml
Killarney Flax Warehouses	Killarney Flax Warehouses	49.18520	-99.66134	http://www.mhs.mb.ca/docs/sites/killarneyflaxwarehouses.shtml
Manitoba Sugar Company	Campbell Soup Plant	49.98208	-98.31013	http://www.mhs.mb.ca/docs/sites/campbellsoupplant.shtml
Manitoba Sugar Company	Manitoba Sugar Company	49.82617	-97.15917	http://www.mhs.mb.ca/docs/sites/manitobasugar.shtml
McKenzie Building	McKenzie Building	49.84895	-99.95021	http://www.mhs.mb.ca/docs/sites/aemckenziebuilding.shtml
Negrych Homestead	Negrych Homestead	51.30710	-100.44973	http://www.mhs.mb.ca/docs/sites/negrychhomestead.shtml
Pine Falls Paper Mill	Pine Falls Paper Mill	50.56854	-96.22705	http://www.mhs.mb.ca/docs/sites/pinefallspapermill.shtml
Pointe du Bois	Pointe du Bois	50.30066	-95.55152	http://www.mhs.mb.ca/docs/sites/pointeduboisturbine.shtml
Scallion Farm	Scallion Farm	49.89062	-100.94849	http://www.mhs.mb.ca/docs/sites/scallion.shtml
St. Peter Dynevor Rectory	J. R. Watkins Building	49.90348	-97.12240	http://www.mhs.mb.ca/docs/sites/watkinsbuilding.shtml
St. Peter Dynevor Rectory	St. Peter Dynevor Rectory	50.18181	-96.84655	http://www.mhs.mb.ca/docs/sites/stpeterdynevorrectory.shtml
St. Vladimirs College	St. Boniface Normal School	49.89145	-97.12041	http://www.mhs.mb.ca/docs/sites/stbonifacenormalschool.shtml
St. Vladimirs College	St. Vladimirs College	51.23626	-101.34960	http://www.mhs.mb.ca/docs/sites/stvladimirscollege.shtml
Winnipeg Masonic Temple	Winnipeg Masonic Temple	49.89490	-97.14394	http://www.mhs.mb.ca/docs/sites/masonictemple.shtml
York Factory	York Factory	57.00271	-92.30443	http://www.mhs.mb.ca/docs/sites/yorkfactory.shtml

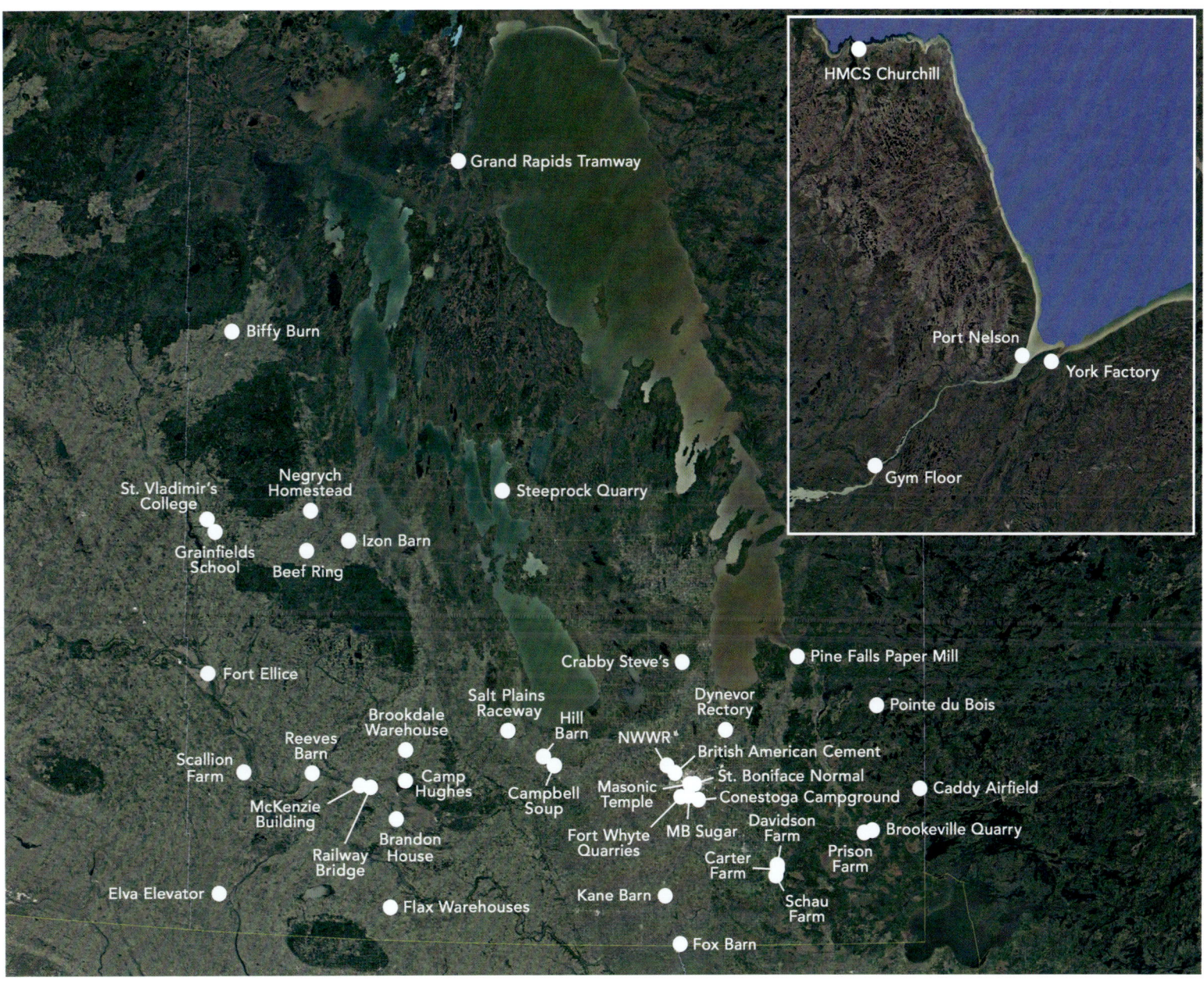

HMCS Churchill

Port Nelson

York Factory

Gym Floor

Grand Rapids Tramway

Biffy Burn

St. Vladimir's College

Negrych Homestead

Izon Barn

Grainfields School

Beef Ring

Steeprock Quarry

Fort Ellice

Crabby Steve's

Pine Falls Paper Mill

Dynevor Rectory

Pointe du Bois

Salt Plains Raceway

Hill Barn

NWWR"

British American Cement

Brookdale Warehouse

St. Boniface Normal

Caddy Airfield

Reeves Barn

Camp Hughes

Campbell Soup

Masonic Temple

Conestoga Campground

Scallion Farm

Davidson Farm

Brookeville Quarry

McKenzie Building

Fort Whyte Quarries

MB Sugar

Prison Farm

Brandon House

Carter Farm

Railway Bridge

Elva Elevator

Flax Warehouses

Kane Barn

Schau Farm

Fox Barn

Index

TOPICS